Prentice-Hall, Inc.
Englewood Cliffs, New Jersey

Norris G. Haring

University of Washington

E. Lakin Phillips

The George Washington University

ANALYSIS AND MODIFICATION OF CLASSROOM BEHAVIOR

Special Education Series
William M. Cruickshank, Series Editor

© **1972 by Prentice-Hall, Inc.**
Englewood Cliffs, New Jersey

ISBN: 0–13–032680–1

Library of Congress Catalog Card Number 76-172064
10   9   8   7   6   5   4   3   2

Prentice-Hall International, Inc., London
Prentice-Hall of Australia, Pty. Ltd., Sydney
Prentice-Hall of Canada, Ltd., Toronto
Prentice-Hall of India Private Limited, New Delhi
Prentice-Hall of Japan, Inc., Tokyo

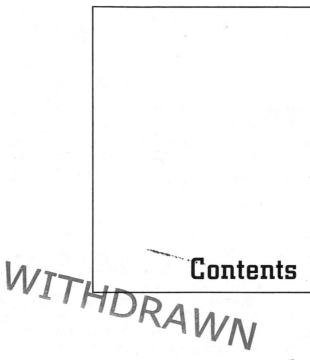

Contents

WITHDRAWN

4

5

6

7

8

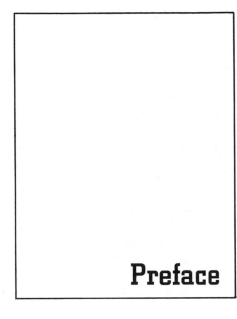

Preface

It has been a decade since our first book, *Educating Emotionally Disturbed Children,* was written, and the experimental and clinical work that preceded the writing was done another five years earlier. Now, after a decade and a half, there have been great changes in our thinking and in the work of others who have contributed materially to the study of behavior disorders and learning problems among children. The changes have been so vast and sweeping that no single volume today can even attempt to encompass them.

Three years ago we began with the idea of revising our book but soon realized that what was needed was not revision but an entirely new book. Even the title no longer seemed appropriate, for the methods we wanted to describe are not limited in application to *one* classification of children; they offer the teacher a powerful method to use in teaching *many* different types of children.

In one sense, education can be considered a commodity which must be sold to the voters, who have the final word on school bond issues, and to parents, who want the best in education for their children. The educational system in the United States today has come under increasing attack from parents and other concerned people who ask, "Do children with academic deficits have learning disabilities or are they the victims of poor instruction?" They also want to know why teachers in ghetto area schools apparently do not teach their students anything. It is the classroom teacher who is generally on the firing line. If the teacher can increase his skills to deal with the learning and behavior problems he encounters in the classroom, he will have gone a long way toward improving public relations.

Analysis and Modification of Classroom Behavior attempts to introduce new scientific skills to teachers. The procedures it offers can easily be adapted to any classroom. They entail no drastic changes in classroom organization or teaching methods, but require merely that the teacher be aware of basic principles of human behavior and utilize them in a consistent manner. Those principles have been determined empirically in laboratory settings and their validity has been demonstrated in the classroom. The wealth of recent literature on behavior modification procedures and the emphasis in teacher training classes on them have resulted in further refinements of the tools for measurement and of the behavior management procedures themselves. With these there has also emerged an increasing regard for the teacher as a systematic observer and modifier of children's behavior. This book is addressed to both the novice and the experienced teacher, who will, we hope, find in behavior modification a way to make their teaching more meaningful and more effective.

Each of the authors has been influenced and stimulated by the other. In addition, peers and students over the past decade have served as watchful critics and encouraging colleagues. We wish to acknowledge with gratitude the assistance of several people. At the University of Washington, Mrs. Mary Ann Hauck assisted in compiling materials for the first draft of this manuscript. Miss Clara Sue Kidwell and Mrs. Ruth Jacobsohn, as editors, are responsible for the final format and the accuracy of the bibliography. At The George Washington University, our colleagues Drs. Sally A. Sibley and David L. Williams of the Psychological Clinic were most encouraging. Staff members of the Experimental Education Unit, Child Development and Mental Retardation Center, University of Washington, provided invaluable assistance, as did staff members at the School for Contemporary Education, McLean, Virginia. A longer-range intellectual debt is owed to Charles B. Ferster, Ogden Lindsley, Leopold Walder, Shlomo Cohen, and Donald K. Pomroy.

Introduction

"Human history," H. G. Wells observed, "becomes more and more a race between education and catastrophe." Never has the truth of this statement been so glaringly evident as it is today, when the threat to life itself has become so frighteningly urgent. If we don't stop polluting our earth, we may not be able to live on it. If we don't stop polluting our seas, we will destroy a vital source of our food supply. If we don't stop polluting the atmosphere, we won't be able to breathe.

Today's children will be the inheritors of our universe, and if it is to be habitable, they must be educated to act with some respect for the existing contingencies. Society looks hopefully to education to find solutions for survival. Our young people must be educated if they are to acquire the knowledge that will enable them to make wise decisions concerning their destiny. And in our technological society, they must also learn the skills needed to implement their decisions.

Time is running out. No longer is the leisurely pursuit of education possible—if indeed it ever was. Technological development has made it necessary for our young people to learn more and to acquire that knowledge more quickly than ever before. In short, education has to become more thorough and more effective.

We tend in the matter of education to think in global terms.

But, in the final sifting, it is the individual child within the framework of his classroom environment who is important. All too often, the individual child is the victim of our present educational system, for success within that system is based not on the child's particular needs and capabilities but on artificial criteria.

We do not deny that education has responded to some extent to the exigencies of our times. Good instruction is provided to many of our children, particularly in the wealthy suburbs where school taxes are high and in private schools where tuition is costly. But the advances have been selective. Large numbers of our children have not been effectively educated. This is especially true in our hard-core urban poverty centers and in our scarcely less poor, scattered rural settlements. We have children with serious learning deficits and children who exhibit a variety of maladaptive social behaviors. These are the children who are unable to perform adequately as a result of the poor or inefficient education they have received, and they present a serious challenge to educators.

It must be said that educators have recognized the failure to educate such children and have made some attempts to overcome it. Aided by such disciplines as psychology, they have tried to identify and diagnose these children. However, diagnosis is frequently accompanied by labels which, however relevant to a medical case history, are of questionable value to the classroom teacher. One reason is that the child's label ("culturally deprived," "hyperactive," "learning disabled") tells the teacher nothing about how to teach that child effectively. Another is that the diagnostic label too often is used to rationalize what is in fact ineffective teaching.

There is no reason today to accept or excuse ineffective instruction. Over the past few years a number of educators using scientific instructional procedures have been successful in educating a wide variety of children, even those with behavior and learning disorders.

Analysis and Modification of Classroom Behavior deals with two basic procedures: one, analysis, pinpoints the relationship between the child's observable behavior and the factors in the environment that evoke it; the other, behavior modification, is the process of altering those conditions or events which are related to the behavior of concern so that it will change in the desired direction. It is a strategy that demands a structured environment which the teacher can change according to both the child's responses and those the teacher wishes to evoke in order to accomplish an educational or behavioral objective.

Any behavior—whether academic, social, or verbal—is a response. One child may throw chairs; another may fail to interact with his peers. But if any sort of behavior is to be changed, it must be precisely analyzed, and to that end it must be defined according to its quantifiable properties, i.e., its movement cycle or basic unit, whether the behavior be "out-of-seat," "talking-out," expressed in the initiation of contacts, or in inappropriate responses, or in hitting or spitting. Measurement can be carried out on the rate, or frequency, or duration of the response, depending on what will give the best data. By concentrating on basic behavioral movements, it is possible to describe behavior accurately, measure it precisely and continuously, and, from these measurements, determine the effects that environmental conditions and events may have on it.

For this reason, our book deals with the child's observable behavior rather than with medical diagnosis. For instance, a child may have tantrums, fail to interact with his peers, and seem not to be attending to the teacher. Taken together, these behaviors are characteristic of what is labeled "autism." If someone were to ask *why* the child behaves in these ways, the teacher might reply: "Oh, he's autistic." The label has been used to explain the behavior. Even though the medical diagnosis is correct, it is of little use, for it fails to provide directions for changing the behavior or for helping the child acquire subject-matter skills. Not only does the label not tell the teacher how to teach the child, but it fails also to tell him what, when, and how much to teach. In addition, it gives him no information about what responses to expect from the child.

If the teacher views the classroom as an environment within which the child acts, and if he uses his knowledge concerning principles of behavior to arrange the events in that environment, he can modify the child's behavior in a predictable direction. By using the techniques of behavior analysis, he can determine how the environment affects the child—whether he responds to it appropriately or inappropriately, or whether the environment evokes any response at all, a lack of response being possible when the child is withdrawn.

He can determine at what level of academic skill the child is functioning and then know at what level to introduce new materials. And on the basis of behavior analysis, the teacher can make still other decisions regarding the child—what goals or terminal objectives should be set, which behavior should be encouraged as appropriate, and which should be discouraged as inappropriate. By considering the environment as a set of independent variables which act as stimuli to the child's behavior (his responses), and by viewing the child's responses as the dependent variables, the teacher has a system within which he can manipulate the independent variables and observe their effects on the dependent variables. The effects will be readily apparent because of continuous measurement and recording of data, both of which are essential to analysis and modification procedures.

Continuous measurement provides the teacher with an ongoing record of the child's behavior in the classroom. The teacher need no longer depend on indirect tests administered and analyzed by psychologists, because the data he has continuously collected provide him with reliable information on which to base decisions for individualized instruction for all his students.

The concept of reinforcement is integral to the practice of behavior modification, and it is remarkable both in its simplicity and in the fact that few teachers realize that reinforcement techniques, properly used, are powerful tools in shaping behavior. In behavioral terms, reinforcement means simply that if a pleasant or rewarding consequence follows a particular kind of behavior, that behavior will tend to recur. Teachers often tend to ignore the child who is working quietly ("But that is what he is supposed to be doing!") and concentrate their attention on the unruly child in an attempt to maintain control over him. But social reinforcement in the form of attention from the teacher will most likely maintain the unruly behavior (and thus give the child control over the teacher). Use of social reinforcement requires that the teacher realize that his attention serves to reinforce the behavior of his students. If he ignores that behavior which is not appropriate and the child is thus denied reinforcement, the inappropriate behavior will tend to diminish. With this simple principle in mind, the teacher can easily modify almost any behavior. If the child's behavior is inappropriate, it can be changed. If his behavior is appropriate, but occurs infrequently, it can be made more frequent, and if it is nonexistent, it can be developed.

The advantages and limitations of social and other reinforcement, the concepts of independent and dependent variables, stimuli and responses, contingencies and reinforcement, are all dealt with in detail in this book. The procedures we describe constitute an empirically scientific approach to education. They combine with, and can be supplemented by, the products of educational technology—programmed instruction, computer-assisted instruction, and teaching machines. But while these technological innovations offer invaluable assistance to the teacher who is trying to keep accurate data on pupil response rates and can relieve him of the chore of routine presentation of drill material, the ultimate responsibility for the child's educational program cannot be left to a machine. It rests with the teacher. The procedures outlined in the following chapters offer him the means to fulfill that responsibility.

Vocabulary and Methodological Concepts

The ordinary classroom is an environment rich in stimuli that affect behavior. There are windows to look out of, chairs to sit in, books to read, chalk to be thrown, tables to be overturned. When a child walks into the classroom and sees a chair, he may walk over to it and sit down, or he may pick it up and throw it at the teacher. The teacher would consider the first action appropriate and the second totally inappropriate. The point is that the chair is a stimulus which evokes a response from the child.

The child with whom the teacher will be most concerned is the one who throws the chair instead of sitting on it, cries instead of doing arithmetic, daydreams instead of working, or exhibits any of a number of other types of behavior that the teacher deems undesirable. He is the child whose repertoire of responses is controlled by the environment in ways that cause his behavior to be disruptive or inappropriate. Or he is the child with the short attention span—the environment simply does not control his behavior appropriately for any length of time; perhaps he will do one arithmetic problem before he begins to daydream.

The child with learning or behavior problems needs a highly structured environment. For the child who throws chairs (an extreme example), the structure may require that his chair be bolted to the floor (an extreme solution). For the child who has trouble paying attention to math, the structure may involve using a programmed textbook in which the material is arranged in a sequence of steps, with each step slightly more difficult than the previous one, and in which each correct answer that the child gives is rewarded by praise or other reinforcement. The behavioral approach to educating children, with its emphasis on the relationship between environment and behavior, works in a situation where the environment is as controlled as possible and the child knows or learns what responses are expected of him.

Basic to the behavioral approach to learning is the Skinner paradigm of stimulus-response-reinforcement (Skinner 1953) which is, in itself, a highly structured concept. It asserts the unvarying relationship that exists when a stimulus is presented, when that stimulus evokes a response, and when that response is reinforced. This relationship can be presented as a law of behavior. When a stimulus evokes a response and that response is reinforced, the stimulus will evoke the same response or one similar to it in succeeding instances.

The structure of the stimulus-response-reinforcement relationship is evident in the classroom when a teacher hands the child a book and asks him to read. The child reads correctly, whereupon the teacher praises him. According to the law, the praise reinforces the child's correct reading, and he will probably read correctly when again given a book. This statement, of course, is highly simplified, but it will serve as an illustration.

One of the most important features of the behavioral approach in education is the necessity for *structure* and *consistency*. The teacher must respond consistently to the child so that the child knows what to expect in any given situation. The lawfulness of the relationship rests on the fact that within any situation, the same stimulus must evoke the same or a similar response, which is then always followed by reinforcement.

Behavior modification as a procedure for educating children can be considered scientific because a basic law of behavior is followed and the conditions under which the law functions are structured. There are independent variables (stimuli) and dependent variables (responses), and there is a vocabulary of terms that must be precisely defined in order to maintain the unvarying conditions of the law. An understanding of the following terms and concepts, beginning with the Skinner paradigm, is essential to the application of behavior modification techniques.

Skinner Paradigm

Stimulus————————⟶ Response————————⟶ Reinforcement

A *stimulus* is anything in the environment that serves to evoke a response. A chair is a stimulus to a sitting behavior (or perhaps a throwing behavior). The child cannot sit or throw if there is nothing to sit on or throw. A *response* is an observable behavior. The teacher cannot tell if the child is thinking of sitting or throwing. He can only observe the child's behavior of sitting or throwing when the child actually sits or throws. *Reinforcement* is the presentation of a desirable or rewarding consequence for a response. It serves to increase the probability that the same type of response will be made to the same stimuli in succeeding instances.

For purposes of discussing the relationship between stimulus and response, the concept of independent and dependent variables in the classroom must be understood. Independent variables furnish the stimuli, and responses to those stimuli are the dependent variables. The child's classroom environment changes all the time. Every time a child is given a new book, or a picture on a bulletin board is changed, or new instructions are given, the child's environment has varied. The environment is the source of the independent variables which affect behavior.

Everything that the child does can be said to depend on the stimuli of the classroom. Writing spelling words or arithmetic answers, pointing to letters in response to directions, sharpening his pencil, hitting another child, or staring out of the window—all these are part of his behavior in the classroom, and all can be classified as responses to classroom stimuli. The child's behaviors, therefore, are dependent variables.

Anything in the child's environment can be a stimulus to a response. However, the teacher may wish to evoke a specific response from the child. To do this, he uses a *cue*. He may say, "Johnny, do this arithmetic problem," thus "causing" him to do the problem. A cue is anything used as a stimulus with the intent of evoking a response. It may be a verbal command, a gesture (such as pointing at a child to indicate that he is expected to answer), a book from which the child is supposed to read, a flashcard to which he responds by saying a word. Cues constitute the teacher's way of controlling the environment by presenting those stimuli to which the child is expected to respond.

Conditioning

The twentieth century marked the beginning of the scientific application of stimuli to elicit specific responses. Pavlov's (1927) experiment in conditioning a response is famous. Making use of the observation that dogs salivate at the scent of food, Pavlov first presented a dog with meat powder to produce the response of salivation and then paired the presentation of the meat powder with the ringing of a bell. This also elicited a salivation response. After a number of trials, the meat powder was withdrawn and the bell-ringing only was presented. The dog still continued to respond by salivating. Pavlov's experiment successfully demonstrated that a response could be conditioned by a stimulus. Watson and Rayner (1920), in their case study of Little Albert and the white rat, successfully conditioned Albert's fear response to the rat by pairing the presentation of the rat with a loud noise which had previously produced the fear response. Albert then began to fear the rat.

It is important to realize that not all responses can be conditioned. For example, a hammer tap on the patellar tendon will produce a reflex knee jerk. This is an automatic and normal neurological response, and as Bijou and Baer (1961) point out, no amount of bell-ringing or loud noise or any stimulus other than the hammer tap will produce that response. However, classroom behaviors that are under the control of the child can be conditioned by stimuli in the classroom—the variables of the classroom environment.

Learning may be considered an example of responses conditioned to stimuli. Responses become conditioned by the use of reinforcing stimuli. When a response to a stimulus is reinforced by the subsequent occurrence of a pleasurable or rewarding event, that response will tend to recur in the presence of the same stimulus. For example, if a child is smiled at by the teacher after he has made a correct response in arithmetic or is complimented for following the rules in a baseball game, the probability is high that he will again make that response in the teacher's presence. If the child is rewarded for answering "four" to the stimulus "$2 + 2 = -$," his response may be said to be conditioned so that the stimulus "$2 + 2 = -$" will always evoke the response "four."

Learning is not limited to the process of making responses that have been conditioned. It involves *stimulus generalization* and *stimulus discrimination* as well. Behavior generalizes from specific stimuli, to which it has been conditioned, to similar stimuli. Stimulus generalization is observed in the very young child who calls all four-legged creatures "bow-wow" or "doggie." The child's verbal response is originally conditioned to dog. Then the stimulus becomes generalized, and all four-legged creatures become stimuli to evoke the response "bow-wow" or "doggie."

Acquisition of the concept of "greenness" is a second illustration of the process of generalization. When the teacher holds up a red circle and a green circle and asks the child to point to the green circle, the teacher will smile at him, or say "Good" or "That's right," when the child points to the green circle. The child can then generalize the concept of greenness to other green objects. If the child points to the red circle or does not point to either circle, the teacher's response will be different, for instance "No" or "Wrong." The teacher's varying responses are examples of *differential reinforcement*, i.e., positive reinforcement for correct responses, negative or no reinforcement for incorrect responses. The teacher develops *stimulus discrimination* in the child by differentially reinforcing the correct response. Stimulus discrimination is another element of the learning process. The green circle can be discriminated from the red one because of the history of reinforcement for the correct response. The green circle and the teacher's direction to "point to the green circle" have become discriminative stimuli (S^Ds), and in their presence the child will make the response (R) of pointing to the green circle. Stimulus discrimination results when the same response is always made to a particular stimulus because the response has been reinforced in the presence of the stimulus (Skinner 1953).

$$S^D \longrightarrow R \longrightarrow S^r$$

The environmental conditions (stimuli) present when the response was reinforced become discriminative stimuli which control the response (Terrace 1966). Without the development of stimulus discrimination, no human—child or adult—would exhibit any predictable pattern of behavior to anything that is commonly part of the environment.

The process of stimulus generalization is part of learning, as in acquiring the concept of "greenness," but it impairs early discrimination, as in the case of the child who calls all four-legged animals "bow-wow." This generalization finally becomes extinguished as refined discriminations take over. For the young child, responses of overgeneralization need to be extinguished. An apt differentiation between processes of generalization and discrimination has been made by Keller: "Generalization we have seen to be merely a kind of bonus derived from *conditioning,* and discrimination (the breakdown of generalization) is largely a matter of extinction" (1954, p. 17).

Establishment of stimulus discrimination leads to stimulus control over behavior. The stimulus present when the response is repeatedly reinforced eventually will exert stimulus control over the response. The teacher is the primary source and manager of stimulus control in the classroom, sometimes acting as the controlling stimulus as he gives instructions, directions, and other information to the class or to individuals, and sometimes relinquishing stimulus control to books, to problems on the blackboard, or to the many other instructional materials used throughout the day.

Operant behavior is learned behavior. Learning is the process of discriminating and generalizing from stimuli in the environment. Two kinds of behavior can be distinguished: *respondent behavior* and *operant behavior.* Respondent behavior is that over which control is exercised by antecedent stimuli. Operant behavior is that which is maintained by subsequent stimuli in the form of reinforcing events (Skinner 1966). Both types of behavior can be conditioned.

In respondent behavior, a response can be conditioned to occur in the presence of any number of stimuli simply by pairing a neutral stimulus with a stimulus already eliciting a specific response when presented to the organism. For example, candy or ice cream, which elicit salivation in a child, can be paired with a bell sound or musical tone, as is often heard from neighborhood ice cream trucks. The bell sound is a stimulus which will elicit salivation after a number of pairings with ice cream or candy (shades of Pavlov!). You may remember that Little Albert's fear response to the rat was conditioned by presenting the rat together with the loud noise that originally caused the fear.

Operant conditioning brings behavior under the control of reinforcing stimuli. The behavior is evoked by the antecedent stimulus because it has been reinforced by subsequent stimuli in the presence of that antecedent stimulus. If candy is reinforcing to a child, then giving him an M & M after he has answered a question correctly will increase the likelihood that he will again answer a question correctly when it is asked (provided, of course, that he knows the answer). Assume for the sake of argument that he does know the answer: If he is unaware that his answer will produce any consequences, the question by itself may not cause him to respond. The anticipation of an M & M, however, will do so.

Reinforcement does not necessarily mean that the child will go through life munching M & Ms. Just as one antecedent stimulus can be substituted for another through conditioning, so can one reinforcing stimulus be substituted for another. Any number of things can be reinforcing to children—food, trinkets, toys, social approval, praise. But the child who is mentally retarded or emotionally disturbed, or who somehow does not react to stimuli in a "normal" way, may not find reinforcing the same things that other children do. It is necessary to condition him to react to reinforcers. The process of conditioning him to a reinforcing stimulus takes place, for example, when food, which is generally a basic reinforcer, is paired with praise from the teacher. As the food is gradually withdrawn, the praise itself becomes reinforcing.

Responses

A stimulus evokes a response, and a response is defined as an *observable behavior*. The child who is looking at a book may be reading silently or he may be daydreaming. If the teacher's objective is to teach the child to read, it is obviously desirable that the child be reading to himself, but the teacher has no way of knowing if this is indeed the case. The only responses that are meaningful to the behaviorist are those that involve observable action. It is not enough to say that the child may be thinking of reading. He must perform some overt act; he must engage in some *behavior*—read orally, write answers to questions, turn pages—that can be observed. Attention span is generally taken as an indication of capacity to learn, and a short attention span is generally considered a deterrent to the learning process. "Attending" labels the behavior of "looking at" or "noticing" a thing or event. If one observes a child looking at a book or watching the teacher or watching a television screen, one infers that the child is attending. However, the validity of the inference is verified only when the child makes an active response to the thing or the event.

A child's attention is observable in all his behavior—smiling at his mother for the first time, holding a bottle of milk, saying his first word, writing an answer to an arithmetic problem, or solving for an unknown chemical in a science experiment. The acquisition of these and all other sorts of behavior requires attending to something in the immediate environment and responding to it in a particular pattern. Regardless of the behavior pattern observed, the child is attending to some specific condition, event, or person in the environment and is responding to it. He may be attending to an untied shoelace and respond by tying it, or he may be attending to the teacher's saying "Spell dog" and respond by writing the word.

Measurement

Events in the classroom can be viewed in temporal terms. The teacher directs and Alexander responds. Alexander then gets a silver star. But the temporal relationship of events does not imply a causal relationship. Antecedent and subsequent events occur throughout the day, but they are not necessarily related by anything other than time. To discuss behavior in terms of stimulus and response, however, implies a causal rather than a temporal relationship. The stimulus evokes the response.

The Skinner paradigm implies a direct relationship between stimulus and response. There exists in the classroom a temporal arrangement of events—antecedent and consequent stimuli—but, as we have said, a simple temporal relationship between two events does not necessarily indicate a causal relationship between them. The effect of a stimulus in eliciting a response is indicated by the rate at which the response occurs in the presence of the stimulus. If a teacher places a textbook on Alexander's desk and Alexander picks up the book and throws it across the room, the two events are temporally, but perhaps not causally, related. The next time she places the book on his desk, Alexander may begin to work from it. If, when the teacher places the book on his desk, Alexander begins to do the arithmetic problems from the book, and the teacher praises him, again the events are temporally related, but no causal relationship has been established. If, however, the teacher notes that *every* time she places the book on his desk, Alexander throws it across the room, then she can say with some reliability that there is a relationship between the two events. If she notes that every time she places the book on his desk Alexander begins to work, another relationship has been established, and if she notes that her praise for one problem done correctly leads Alexander to do the next problem correctly, she has completed the paradigm.

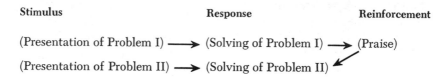

Stimulus	Response	Reinforcement
(Presentation of Problem I) ⟶	(Solving of Problem I) ⟶	(Praise)
(Presentation of Problem II) ⟶	(Solving of Problem II) ↙	

The validity of the paradigm is a function of the control exerted by the stimulus over the response, and the control is indicated by the regularity with which the stimulus evokes the response. Measurement of the response rate in the presence of the stimulus is a crucial factor in determining the relationship between the two. Another factor that increases the response is reinforcement. The degree of control exerted by a given stimulus over a particular response is altered by manipulation of the consequence (the reinforcement of the response).

The *response rate*—the number of responses per unit of time that the child makes under specified conditions—is the critical measure of the effects of any independent variable on the child's performance. If the teacher wants to change the child's response rate, he can experiment by changing the type of material or by changing an event that occurs during or immediately after the child's performance. If this change in environmental conditions affects performance, the change will be observable in the child's altered response rate.

Before the emissions of a response can be counted, the response must be defined as a movement cycle, that is, as a discrete unit with a beginning and an end. And it must be repeatable. For example, out-of-seat behavior can be defined as a movement cycle beginning when the child gets out of his seat, i.e., when no part of his body is touching the chair, and ending when he returns to the chair and sits down. With the cycle completed, the behavior can be counted as one out-of-seat response.

Academic responses must be similarly defined. Response requirements for solving addition problems must change with the complexity of the material. For instance, more time is needed to solve two-place addition problems than one-place problems, and even more time must spent on three-place problems. The rate of response therefore may be expected to decrease as the problems increase in complexity—the more difficult the problem, the fewer the responses. However, in answering addition problems it is the writing of numbers that is the basic unit of response, and the units of measurement are comparable for all addition problems, whatever their complexity or the conditions under which the response is to be made. In each case, the response can be quantified in terms of its movement cycle unit. The same physical output is required; only the prerequisite for making the response is altered. For purposes of counting, the particular type of behavior should be broken down into its smallest discrete units. Thus, in arithmetic the response would be writing numbers rather than complete answers, and each number would be counted. A rate of oral reading would be the number of words said in a minute. The child who is out of his seat (and back in it) fifty times in twenty-five minutes has an out-of-seat rate of two responses per minute.

There are many instances when the response rate does not provide a reliable picture of a behavior pattern. Sometimes tantrums, crying, or contact with peers or teachers (or lack of it) are units of behavior that extend over a long period of time per unit of occurrence. It may be twenty minutes before Henry returns to his seat after having left it. Such behavior may require that data be recorded in terms of percentage of time during which the behavior occurs. For example, an observer might break down an observation period into very small units of time, such as ten-second intervals, and observe the number of ten-second intervals during which the child is out of his seat. The units of time during which the behavior occurs can then be converted to a percentage of the total time during which it occurs. Percentage of time, however, is a less than precise form of measurement, and it should not be used when the behavior permits a precise enough definition of movement cycle for a rate measurement to be taken.

Before a teacher can design any program to change a child's behavior by manipulating the independent variables of the environment, he must have response data. In order to tell whether the independent variables are changing the rate of the behavior, he must know what the original rate was. In addition, a teacher cannot, on observing a child with a number of disruptive behaviors, decide to change all of them at once. The response data can indicate which behaviors are occurring at a high rate, and he can pinpoint one of these to be altered. Sometimes, after examining the response data, the teacher finds that a behavior which seemed to him to occur very frequently actually occurs with less than the expected frequency and is not as much in need of modification as other behaviors. The teacher may think that Victoria is always jumping out of her seat to sharpen a pencil or talk to another child, but when he has objective response data he *knows* how many times in a specified period the child is actually out of her seat. He knows the rate at which she is emitting that behavior.

Once modification procedures are instituted, continuous measurement of the child's responses must be taken and the response data evaluated. If the data indicate a desirable change in frequency (acceleration of an appropriate behavior or deceleration of an inappropriate one), the teacher can consider the procedural design successful. If not, a change in the modification design is necessary; perhaps a different antecedent stimulus (e.g., a different textbook) or a different consequence (e.g., the awarding of silver stars) should be introduced. No matter what the decision, however, it is always based on the response data.

Every child will exhibit a unique pattern of responses. Although his behavior may be the same as that observed in other children, the rate of occurrence will be different. George may write two numbers a minute, while Eldridge may write twenty. The teacher may wish to accelerate George's rate and be perfectly satisfied with Eldridge's. A program of modification can be designed for each child on the basis of that child's response data. The *terminal objectives* for each child are realistically identified according to what he should be able to do and the successive approximations that should lead him to do it. The child is not expected to conform to a norm. His progress is determined solely on the basis of the response data obtained—where he was and where he is going. His progress is always determined by the criteria of his own past performance as shown by the data.

Reinforcement

The third component of the Skinner paradigm, the reinforcing stimulus, is the key to successful behavior modification. The classroom teacher faces a heterogeneous population of children with a variety of behaviors. Some children will make appropriate responses much of the time, while others will respond inappropriately most of the time. Using techniques of reinforcement, the teacher can accelerate rates of appropriate behavior and diminish the frequency of inappropriate behavior. Reinforcement is always contingent on the emission of a response. The offering of a positively reinforcing stimulus—candy, free time, teacher praise—is contingent on the child's emission of a response judged appropriate by some predetermined criteria. The teacher may give an M & M for each word spoken correctly, a gold star for ten correct arithmetic responses, or praise for ten minutes of sitting quietly in one's seat.

Reinforcement is an extremely effective technique, but its use demands sensitivity on the teacher's part, both in the selection of the reinforcer and in the timing of its presentation. The selection of appropriate reinforcers is necessary for a successful modification program. The teacher can use reinforcers that are readily available in the classroom. Social attention and praise are effective reinforcers for most children. But more powerful extrinsic reinforcers may be necessary for children with inappropriate social behavior. Ultimately, however, the effectiveness of the reinforcer chosen depends on the knowledge of the teacher. Food or candy obviously will not be particularly reinforcing to the child who has just eaten lunch with a dessert of candy or ice cream. Moreover, what is reinforcing to one child may not be to another. Grover may be reinforced by receiving a smile from the teacher, while Franklin may need a more tangible reward, like a toy. The choice here, as with the choice of an antecedent stimulus, depends on the teacher's recognition of the child as an individual with likes and dislikes peculiarly his own.

Reinforcement takes several forms. *Positive reinforcement* is the presentation of a pleasurable or desirable consequence for behavior. Candy, praise, tokens, green stamps—all can be positively reinforcing for most children. One concept of positive reinforcement is contained in what Premack termed "a generalization, not a theory" (1959). This principle has been restated as a differential probability hypothesis (Premack 1965; Homme 1966), whereby any behavior will reinforce any other behavior if the former occurs more frequently (i.e., has a higher probability of occurrence) than the latter. If low probability behavior is rewarded by the opportunity to engage in high probability behavior, the former will be reinforced. High probability behavior (such as play) can be used to reinforce low probability behavior (such as doing arithmetic). If a child appears to enjoy arithmetic but does not like to read, the teacher may arrange his schedule so that completion of a reading assignment will be followed by arithmetic. If the child's response rate in reading increases under this arrangement of the environment, the teacher has an indication that his modification procedures are working.

Negative reinforcement is the type that appears most often in ordinary classrooms. A response is emitted in order to effect the removal of a real or threatened aversive event. The child who is told that he will be punished unless his arithmetic is completed will respond to the task so that the threat of being punished is removed. Negative reinforcement temporarily strengthens the response rate. The mother who nags her child to practice the piano is practicing negative reinforcement. When the child practices, the mother stops nagging. The teacher who scolds a child for mispronouncing a word increases the probability that the child will pronounce the word correctly to avoid being scolded. However, negative reinforcement can also cause a drop in the response rate. If the class laughs at a child who stumbles over a word, the child's rate of oral response may decrease.

Extinction of a behavior is a deliberate strategy of withdrawing all reinforcement, positive or negative. Although responses conditioned by negative reinforcement are extremely resistant to extinction, withdrawal of either type of reinforcement is designed to eliminate a specific conditioned behavior.

Teachers often unwittingly reinforce the very behavior they wish to eliminate by giving attention to it. A child who misbehaves in school often gets much more attention from the teacher than the child who behaves appropriately. The teacher thus conveys the idea that he will notice only the child who misbehaves. The teacher would no doubt deny any such intention, but an examination of his behavior would reveal that this state of affairs does exist. The child misbehaves, the teacher warns, the child continues to misbehave. The teacher's behavior toward the child has become conditioned; the child's misbehavior is a stimulus controlling the teacher's behavior. To alter this situation, the teacher must find ways to reinforce the child when he behaves properly and to ignore, insofar as possible, his misbehavior. This is extinction, which is a learning process—the child learns not to emit a behavior that will not gain him satisfactory consequences.

Behavior should be reinforced differentially. Reinforce the desired behavior; ignore the unwanted behavior. Usually it is possible to ignore a large amount of the child's undesirable behavior if, at the same time, one positively reinforces the wanted behavior. A line is then drawn quite clearly between desirable behavior and unwanted, unreinforced behavior.

Contingency Management

The basis of behavior modification procedures is contingency management. What happens after the child has done an arithmetic problem? Is he praised, ignored, or punished? The event that occurs after the child's response is said to be contingent on that response. The term *contingent* implies that there is a relationship between what the child does and what happens afterward, a relationship that is resultant rather than merely temporal. The result does, of course, follow the child's behavior, but it happens because of the child's behavior. Most of our behavior, if we stop to think about it, is controlled by contingencies of one sort or another. We occupy our homes contingent on rent or mortgage and tax payments. Our salaries are contingent on job performance. A teacher's credentials are contingent on completion of a course of study. The praise we receive in recognition of our service to others is gratifying enough for most of us to keep on making the appropriate responses in order to ensure its continuation. The contingencies of our environments, then, control our behavior and can predictably influence our responses.

In a classroom, a teacher can manage a child's behavior by arranging contingencies. The child can be cued to make certain responses and can be reinforced for those responses. Responses can be accelerated, decelerated, maintained, or extinguished by appropriate contingency management. As far back as 1943, Warren and Brown described the effect of contingencies on child behavior: if a contingency is established between the child's behavior and his environment, a powerful effect on the child's behavior will be observed. For the teacher, then, the procedures of contingency management involve selecting and arranging the stimuli in the environment (the independent variables) to reinforce (or to extinguish) the child's responses (the dependent variables). "In principle, the development of complex behavior is most easily accomplished by carefully designing the environment so that it favors the occurrence of early stages of the behavior, and can be gradually converted into the environment where the final behavior must occur" (Michael 1963, p. 86). If the teacher has determined in advance what responses he will reinforce, the child's repertoire of responses will be effectively shaped. The sooner the child discovers the contingencies in his environment, the sooner his behavior will come under the control of the environment. By careful planning of terminal behaviors to be shaped and successive approximations to be reinforced, we greatly shorten the adaptation period in the child's acquisition of a social response repertoire, greatly decrease the number of irrelevant responses emitted, and thereby reduce the necessity to extinguish inappropriate behavior. When contingencies between appropriate responses and reinforcing stimuli become established, appropriate responses to discriminative stimuli rapidly increase and inappropriate responses are extinguished. Effective contingency management thus eliminates irrelevant and inappropriate responses.

If a particular inappropriate response occurs at a very high rate or more frequently than others, then simply by virtue of being emitted more often, it will probably be reinforced at a higher rate than the others. Herrnstein explains that "in any situation in which accidental contingencies are operating, the net result may simply be an accentuation of a response already dominant" (1966, p. 49). Therefore, if the child's repertoire of social responses has not been objectively measured, and if specific goals of terminal behavior have not been objectively measured, and if specific goals of terminal behavior have not been established for him, and if successive approximations of the terminal behaviors have not been specified for reinforcement, there is a high probability that accidental contingencies will predominate and function only to maintain the inappropriate responses that are already dominant. If the contingencies in the environment are not clearly defined, the child may emit many random and irrelevant responses before making the appropriate response to be reinforced.

Contingency management is a systematic approach to the use of reinforcement. It involves a statement of the functional relationship between the child's responses and their consequences—that is, a statement of what type and frequency of reinforcement will follow a particular response.

Although the concept of reinforcement stems from Skinner's paradigm, that paradigm describes a laboratory situation. A more explicitly class-room-oriented version of Skinner's paradigm has been developed by Lindsley (1964), who identifies *four components of a contingency management system*. E^A is the *antecedent event*, M is the *movement* (the response to be measured), A is the *arrangement of reinforcement* (its presentation schedule), and E^S is the *subsequent event* designated as a consequence (reinforcement) of the response.

| E^A | M | A | E^S |
| Antecedent Event | Movement | Arrangement | Subsequent Event |

Many complex schedules of reinforcement have been worked out (Bijou and Baer 1966), but the four basic schedules (Ferster and Skinner 1957) shown in table 1.1 are *Fixed Ratio* (FR) and *Variable Ratio* (VR), based on number, and *Fixed Interval* (FI) and *Variable Interval* (VI), based on time. Reese (1966) and Ferster and Skinner (1957) have provided excellent examples of typical response patterns occurring under these schedules.

Table 1.1. Schedules of Reinforcement

	Fixed	Variable
Ratio	FR	VR
Interval	FI	VI

On a fixed ratio schedule, reinforcement follows a specific number of responses, and the schedule is identified according to the number of responses required before reinforcement is presented. For example, FR1 is identified as a fixed ratio of one and is the same as Continuous Reinforcement (CRF). Under FR1 or CRF, reinforcement is presented directly after every correct response. On an FR10 (fixed ratio of ten), reinforcement would be presented after ten correct responses.

A variable ratio schedule means that the number of responses emitted before reinforcement is not fixed. Most reinforcement in the ordinary classroom occurs on a variable ratio schedule. This is particularly true of academic work. For instance, ten arithmetic problems may have to be completed correctly to earn an A, while twenty spelling words have to be spelled correctly to earn an A.

Reinforcement on a fixed interval schedule follows the first correct response emitted after the specified interval has elapsed. On an F15 (fixed interval of five) schedule, reinforcement would follow the first correct response emitted after five minutes had elapsed. Similarly, on an FI2 schedule, reinforcement would be presented for the first response given after two minutes had elapsed.

A variable interval schedule means that reinforcement comes at irregular intervals. Trying to hail a taxicab would be an example of seeking reinforcement on a variable interval schedule.

The various schedules of reinforcement produce different patterns of response. A low fixed interval schedule, for instance, produces what is known as a scalloped curve. At the beginning of the interval, there is a low rate of response. As the interval proceeds, the rate accelerates, and by the end of the interval, it is high. When reinforcement is presented, the rate drops to its initial low, again slowly accelerates, and then rapidly accelerates near the end of the interval. A child who has an arithmetic assignment due in fifteen minutes will characteristically show a pattern of low response rate early in the interval, with a gradual increase and then a rapid acceleration as the time comes to an end. The child watching the clock near the end of the day will exhibit a low rate of clock-watching thirty minutes before dismissal time, but his rate will rapidly accelerate as the close of the school day approaches.

Variable ratio and variable interval schedules produce stable performance patterns. Reinforcement on a variable ratio schedule works best when the responses are occurring at a high rate with infrequent pauses. Thus there is little chance of the pause being reinforced instead of the response. Responses usually occur at a higher rate on this schedule than on a variable interval schedule. However, if too many responses are required before reinforcement is presented, a stable performance rate is not maintained.

Once a contingency system begins to operate satisfactorily, it becomes important to spread the same amount of reinforcement over a longer period of time or over a larger number of responses. At the beginning of a contingency management system, it is probably best to reinforce the child every time he responds appropriately (FR1 or CRF). When the behavior pattern begins to stabilize, reinforcement should be less generous. On a fixed ratio schedule, the child can be given a piece of candy after he correctly solves five problems (FR5) or correctly spells ten words (FR10). Fixed ratio schedules are generally more satisfactory than fixed interval schedules because the rate of reinforcement depends not on the arbitrary variable of *time*, but on the *child's performance*. Eventually, the child can be put on a VR schedule where reinforcement is presented after a random number of responses.

Shaping

With a child who makes few appropriate responses that can be reinforced, it is necessary first to evoke behavior which approximates the appropriate kind and then shape it through a series of approximations until the final appropriate behavior becomes conditioned. Shaping procedures must be carefully planned. The terminal behavior must be identified, successive approximations to that behavior must be defined, and the approximations must be immediately reinforced. Shaping procedures work because "during shaping, reinforcement not only strengthens the particular response that is reinforced but also increases the likelihood that a closer approximation will occur" (Reese 1966, p. 13). If the terminal objective for a child is to have him sit quietly in his seat, successive approximations might include the child's presence in the vicinity of the desk, his touching the chair, any sitting (no matter how brief), and finally sitting for increasingly longer periods of time.

Chaining

A *chain of behavior* is a series of responses in which each response functions as the discriminative stimulus for the next response. Chaining procedures promote the effective development of complex responses by joining conditioned responses as components of a chain. Behavior is evoked by stimuli and reinforced by stimuli. A stimulus that reinforces one behavior can also serve to evoke the next behavior. Looking at a pencil, reaching for it, grasping it, raising it to a writing position, and moving it to make a mark are responses in a series that constitutes the act of writing. Each response in the chain provides the discriminative stimulus for the next response as well as the conditioned reinforcer for the previous one. A chain is made up of a number of responses that must be emitted before the final reinforcement occurs. Barnaby, a white rat, was trained to go through an arch, up a ladder, across a drawbridge, up a staircase, along a handcart, and up a spiral staircase, at the top of which he hit middle C on a piano, which opened a gate blocking a tunnel. Barnaby then entered a plastic elevator, where he pulled a latch; the latch released the elevator to the bottom of the apparatus, where he pressed a lever five times and obtained food. The chaining process proceeds backward by conditioning the last behavior first. Barnaby was conditioned to lever-pressing first of all. Then he was placed in the elevator from which he could see the lever. He learned to work the elevator to get at the lever, which had become a discriminative stimulus indicating food. When the elevator operation was conditioned, he was placed in the tunnel through which he had to pass to get to the elevator. The chaining process instilled in Barnaby a complex series of behaviors, all of which were conditioned ultimately by the reinforcement of food (Goldiamond and Dyrud 1966).

In the classroom, the sequence of activities can be considered a chain, with each activity, task, or assignment a component in the chain. If the sequence is reading, arithmetic, recess, spelling, writing, and lunch, the completion of each assignment or activity can be considered as both reinforcement for that assignment and a discriminative stimulus for the next assignment. A behavioral component with a low rate of response can be arranged in the chain so that it becomes the component nearest the primary reinforcer or at least the component preceding a very strong conditioned reinforcer. Chaining procedures can incorporate the Premack principle to good advantage: high probability behaviors can be used to reinforce low probability behaviors in a sequence that ends with the highest probability behavior (for example, lunch). The value of chaining procedures lies in their usefulness for building a complex series of behaviors so that the child will work for fairly long-range goals rather than depend on immediate reinforcement.

Summary

Contingency management in the classroom is based on definite principles of behavior. Consequences that are not neutral in relation to behavior are either reinforcing or aversive. They can be presented following a behavior, or they can be withheld or withdrawn. Each situation will have a different and predictable effect on behavior, as will the schedule of presentation of reinforcement (fixed or variable ratio or interval). Behavior is predictably affected by—

1. presenting reinforcing events;
2. withholding reinforcing events;
3. withdrawing aversive events;
4. presenting aversive events;
5. scheduling stimulus events to occur frequently;
6. scheduling stimulus events to occur intermittently.

These contingency management practices are in operation in almost all classrooms, but few teachers are fully aware of them or apply them in a systematic manner. It is, however, in the systematic use of contingent reinforcement that hope for the success of classroom management lies.

References

Bijou, Sidney W., and Donald M. Baer. *Child Development Volume 1: A Systematic and Empirical Theory.* New York: Appleton-Century-Crofts, 1961.

_____. "Operant Methods in Child Behavior and Development." In *Operant Behavior: Areas of Research and Application*, edited by Werner K. Honig, pp. 718–89. New York: Appleton-Century-Crofts, 1966.

Ferster, C. B., and B. F. Skinner. *Schedules of Reinforcement*. New York: Appleton-Century-Crofts, 1957.

Goldiamond, Israel, and Jarl E. Dyrud. "Reading as Operant Behavior." In *The Disabled Reader: Education of the Dyslexic Child*, edited by John Money, pp. 93–115. Baltimore: The Johns Hopkins Press, 1966.

Herrnstein, R. J. "Superstition: A Corollary of the Principles of Operant Conditioning." In *Operant Behavior: Areas of Research and Application*, edited by Werner K. Honig, pp. 33–51. New York: Appleton-Century-Crofts, 1966.

Homme, Lloyd E. "Human Motivation and Environment." In *The Learning Environment: Relationship to Behavior Modification and Implications for Special Education*, Norris G. Haring and Richard J. Whelan, coordinators, pp. 30–39. Symposium sponsored by the School of Education, University of Kansas, 1965. *Kansas Studies in Education*, 16:2 (1966).

Keller, Fred S. *Learning: Reinforcement Theory*. New York: Random House, Inc., 1954.

Lindsley, Odgen R. "Direct Measurement and Prosthesis of Retarded Behavior." *Journal of Education*, 147:1 (1964), pp. 62–81.

Michael, Jack. *Laboratory Studies in Operant Behaviors*. New York: McGraw-Hill Book Company, Inc., 1963.

Pavlov, Ivan Petrovich. *Conditioned Reflexes*. Edited and translated by G. V. Anrep. London: Oxford University Press, 1927.

Premack, David. "Toward Empirical Behavior Laws: 1. Positive Reinforcement." *Psychological Review*, 66 (1959): 219–33.

_____. "Reinforcement Theory." In *Nebraska Symposium on Motivation*, edited by David Levine, pp. 123–80. Lincoln, Nebraska: University of Nebraska Press, 1965.

Reese, Ellen P. *The Analysis of Human Operant Behavior*. Dubuque, Iowa: William C. Brown Company, Publishers, 1966.

Skinner, B. F. *Science and Human Behavior*. New York: The Free Press, 1953.

_____. *Verbal Behavior*. New York: Appleton-Century-Crofts, 1957.

_____. "What is the Experimental Analysis of Behavior?" *Journal of the Experimental Analysis of Behavior*, 9 (1966): 213–18.

Terrace, H. S. "Stimulus Control." In *Operant Behavior: Areas of Research and Application*, edited by Werner K. Honig, pp. 271–344. New York: Appleton-Century-Crofts, 1966.

Warren, A. Bertrand, and Robert H. Brown. "Conditioned Operant Response Phenomena in Children." *The Journal of General Psychology*, 28, second half (1943): 181–207.

Watson, John B., and Rosalie Rayner. "Conditioned Emotional Reactions." *Journal of Experimental Psychology*, 3 (1920): 1–14.

Behavioral research has strongly influenced educational practices for children with such disorders as mental retardation and delinquency. It is now readily acknowledged that the behavior of children and young adults follows fixed laws of behavior which can be applied successfully in classroom settings when systematically administered under structured conditions. Further, it is becoming apparent that these laws can form the basis for establishing functional instructional procedures.

Results of behavioral research have been applied by several prominent investigators. Each program varies in one or several dimensions from the others. The programs described in this chapter have been selected for their uniqueness, either in the types of reinforcement and the system used to apply them or in the types or categories of behavior modified. They should not, however, be regarded as representing a comprehensive survey of programs in which behavior principles are systematically applied.

Token Reinforcement

Some conditions in the environment, such as food and basic comfort, are natural reinforcers. These are *primary reinforcers.* A variety of other conditions become reinforcers after being paired for a while with the presentation of primary reinforcers. These *conditioned reinforcers*—such as activities, objects, and special events and opportunities—can become potent in developing and maintaining behavior.

Conditioned reinforcers are varyingly effective, depending on the individual's degree of satiation or deprivation of them and on the timing of their presentation in relation to behavior. With one form of conditioned reinforcement—token reinforcement—the tokens earned are exchangeable for other items. The strength of a token reinforcement system lies in the attractiveness of the activities for which the tokens can be exchanged. Tokens—anything from actual tokens to plastic disks, stars, or check marks —become effective as conditioned reinforcers to develop and maintain behavior because they are exchangeable for something of value to the student. They can be exchanged for commercial items or for minutes of time to engage in a choice of activities.

The Premack Principle

Homme and his co-workers (Homme et al. 1963) used a different approach in managing the behavior of preschool children. Instead of systematic social reinforcement, they applied the Premack (1959) principle. This principle, which Lovaas (1968) rightly identified as being as old as child-rearing, explains the relationship between any two activities when one is more likely to be chosen than the other. The probability of responding to the less preferred activity can be increased by making the more frequently chosen activity contingent on it.

Applying this principle to the preschool in which they were involved, Homme's group observed that most of the activities the children engaged in, when given the opportunity, were those—like running and screaming— which the instructors sometimes disliked. After the teachers identified the types of tasks they wanted the children to perform, the daily program was arranged to require the children to do each task for a brief period of time. Then a bell sounded and the children were told what activities they were free to engage in, such as running and screaming. Within a short period of time the teachers had no difficulty with classroom management. Other activities found to be of high strength included pushing the investigator around the room in his caster-equipped chair, throwing a cup across the room, and kicking the wastebasket. These became approved behaviors and served to increase the amount of time the children spent doing exactly what the teachers had planned.

Since this early application of the Premack principle, a number of programs have used Homme's example with refinements, especially in the selection of the high-strength activities to be used as reinforcers.

The programs described below incorporate various combinations of the use of token reinforcement, high-strength activities (according to the Premack principle), and social reinforcement from the teacher.

Each program is described according to the type of child taught, the reinforcement system used, the extent of the curriculum, and the measurement procedures used. As a final note of introduction, we should state that the programs described below emanate from the work that B. F. Skinner (1938, 1953, 1957, 1971, in press) began at Harvard University in the early 1930s.

The Management of Emotionally Disturbed Children

The Engineered Classroom

A frequently used program is that designed by Hewett (1967, 1968), who views his educational approach for emotionally disturbed children as "engineered" education. As standards for learning, Hewett identifies certain behaviors such as adequate attention span; appropriate studentlike behavior in the classroom; direction-following; patience within the limits of available time, space, and activity; effective exploration of conditions in the environment; desire for social approval and avoidance of disapproval; self-care; and development of intellectual skills. The teacher is seen as a behavioral engineer who defines task assignments, provides rewards for learning, and maintains a well-defined structure which specifies the limits of acceptable behavior. Hewett considers these responsibilities to be essential for effective teaching.

Hewett's engineered classroom technique, carried out in public school classrooms in Tulare and Santa Monica, California, as well as in the institutionalized setting of the Neuropsychiatric Institute at the University of California at Los Angeles, is divided into three major areas corresponding to a hierarchy of educational tasks. The primary area is the mastery center. Here academic tasks—reading, written language, and arithmetic—are assigned. Every fifteen minutes of the 240-minute day, a new task is given. The second area, the exploratory center, is designed to develop exploratory skills through activities in science, communication, and art. The science section is equipped for activities dealing with electricity, magnetism, basic chemistry, and animal care. The communications area contains a tape recorder, a listening area, simple games for small groups of children, and Morse Code facilities. The third area, the order center, deals with activities requiring attention, active response, and direction-following. Not all areas are necessarily used simultaneously.

Suitable educational tasks are selected from a hierarchy of seven basic tasks; Hewett considers the achievement of five of the seven necessary before formal schooling begins. To reach the final objectives of instruction, Hewett recommends the acceptance and reinforcement of successive approximations. Reinforcement ranges from tangible reinforcers like candy, small toys, and trinkets to the social approval that teachers ordinarily use. Task completion, sensory stimulation, and task accuracy are additional reinforcers.

At the beginning of each day, a record card with roughly 200 ruled squares is handed to each child. Every fifteen minutes, a row of squares is filled in with check marks (to a maximum of ten), according to the child's task accomplishments and classroom conduct. The child is given—

1. two check marks for starting the assignment;
2. three for carrying out the assignment;
3. five possible bonus marks for "being a student."

To provide extra motivation, additional check marks can be given. Check marks are not contingent on specific outputs of work but on behavior that "looks like that of a good student." At the end of each week, record cards are exchangeable for candy, small toys, and trinkets.

At upper levels in the hierarchy, Hewett introduces other types of rewards in the form of activities which are thought to be reinforcing in themselves. These are used as intervention techniques: to stimulate the child to collect a maximum number of check marks, the teacher is directed to intervene with the child when his behavior is inappropriate and to change his assigned tasks so that he will again display good student behavior. The new assignment is always one step down in the hierarchy— i.e., it is easier and possibly of greater interest. Hewett records the child's performance in terms of the percentage of time the child attends to the tasks. He evaluates the effects of the instructional conditions from the changes that occur in the child's mean percentage of attention to tasks under two different conditions.

Hewett's reinforcement procedures are not contingent on specific instances of good performance or behavior, but on general patterns of good behavior. The teacher is directed to use the more reinforcing activities of the exploratory or order center as a technique for interfering with inappropriate behavior in some other area. Hewett does not use the reinforcing strength of activities in one center for increasing performance or student-like behavior in another. Although the design of Hewett's procedures is not as adaptable to individual needs of students as those of some other programs, its strength lies in the identification of specific tasks to be required, the general focus on reinforcement of positive and constructive behavior, and the identification of specific responses to be made by the teacher under specific conditions.

Modification of Autistic Behavior

Currently there are two approaches for modifying the behavior of autistic children. One uses positive reinforcement to increase the output of appropriate behavior (Ferster 1961; Ferster and DeMeyer [DeMyer] 1961, 1962), while the other adds to this the use of aversive consequences for autistic behaviors (Lovaas 1968; Lovaas et al. 1965; Lovaas, Schaeffer, and Simmons 1965). Lovaas and his associates and Ferster and DeMeyer (DeMyer) consider that even the behaviors of autistic children are learned and can be explained in terms of behavior principles. Ferster states that there is no evidence yet that autistic behavior is related to any genetic abnormality.

Several general patterns of behavior typify the autistic child. He has a very limited set of appropriate responses, most of which are simple and repetitive, and these he emits infrequently. The behaviors he emits most often are of the self-stimulating sort. He also has a very specific set of behaviors to which adults are averse—tantrums, self-destructive behavior, and crying occur frequently and are predictably triggered by only slight changes in environmental conditions. These behaviors are also maintained by adults in the environment. Adults in the environment *strongly* condition the tantrums by attending to the child when he screams, cries, etc. They do so to stop the tantrum because it is so aversive to themselves, but in doing so they reinforce the child for producing it in the first place. Thus, it stops temporarily, but the likelihood that it will recur in future is great. Usually, the adult's role in maintaining these behaviors is a surprise to him. In addition, the child is especially characterized by his complete lack of responsiveness to social stimuli.

The approach that Ferster and DeMeyer (DeMyer) use to modify these extremely inappropriate behavior patterns is to increase gradually the child's level of activity by progressively activating his environment. Their procedures have three basic features: first, an objective identification of the child's behavior; second, a description of the types of responses the therapist or teacher will make to the behavior; and third, the reinforcement of small gains in behavior.

Ferster and DeMeyer (DeMyer) establish an environment to which the child's behavior is expected to conform as the environmental conditions slowly change. They compare these procedures to the gradual process of normal growth and development. The activities used in their program at Indiana University Medical Center (Ferster and DeMeyer 1962) include identifying letters of the alphabet, working in an experimental environment for a later opportunity to swim or play outside as delayed reinforcers, and other types of complex behavior.

The first objective is to sustain some very simple but appropriate behavior and then gradually to evoke a more complex set of responses. For example, their behavior modification procedures conducted under experimental control in a laboratory setting first required the child to press a button (response key). When this response was well established, the child was required to press a window panel on a teaching machine to match one stimulus with another. Ferster's later work in a nursery school setting (in press, 1971) concentrated on *shaping* behaviors specified as appropriate for the setting.

In his early work with autistic children, Ferster used an experimental room furnished with a variety of devices that could be automated by a coin dropped in a slot. The devices included a television set, a pinball machine, a food and trinket vendor, a phonograph, a color wheel, a picture viewer, a telephone set, a set of electric trains, an electric organ, a trained animal, and an eight-column vending machine. Each child spent from 60 to 180 minutes in this room depressing a response key on a coin dispenser. Later the child worked on a match-to-sample machine, which required him to match a sample item with its counterpart. He was reinforced for these responses with coins first on a fixed ratio and then on a variable schedule. He could spend the coins in one or more of the devices available. The objective, moving each child to the point where he was continually active, was accomplished by reinforcing him for responding appropriately to the equipment. Response data, automatically collected and recorded as the child responded, showed that the procedures accomplished the objective.

Ferster's later project (in press, 1971) at Linwood Children's Center with Jeanne Simons was directed at developing in a preschool setting "normal" social behavior for that stage of growth and development. *Shaping* was the basic procedure used to modify the behavior patterns of these autistic children. The clinician placed limits on their behavior, used procedures of differential reinforcement and extinction, and gave or withheld reinforcers like food, attention, automobile rides, and toys. The shaping procedures required the clinician's or therapist's behavior to be exactly contingent on each child's responses, with the added requirement that the response expectations be slightly increased as each reinforcement cumulatively changed the child's behavior. To accomplish these changes, the therapist also manipulated conditions which occurred prior to the child's response, introduced conditions to prevent the occurrence of undesirable behavior, and was careful to avoid reinforcing undesirable behavior when it did occur. When a skillful manager applies these shaping procedures, dramatic changes in behavior may occur.

Lovaas defines his total modification effort as educational, likening it to programmed learning in slow motion. His approach is to engineer a child's activities in speech, play, and the handling of affection, and in intellectual skills like reading and writing. His treatment program has two major features: the identification of conditions that build complex behaviors and the identification of those that give social stimuli the strength of reinforcers. Consequences are manipulated in three ways: with food instead of social reinforcement, with social reinforcers, and with electric shock as an aversive stimulus.

Lovaas uses two types of procedures to develop social reinforcers. First, by pairing social stimuli with food, he encourages the child to respond to the social stimuli—something that autistic children usually do not do. Once the child is conditioned to respond to social stimuli paired with food, the social stimuli can be used as reinforcers to maintain the strength of other behaviors.

His second procedure for developing social reinforcers is based on the fact that any event paired with pain reduction gains the strength of a positive reinforcer. For example, the parent or teacher who aids the autistic child becomes a positive reinforcer. To induce anxiety in the child (Lovaas considers all autistic children deficient in this emotion), he has the child stand in a room equipped with an electrified floor. The child is given a painful electric shock which is stopped when he seeks the company of the attending adult. Results from this procedure show that the persons the child turns to during the shock do become positive social reinforcers. In addition, these children generally increase their physical contact with the attending adults. The nursing staff of the Neuropsychiatric Institute at U.C.L.A. noted that these children not only become more responsive to adults but also seek more affection and become more dependent. During "successful shock avoidance training," these children also appear happy and smile for what is often thought to be the first time.

The third conditioning procedure used by Lovaas and his co-workers takes advantage of the reinforcing strength of play behavior to increase other desirable behavior such as appropriate speech. The investigation of games like chasing or hide-and-seek suggests that these are powerful reinforcers for children.

Summarizing the results of the procedures, Lovaas found that—

1. self-destructive behavior can be extinguished by withdrawing interpersonal contact contingent on its emission;
2. self-destructive and tantrum behavior can be extinguished by the use of painful electric shock contingent on its emission;
3. echolalic speech is decreased and appropriate speech is increased when adult attention is presented only for appropriate speech;

4. appropriate social and verbal behavior seems to exist in an inverse ratio to self-destructive behavior and psychotic speech because, when appropriate behavior begins to strengthen under reinforcement, inappropriate behavior decreases without any direct application of reinforcement techniques.

The Management of
Social Behavior

Working with Preschool Children

Behavior modification procedures for preschoolers have been designed by Florence Harris and her associates (Harris, Wolf, and Baer 1964) at the Developmental Psychology Laboratory at the University of Washington. This group concentrated on the development of normal preschool behaviors, primarily social in nature, through the appropriate use of social reinforcement by adults and peers. They designed their procedures to eliminate crying not due to pain, tantrums (Hart et al. 1964), regressed crawling (Harris et al. 1964), isolate play (Allen et al. 1964), excessive aggression, too much or too little interaction with teacher or peers, and ineffective communication. The basic design for extinguishing such behavior is to withhold adult and peer social reinforcement when a child with a pattern of these undesirable responses exhibits any one of them. It also includes procedures for providing peer or adult attention for the converse of the inappropriate behaviors. When the child plays cooperatively with his peers, interacts appropriately with his teacher or peers, or communicates verbally or by gesture in line with his level of skill, social reinforcement is lavishly given.

The child's progress is measured by the percentage of time during each session that he exhibits inappropriate and appropriate behavior under conditions where social reinforcement is administered incorrectly (before modification) and correctly (during modification). To obtain this percentage measurement, observers record the presence or absence of the behavior during each successive ten-second interval of the session.

These modification procedures, characterized by their emphasis on adult and peer social reinforcement to build preschool social behavior, are also characterized by a reversal control technique to demonstrate that they actually do manipulate the reinforcing condition that is responsible for the child's change in behavior. For example, one investigation (Allen 1967) concerned two young girls with normal speech repertoires but very low rates of initiated verbalization. Procedures for modifying this behavior entailed the collection of several weeks of response data on the frequency of speech directed to self, to teachers, and to other children. Speech directed to self occurred with the highest frequency. The teachers then began giving warm and intensive social reinforcement to either child every time she spoke to a teacher. This technique sharply increased the rates of talking to the teachers. In the second phase of the modification procedure, the teacher gave attention to each girl, not only when she talked to a teacher, but also whenever she talked to another child. The rate of talking to other children did accelerate, but not as dramatically, while the rate of talking to teachers remained high. During a *reversal period*, the teachers changed their pattern of reinforcement, providing attention to each girl only when she was not talking. This change reversed the girls' patterns of response: a low rate of talking to the teacher and to other children returned. In the third phase of the procedure, the teachers again provided social reinforcement for speaking to a teacher but no reinforcement for speaking to other children, a change in conditions that reestablished the original modification pattern.

These research studies demonstrate that adult and peer social reinforcement effectively maintains either desirable or undesirable behavior, depending on the behavior to which it is applied.

**Working with Children with
Developmental Deficits**

Spradlin and his co-workers (Girardeau and Spradlin 1964; Lent 1965) developed a token reinforcement system in a cottage program for mentally retarded adolescent girls. Contingency management was directed primarily at the development of social behavior rather than academic skills. In this program, the social behaviors that should be developed were identified and broken down into components which could be reinforced as successive approximations to the specified terminal social behavior.

Behaviors were classified as those to be decreased (negative behaviors) or accelerated (positive behaviors). Negative behaviors included talking and laughing while working, nonverbal play while working, other nonproductive behavior during work time, defiance of authority, unmannerliness, and grossly immature behavior. These general categories of behavior were also defined by the investigators in terms that enabled any observer to identify the occurrence of a unit of any particular one.

Reinforcement was provided in accordance with the following guidelines:

1. Positive reinforcement was given immediately following a specified desirable behavior or an approximation of it.
2. Positive reinforcement was presented on a continuous schedule while the behavior was being acquired and intermittently when the behavior needed only to be maintained.
3. The reinforcer was used in large amounts at first, but once the behavior was acquired, the amount was gradually reduced.
4. Slight approximations to terminal behavior were amply rewarded until more complex chains of response were developed.
5. To effect its extinction, undesirable behavior was ignored.
6. Reinforcement scheduling was individualized.

Reinforcement was provided by a token system using nonnegotiable coins exchangeable for items like candy, gum, fruit, soda pop, hair clips, perfume, lipstick, jewelry, lace underwear, crayons, and paper. These items were displayed in a school store. Each token coin was equivalent to one cent to be spent on items priced at retail value. Equipment could be rented, but the rental cost was determined for each girl on the basis of her performance.

Tasks receiving reinforcement included: bedmaking and other housekeeping duties; proper showering, shoe-shining and other grooming tasks; group play for thirty minutes; coloring and other school readiness activities; punctuality in arriving at work or speech therapy sessions; and the generally proper use of a twenty-minute period of leisure time. A pay scale indicated the worth of each task, the value varying from one to five tokens.

The program began with a three-month observation period of the girls' patterns of behavior, after which the token reinforcement system was introduced. Token reinforcement was given to each girl for correct responses during daily activities for a ten-day period, after which the pay scale for tasks was set up. This scale was intended only as a guideline, because emphasis was on behavioral improvement and not on task completion without improvement. The introduction of token reinforcement caused only one difficulty: the girls became motivated to respond to more tasks than were available. Because the staff could not set up more homemaking tasks, school tasks were added to satisfy the girls' motivation to work.

As the number of available tasks increased, the girls began to earn more tokens. They also began to save them toward the purchase of more expensive items. The use of token reinforcement spread to the management of problems confronted by the speech therapists, educators, and recreation personnel who periodically worked with these girls. The directors of the program considered the expense negligible when compared to the total cost of the program per child per year.

Academic Behavior

Working with Children Who Have
Developmental Deficits

Behavior modification has also been used to increase the rates of academic performance among children with developmental deficits. The development of the Programmed Learning Classroom (Birnbrauer et al. 1965) at Rainier School, a facility for mentally retarded children in Buckley, Washington, was greatly influenced by the work of Sidney Bijou (1966). The program was designed to help mentally retarded children acquire academic skills, good study habits, and the social conduct necessary for academic learning. The children, most of whom were in residence, were from eight to fourteen years of age.

The token system used depended on marks made by the teacher in three-page booklets belonging to each child. Marks were given for correct academic responses and appropriate social behavior in the classroom. One mark was given for each correct response, ten extra marks were given for error-free assignments, and bonus points were awarded for cooperation or some extra effort. The child's progress was evaluated according to the number of items he completed on tasks, his percentage of error, and the duration of the session spent in "time-out." Systematic procedures were used for counting these responses, for correcting errors, and for managing misbehavior that was too disruptive.

The classroom contained four sections:

1. a work area with six desks, three writing tables, and two all-purpose tables;
2. three private study areas for individualized presentation, especially of auditory stimuli;
3. a time-out area;
4. an observation area.

All instruction in reading, writing, and arithmetic was individualized, using materials that were prepared by the teacher according to programming principles. Each child had classroom instruction for one to two hours daily.

The token system produced significant changes in the academic and social behavior of these children and was extended to other areas of daily activity for some of them. The program has been a model for surrounding school districts and institutions, demonstrating the extent of skill development possible for mentally retarded children in a properly programmed environment.

The foregoing studies demonstrate the application of behavior principles in different settings. With each type of application, significant changes in performance have been observed. Each program, except possibly that of Lovaas, includes at least some approximation of token reinforcement. For example, Hewett's use of a record card and check marks redeemable for commercial items is a type of token reinforcement. However, his program emphasizes changes in antecedent conditions and the development of what he identifies as good student behavior. The program at the Developmental Psychology Laboratory for preschool children, even with its strong emphasis on the application of social reinforcement, has also used token reinforcement occasionally to modify behavior.

Research on Classroom Behavior

The final portion of this chapter on research is devoted to several recent studies which have been conducted in regular school classrooms for children at different age levels. It is their application to "normal" children that distinguishes them from most research, which necessarily concentrates on children with special problems and deficits. For instance, there is an abundance of research on children with physical handicaps, learning deficits, and economic or social disadvantages. While the teacher of "normal" children in a regular public school faces, in less intense form, some of the same problems that the teacher of exceptional children does—disruptive behavior, variable rates of learning ability, inattention—the applicability to the regular classroom of research on exceptional children is frequently limited. The studies that follow demonstrate the usefulness of several kinds of reinforcement applied systematically in the regular classroom to improve academic performance and reduce asocial, disruptive, or inattentive behavior.

One of the most frustrating problems that the average urban public school teacher has to deal with is disruptive classroom behavior. Children push one another, talk out of turn, throw objects—the list could go on and on, for students from kindergarten through high school are quick to sense when the teacher is not in control, and the variety of disruptive behaviors that children can exhibit is limited only by their imagination. Given the opportunity, even one or two disruptive children can turn a classroom into bedlam, making it impossible for the teacher to teach or for students to work, even if they want to.

Earlier we pointed out that attention to appropriate behavior not only tends to reinforce that behavior but often results in a decrease of inappropriate behavior, simply because the latter is incompatible with the former. Thomas, Becker, and Armstrong (1968) demonstrated that disruptive classroom behavior can not only be eliminated but can also be produced contingent on the teacher's behavior. They investigated the effects of the teacher's behavior on children's classroom behavior by systematically varying approving categories of teacher behavior (praise, smiles, and contacts) and disapproving ones (verbal reprimands, physical restraint). The study involved a middle-primary public school class of twenty-eight children. Both teacher and child behaviors were measured; a sample of ten children was observed each day. Data showed that approving responses from the teacher served a positively reinforcing function in maintaining appropriate classroom behavior, whereas disruptive behavior increased each time approving teacher behavior was withdrawn. When the amount of the teacher's disapproving behavior was tripled, disruptive behavior increased, particularly in the gross motor and noise-making categories. The authors point out that although a teacher's display of approval to reinforce good student behavior generally results in an increase in the frequency and duration of appropriate behavior, teachers must be careful to avoid attending to inappropriate behavior. The teacher who "cuddles the miscreant, tries pleasantly to get a child to stop behaving disruptively, talks with a child so that he 'understands' what he was doing wrong, or who pleasantly suggests an alternate activity to a child who has been performing inappropriately is likely to find an increase in the very behavior he had hoped to reduce" (p. 44).

Occasionally, a teacher's repertoire of social reinforcers is inadequate to make such reinforcement successful. In such cases, some other workable reinforcer that is available in the classroom must be found. Barrish, Saunders, and Wolf (1969) report the use of a very simple technique for reducing disruptive classroom behavior. Their study was carried out in a fourth-grade public school classroom of twenty-four students. Of these, seven had been referred to the principal several times because of their disruptive behavior, and the principal realized that the classroom had a general behavior problem.

Baseline rates of inappropriate behaviors were obtained, and two types of behavior—out-of-seat and talking-out—were selected for modification. During the daily math period, the class was divided into two teams in order to play a game. The teacher explained the game to the students, emphasizing that each out-of-seat or talking-out response by any student would result in a mark on the blackboard for that student's team and a possible loss of privileges for all members of the team. Whichever team received the lower number of marks would win the game and receive certain privileges. Privileges were events available in any classroom, such as extra recess, first turn to line up for lunch time, stars, and name tags. Not only would privileges function as reinforcers; the very act of winning would itself be reinforcing.

The individual contingencies for group consequences were successfully applied first during a math period and then during a reading period. The authors noted that "the program was apparently popular with students and school officials. Every professional involved in the study . . . stated that in general the students seemed to enjoy playing the game. The teacher stated that some students went so far as to request that the game be played every period" (p. 123).

Token reinforcement is another effective procedure in overcoming disruptive behavior. An investigation of the effects of a token reinforcement program on disruptive behavior in a public school classroom was undertaken by O'Leary, Becker, Evans, and Saudargas (1969). The study had three objectives: (a) to analyze the separate effects of classroom rules, educational structure, teacher praise, and a token reinforcement program on children's disruptive behavior; (b) to determine whether a token reinforcement program used only in the afternoon had any effect on the children's behavior in the morning; (c) to examine the extent to which the effects of the token reinforcement program persisted when token reinforcement was discontinued. Seven members of a second-grade class of twenty-one children from lower middle-class homes were selected for study because they exhibited a great deal of undesirable behavior.

Rules, educational structure, and the praising of appropriate behavior while ignoring disruptive behavior were introduced successively, but none of the procedures consistently reduced disruptive behavior. However, a combination of them nearly eliminated the disruptive behavior of one child. When the token reinforcement program was introduced, the frequency of disruptive behavior declined in five of the six remaining children. The withdrawal of token reinforcement increased the disruptive behavior of these five children, and its reinstatement reduced the disruptive behavior of four of them. Data indicated that although rules, educational structure, and "praising and ignoring" had no consistent effects on behavior, token reinforcement was definitely associated with a reduction of disruptive behavior. Increased attendance also seemed to be associated with the token reinforcement phases, and improved academic achievement during the year may possibly have been related to token reinforcement. Token reinforcement was administered only during the two-hour afternoon period, and data showed that the decrease of disruptive behavior in the afternoon session did not generalize to the morning session. Commenting on this aspect of the study, the authors emphasize that " 'generalization' is no magical process, but rather a behavioral change which must be engineered like any other change" (p. 13).

School teachers, particularly those who teach in urban schools, are constantly faced with the problem of how to get children to pay attention in order that they may learn. If the student responds appropriately, the teacher assumes that he has been attending. Packard (1970) developed and examined a simple, economical, and reliable method by which a teacher can increase those behaviors he considers attentive by applying group contingencies for a whole class. Cumulative time measures of classroom attention were taken of four elementary classes: kindergarten, thirty-two children; third grade, thirty-four children; fifth grade, twenty-five children; and sixth grade, thirty children. Measures were also taken for sixteen randomly chosen students in these same classes. Each class was considered an individual responding organism. Base rates showed considerable variation. Explicit instructions regarding student attention produced a temporary increase in attention for some students and for some grades. However, group contingencies, which required the attention of every student in the class, and token reinforcement for class achievement of a gradually increasing criterion of attention raised group measures to a consistent 70–85 percent level of "time attending to task as instructed" and raised individual student measures to a stable 90–100 percent level. Reversals and other data demonstrate that the elementary teacher can obtain the maximum attending behavior from all students in the class by providing contingent reinforcement for the class as a whole.

Closely linked to the problem of attention is that of study behavior. Hall, Lund, and Jackson (1968) investigated the effects of making the attention of the teacher contingent on children's study behavior. Studies were carried out in classrooms of two elementary schools whose students came from the most economically deprived section of the city.

Individual rates of study were recorded for one first-grader and five third-graders who had high rates of disruptive or dawdling behavior. The behavior included, among many other things, rolling pencils on the floor, chewing and licking pages of books, blowing bubbles and making noises while drinking milk, punching holes in the milk cartons so that milk would run out on the desk, and the more usual out-of-seat and talking-out types of behavior. A reinforcement period, in which study behavior was reinforced by the teacher's attention while non-study behavior was ignored, resulted in sharply increased study rates. A brief reversal of the contingency, in which attention was given only after periods of non-study behavior, brought back low rates of study. Reinstatement of the teacher's attention contingent on study again markedly increased study behavior. The investigation is important, for it demonstrates how effective appropriate behavior on the part of the teacher can be in developing desirable classroom behavior.

Ultimately, the teacher's task is to increase the academic performance of his students. The students are supposed to learn enough so that by the end of the term they can progress to the next class. The study reported by Lovitt, Guppy, and Blattner (1969) used a free-time contingency to increase the spelling accuracy of students. A public school classroom of thirty-two fourth-graders provided the setting for the study. Spelling performance was assessed under three conditions: (a) when traditional procedures were in effect; (b) when contingent free time was individually arranged; and (c) when a group contingency, listening to the radio, was added to the individual free-time contingency. As a result of the contingencies, the majority of the pupils increased their spelling performances, demonstrating that contingent free time and radio-listening were effective reinforcers.

Even students who have no performance problems can be motivated to improve their performances by receiving reinforcement. In Glynn's (1970) investigation of the effects of different treatments of token reinforcement—self-determined, experimenter-determined, and chance-determined token reinforcement—each was compared with nonreinforcement for its effectiveness in improving the learning of history and geography materials in the classroom. Four classes of ninth-grade girls, a total of 128 students, served as subjects. The girls had been assigned to the classes alphabetically, so that each class represented a heterogeneous group. Self-determined reinforcement used in one class proved as effective as experimenter-determined reinforcement in another for improving academic performance. Even after token reinforcement was withdrawn, performance in these two classes remained slightly superior to that of the nonreinforced class. Throughout the study, performance in the chance-reinforced class remained below that of the nonreinforced class.

Orme and Purnell (1970) applied operant procedures to an out-of-control public school classroom. Teachers who are about to throw up their hands in despair because of the apparent impossibility of controlling their classrooms may take heart after reviewing this study.

The purpose of the investigation was to adapt behavior modification procedures so that they could eventually be used by a single teacher working in a regular classroom. The subjects were eighteen pupils in a combined third- and fourth-grade classroom in an urban elementary school. The regular teacher (T_1) and the intern teacher (T_2) shared morning teaching duties and agreed that most of the behavior in the classroom was disruptive—impulsive, aggressive, and destructive.

The classroom was divided into two smaller rooms in an attempt to establish "total" milieu control in one room (Room B) through conditioning and modeling procedures. Experimental conditions were organized so that desirable changes in pupil behavior could be expected to *transfer* to Room A. The testing of this transfer-of-control hypothesis constituted one of the basic experimental aims of the study.

The six-week study involved a program of earned reinforcement and teacher-training (including training in the manipulation of surrounding conditions and curriculum variables). It also made use of videotapes for both training and subsequent measurement and analysis.

Following an initial week of pretreatment observation, pupils were randomly divided into two sections, each of which was assigned to Room B on alternate mornings. Room B was transformed into a highly desirable environment, and after the first week each student's entry into it was contingent on points he had earned in Room A. Once admitted to Room B, pupils could earn points to be spent on candy, balloons, comics, math puzzles, a "conversation" with a computer, and other reinforcers from the "store" located there. These tangible reinforcers were used because of the strength and frequency of the pupils' disruptive behavior and the teachers' lack of social reinforcement value in the classroom. Except for the edibles and small trinkets, which were included because the teachers felt students might respond only to these, all reinforcers were selected for their value in supplementing the regular curriculum. The students responded enthusiastically to the latter and were given an opportunity to determine portions of their own curricula by earning time.

The systematic application of teaching techniques designed to evoke and reinforce specific forms of social and academic behavior incompatible with disruptive activities led to a relatively stable and desirable modification of the disruptive behavior.

Several important factors contribute to the uniqueness of the study. First, the experiment involved the simultaneous manipulation of a great number of variables; these concerned curriculum, teacher-training, contingencies (both teacher-managed and self-imposed), a "menu" listing the reinforcers available, the "store," the taking of data, and classroom arrangement. Second, the contingencies chosen were not contrived reinforcers but those available to any public school classroom. The imaginative selection of contingent reinforcers made them desirable to the students, but their selection was governed by the teachers' desire to broaden the curriculum. For example, putting together a model plane could lead to a discussion on the laws of physics. Finally, although the study was carried out by two teachers, it was designed for, and could easily be adapted for use by, only one teacher in an ordinary public school classroom.

Many other investigators have been successful in using behavior modification procedures. Lack of space precludes a discussion of all the studies here, but mention should be made of several concerning delinquents (Burchard and Tyler 1965; Tyler and Brown 1967), parents (Patterson and Reid 1970); teachers (Thomas, Becker, and Armstrong 1968; Becker et al. 1967; Haring and Lovitt 1969), and college students (Raygor, Wark, and Warren 1966).

Summary

Our intent in this chapter has been to show the powerful effects that can be achieved when projects involving behavior intervention are systematically planned. Critical to behavior management in the classroom and in the home is the establishment of the relationship between the behavior and its consequences. The precise specification of the conditions which will prevail, the specification of the contingency that exists, and the careful and precise management of this contingency based on reliable records of the behavior are essential. Studies have demonstrated beyond a doubt that with these essential elements, intervention can be effective. Extremely difficult behavior patterns established by children over a period of time can be reversed in a positive, productive direction when conditions for changing behavior have been well planned and systematically carried out.

The principles of behavior are not based on theory alone; they are the outgrowth of experimental studies carried out in the laboratory setting and in the classroom. Their successful application requires that the procedures for their implementation be adapted to the requirements of the setting and that they be administered precisely and systematically.

Continuous response data are essential if the need for precision is to be met. The teacher who wants to implement a program of behavior modification must have ongoing data on the children's responses in order to know whether his procedures are effective.

Eventually, the teacher will assume the role of behavior manager. Not only will he be the source of instruction, direction, and information, but he will manage the contingencies on his students' performances as well.

Good teaching—good management—is based on principles of behavior modification. The studies described here serve to demonstrate the validity of this statement. They are only a few of the rapidly growing number of research projects which attest to the successful application of behavior principles in the management of behavior.

References

Allen, K. Eileen. "The Strengthening of Adjustive Behaviors through Systematic Application of Reinforcement Procedures." In *1967 International Convocation on Children and Young Adults with Learning Disabilities Proceedings*. Pittsburgh: Home for Crippled Children 1967, pp. 351–71.

Allen, K. Eileen, Betty Hart, Joan S. Buell, Florence R. Harris, and Montrose M. Wolf. "Effects of Social Reinforcement on Isolate Behavior of a Nursery School Child." *Child Development*, **35** (1964): 511–18.

Barrish, Harriet H., Muriel Saunders, and Montrose M. Wolf. "Good Behavior Game: Effects of Individual Contingencies for Group Consequences on Disruptive Behavior in a Classroom." *Journal of Applied Behavior Analysis*, **2** (1969): 119–24.

Becker, Wesley C., Charles H. Madsen, Jr., Carole Revele Arnold, and Don R.

Thomas. "The Contingent Use of Teacher Attention and Praise in Reducing Classroom Behavior Problems." *The Journal of Special Education,* 1 (1967): 287–307.

Bijou, Sidney W. "Application of Experimental Analysis of Behavior Principles in Teaching Academic Tool Subjects to Retarded Children." In *The Learning Environment: Relationship to Behavior Modification and Implications for Special Education,* coordinators, Norris G. Haring and Richard J. Whelan. Symposium sponsored by the School of Education, University of Kansas, 1965. *Kansas Studies in Education,* 16:2 (1966): 16–23.

Birnbrauer, J. S., M. M. Wolf, J. D. Kidder, and Cecilia E. Tague. "Classroom Behavior of Retarded Pupils with Token Reinforcement." *Journal of Experimental Child Psychology,* 2 (1965): 219–35.

Burchard, John, and Vernon Tyler, Jr. "The Modification of Delinquent Behaviour through Operant Conditioning." *Behaviour Research and Therapy,* 2 (1965): 245–50.

Ferster, C. B. "Positive Reinforcement and Behavioral Deficits of Autistic Children." *Child Development,* 32 (1961): 437–56.

_____. "Operant Reinforcement of Infantile Autism." In *The Improvement of Instructions,* edited by Norris G. Haring and Alice H. Hayden. Seattle: Special Child Publications, Inc., in press, 1971. (Reprinted from *An Evaluation of the Results of the Psychotherapies* by Stanley Lesse. Springfield, Ill.: Charles C Thomas, Publisher, 1968.)

Ferster, C. B., and Marian K. DeMeyer. "The Development of Performances in Autistic Children in an Automatically Controlled Environment." *Journal of Chronic Diseases,* 13 (1961): 312–45.

Ferster, C. B., and Marian K. DeMyer. "A Method for the Experimental Analysis of the Behavior of Autistic Children." *American Journal of Orthopsychiatry,* 32 (1962): 89–98.

Girardeau, Frederic L., and Joseph E. Spradlin. "Token Rewards in a Cottage Program." *Mental Retardation,* 2 (1964): 345–51.

Glynn, E. L. "Classroom Applications of Self-determined Reinforcement." *Journal of Applied Behavior Analysis,* 3 (1970): 123–32.

Hall, R. Vance, Diane Lund, and Deloris Jackson. "Effects of Teacher Attention on Study Behavior." *Journal of Applied Behavior Analysis,* 1 (1968): 1–12.

Haring, Norris G., and Lovitt, T. C. *The Application of Functional Analysis of Behavior by Teachers in a Natural School Setting.* Final Report, Grant No. OEG-0-8070376-1857 (032), U.S. Department of Health, Education, and Welfare, Office of Education, Bureau of Research. Washington, D.C., November, 1969.

Harris, Florence R., Margaret K. Johnston, C. Susan Kelley, and Montrose M. Wolf. "Effects of Positive Social Reinforcement on Regressed Crawling of a Preschool Child." *Journal of Educational Psychology,* 55 (1964): 35–41.

Harris, Florence R., Montrose M. Wolf, and Donald M. Baer. "Effects of Adult Social Reinforcement on Child Behavior." *Young Children,* 20 (1964): 8–17.

Hart, Betty M., K. Eileen Allen, Joan S. Buell, Florence R. Harris, and Montrose M. Wolf. "Effects of Social Reinforcement on Operant Crying." *Journal of Experimental Child Psychology,* 1 (1964): 145–53.

Hewett, Frank M. "Educational Engineering with Emotionally Disturbed Children." *Exceptional Children,* 33 (1967): 159-67.

_____. *The Emotionally Disturbed Child in the Classroom: A Developmental Strategy for Educating Children with Maladaptive Behavior.* Boston: Allyn & Bacon, Inc., 1968.

Homme, L. E., P. C. deBaca, J. V. Devine, R. Steinhorst, and E. J. Rickert. "Use of the Premack Principle in Controlling the Behavior of Nursery School Children." *Journal of the Experimental Analysis of Behavior,* 6 (1963): 544.

Lent, J. R. "The Application of Operant Procedures in the Modification of Behavior of Retarded Children in a Free Social Situation." (Paper presented at the American Association for the Advancement of Science Annual Meeting, Berkeley, California, December, 1965.)

Lovaas, O. Ivar. "Some Studies on the Treatment of Childhood Schizophrenia." In *Conference on Research in Psychotherapy,* Vol. 3., edited by J. M. Shlien, pp. 103-21. Washington, D.C.: American Psychological Association, 1968.

Lovaas, O. Ivar, Gilbert Freitag, Vivien J. Gold, and Irene C. Kassorla. "Experimental Studies in Childhood Schizophrenia: Analysis of Self-Destructive Behavior." *Journal of Experimental Child Psychology,* 2 (1965): 67-84.

Lovaas, O. Ivar, Benson Schaeffer, and James Q. Simmons. "Building Social Behavior in Autistic Children by Use of Electric Shock." *Journal of Experimental Research in Personality,* 1 (1965): 99-109.

Lovitt, Thomas C., Tal E. Guppy, and James E. Blattner. "The Use of a Free-time Contingency with Fourth Graders to Increase Spelling Accuracy." *Behaviour Research and Therapy,* 7 (1969): 151-56.

O'Leary, K. Daniel, Wesley C. Becker, Michael B. Evans, and Richard A. Saudargas. "A Token Reinforcement Program in a Public School: A Replication and Systematic Analysis." *Journal of Applied Behavior Analysis,* 2 (1969): 3-13.

Orme, Michael E. J., and Richard F. Purnell. "Behavior Modification and Transfer in an Out-of-Control Classroom." In *Behavior Modification in the Classroom,* edited by George A. Fargo, Charlene Behrns, and Patricia Nolen, pp. 116-138. Belmont, Calif.: Wadsworth Publishing Company, Inc., 1970.

Packard, Robert G. "The Control of 'Classroom Attention': A Group Contingency for Complex Behavior." *Journal of Applied Behavior Analysis,* 3 (1970): 13-28.

Patterson, G. R., and J. B. Reid. "Reciprocity and Coercion: Two Facets of Social Systems." In *Behavior Modification in Clinical Psychology,* edited by C. Neuringer and J. L. Michael. New York: Appleton-Century-Crofts, 1970.

Premack, David. "Toward Empirical Behavior Laws: 1. Positive Reinforcement." *Psychological Review,* 66 (1959): 219-33.

Raygor, Alton L., David M. Wark, and Ann Dell Warren. "Operant Conditioning of Reading Rate: The Effect of a Secondary Reinforcer." *Journal of Reading,* 9 (1966): 147-56.

Skinner, B. F. *The Behavior of Organisms: An Experimental Analysis.* New York: Appleton-Century-Crofts, 1938.

_____. *Science and Human Behavior.* New York: The Free Press, 1953.

_____. *Verbal Behavior.* New York: Appleton-Century-Crofts, 1957.

—————. "Teaching: The Arrangement of Contingencies under which Something is Taught." In *The Improvement of Instruction*, edited by Norris G. Haring and Alice H. Hayden. Seattle: Special Child Publications, Inc., in press, 1971.

Thomas, Don R., Wesley C. Becker, and Marianne Armstrong. "Production and Elimination of Disruptive Classroom Behavior by Systematically Varying Teacher's Behavior." *Journal of Applied Behavior Analysis*, 1 (1968): 35–45.

Tyler, Vernon O., Jr., and G. Duane Brown. "The Use of Swift, Brief Isolation as a Group Control Device for Institutionalized Delinquents." *Behaviour Research and Therapy*, 5 (1967): 1–9.

When a new child enters the classroom, the teacher is confronted with an unknown entity. After Gene has walked into the room and the teacher has said "Hello," what does she do? How will Gene fit into the classroom environment? What does he know and what does he need to learn? Every teacher is faced with a classroom full of Genes and Jeanettes, all of whom must be taught. The teacher should know how the environment of the classroom will affect each child and under what conditions each will learn best. The process of evaluating the relationship between classroom conditions (stimuli) and a child's behavior (responses) is *behavior analysis*. Essentially, behavior analysis tells the teacher where the child is in the learning process, what classroom conditions affect his behavior, and what the terminal objectives for him should be.

Behavior analysis is probably best explained by describing its three basic steps: (a) direct observation of the child's responses, (b) continuous measurement of those responses, and (c) systematic changes in the environment. In an analysis of behavior, the independent (environmental) variables and the dependent (behavioral) variables are carefully defined and their relationship is established. New independent variables are introduced under carefully controlled conditions, and their effect on the dependent variables is determined on the basis of changes in the rate of response.

The behavior which is to be observed must be precisely defined in terms of movement cycles. Examples of observable behavior are: sitting in a seat, lifting a desk top, reaching for a book, turning pages, writing letters or numbers, reading words orally, and whispering to a neighbor. All of these are responses. They can be further identified as desirable or undesirable, appropriate or inappropriate, and as responses which should be increased, decreased, maintained, or eliminated.

Measurement

The rate of the response is what determines the conditions the teacher will set up to change a child's behavior. Measurement of behavior is the critical factor in teaching. It provides essential information concerning placement of the child in the classroom and prompts the choice of those conditions which will be most effective in modifying the child's behavior and performance, directing it toward terminal objectives. Continuous measurement is the process whereby the child's responses to selected stimuli are measured over a period of time. This data-collecting process requires that the behavior be defined and then measured in terms of rate or duration of response. For instance, a child who is exhibiting out-of-seat behavior can be observed in at least two ways: how often in a given block of time he is out of his seat and for what length of time he exhibits this behavior.

All observable responses can be counted. For example, over a period of specified duration, the teacher can count the number of times the child writes letters or numerals correctly or incorrectly in his programmed reading and math materials. Or a count can be made of the number of problems completed, comprehension questions answered, words read or spelled, or pages read. When such a count is totaled and recorded, a behavioral measurement per unit of time has been obtained. From the recorded data, the response rate for each session can be calculated and plotted on a graph.

An example of when it would be more appropriate to measure the duration of a response rather than its rate would be when a physical therapist is working on certain areas of a child's muscular development. As the child develops greater control, he will be able to hold a muscle position for longer periods of time. Consequently, the response will decrease in rate of occurrence as the cycle of movement extends over longer periods. With this type of response, duration is the important indication of progress. Similarly, if the terminal objective is to have Andrew sit in his seat for ten minutes, then duration of in-seat behavior is the important factor.

Criterion behaviors (successive approximations of terminal objectives) can be measured to determine the child's stage of development. When the child achieves a high, stable, error-free response rate for a particular behavior, it can be said that he has mastered that behavior. Once a child has achieved the terminal objective through such mastery, there is no further need to obtain data, unless some change occurs.

Baseline

All procedures of behavior analysis, whether for assessment of skills or classroom instruction, begin with a baseline measurement of performance. This is the initial measurement of a behavior under a stable set of conditions. However, for response measurement to be useful, the conditions under which it is conducted must be well defined. Before a baseline measurement of performance can be taken, the response to be measured must be precisely specified, the response of the teacher must be exactly determined, and the materials to which the child will respond must be planned so as to require equal response units. The independent variables must also be carefully planned and specified. Once these conditions have been met, observation and recording of the child's responses can begin. When taking the baseline measurement, the teacher manipulates nothing; he only observes and records.

The teacher must remember that his attention as a social reinforcer can significantly influence behavior and must therefore be held constant. Thus, if he is taking a baseline measurement of José's hitting behavior, he must make sure that his responses (i.e., his instructions and comments) remain the same during each day of the baseline period. If he has always reprimanded José in the past, he must continue to do so after every incident, and he must record every incident. In addition, he must hold other conditions of the classroom constant. When he has determined that José hits other children on an average of two times an hour over a number of days, he has a baseline measurement.

If academic performance is to be assessed, the material to which the child responds must require the same type of response (such as writing numbers) as will be required in the program to be set up for him. Thus, if the teacher wants to know the complexity of the child's responses to addition problems, the child can be given problems ranging from the simple "4 + 4" type to more complex ones of adding three-digit numbers. Several problems at each level of complexity must be given if the responses are to be representative of the child's skills. For example, the assessment of skills in addition involves determining whether the child can add one-place, two-place, or three-place columns of numbers with and without carrying. One problem presented at each skill level will not furnish adequate information about the child's ability to add; several problems will. For the most reliable assessment, ten or more problems of each type should be introduced. The child's rate and accuracy of response at each level of difficulty show his skills at that level.

Some commercial materials have their own placement tests based on criterion measures of performance. These tests indicate at what level the child should be placed. For commercial materials without placement tests, the teacher can select criterion pages or problems to use for assessment. For example, if basal readers are used to teach reading, the teacher can take a sample of content one-fourth of the way into each book level. For this assessment, the child is asked to respond orally. His placement is determined by the level at which he mispronounces from three to five percent of the words.

In addition, there are several types of standardized tests whose subtests may be useful for assessment if they are expanded to allow reliable measurements. The teacher might expand the arithmetic subtests of the Wide Range Achievement Test (Jastak, Bijou, and Jastak 1965) by adding several problems of each type presented. Cues to evoke desired responses for assessment (controlled cues) must be sequentially arranged to avoid contaminating the assessment data with a compounding of cues. An example of the use of controlled cues to determine what concepts are part of a child's receptive language is provided by the following procedure given by Chalfant, Kirk, and Jensen (1968) for assessing the child's understanding of the concept "touch."

The child's imitative motor behavior must first be assessed to determine whether he possesses this skill. The authors describe a ball-rolling procedure which is presented to the child for imitation; if he imitates it, reinforcement is given. The next step is to direct the child to touch something on the table to which the teacher points. If the child responds by touching the object, the teacher skips the next three steps and presents the directions for the sixth and final step. If the child does not respond correctly to step two, he must be taught to touch by imitation, then be asked to touch one object, and then many different objects. The sixth step is the point at which the recognition of object words (glass, spoon, plate) can be assessed. When the child can respond to the command to touch certain objects, the teacher can determine what object names the child has already learned. These steps show the controlled introduction and repetition of cues that provide a reliable measurement of skills.

Sidman (1960) considers obtaining a baseline measurement of performance a prerequisite to "any manipulative study. Manipulation of new variables will often produce behavioral changes, but in order to describe the changes we must be able to specify the baseline from which they occurred; otherwise we face insoluble problems of control, measurement, and generality" (p. 238).

Baseline measurements are valid response data because the specified responses are measured directly and the measurement is continuous during a time when variables are held constant. Sidman requires a true baseline response pattern to be a steady state, one that "does not change its characteristics over a period of time" (1960, p. 234). A baseline measurement of performance provides an assessment of skills based on a measurement of response rates. The first criterion for such a measurement is that it provide a reliable pattern of the rates of correct and incorrect responses for a specified type of response prior to the manipulation of variables, i.e., to changes in the learning conditions. The teacher's objective in taking a baseline is to determine the child's level of skill so that he can establish a set of conditions in which the child performs without error. Assessment of skills prior to instruction, therefore, is essential, so that when instruction begins, the child will find himself in a stable environment designed for his needs.

Determining Conditions and
Evaluating Their Effectiveness

After the teacher has obtained a baseline and analyzed the child's behavior to find out where he is in the learning process, he must determine the instructional and reinforcing conditions that will initiate and maintain performance most effectively. Performance or behavior patterns vary under different conditions; each time an instructional condition is changed, the pattern may be altered. The behavioral change is a consequence of the alteration of a condition or the introduction of a new one.

In order to obtain useful data, therefore, it is important to select a response that can be continuously recorded under each change in conditions. The response rate, calculated by dividing the number of responses by the length of time (usually stated in minutes), shows the influence of each different instructional condition on a particular behavior. This information enables the teacher to set up those conditions which are most conducive to the child's attaining the behavioral objectives established for him.

For example, if the teacher wishes to determine whether immediate feedback of answers is a more effective reinforcer than special activities contingent on good performance, the child's response data will furnish this information. If Spiro's rate of performance is two correct responses per minute when he learns immediately about his accuracy and five correct responses per minute when he is given time to engage in pleasant activities following a good performance, the latter reinforcer obviously is the more effective one.

The effects on performance of a change from a nonlinguistic basal reader to a linguistic one could be evaluated by measuring the rates of correct and incorrect responses to first one reader and then the other. In both cases, the consequences reinforcing performance should be the same. In addition, the same type of response should be measured for both materials, e.g., orally reading a selected number of lines of print, reading a list of words, and answering comprehension questions. For another example, the teacher may be interested in comparing the motivating effects of token reinforcement with those of social reinforcement from the teacher. In either case, adherence to specific design is necessary in order to obtain reliable information about these instructional conditions.

Any evaluation of conditions influencing behavior must be carried out by changing one condition at a time and measuring the behavior under that condition. Furthermore, the effects of the condition introduced cannot be assessed after only one treatment period, since the predictable behavior pattern may not fully emerge after only one session. If materials are to be evaluated, one change should be made in the conditions antecedent to the child's response, but all conditions subsequent to it should be held constant. If a reinforcer is to be evaluated, one event subsequent to the performance should be changed, but all conditions occurring before it should be held constant. Whether the change is antecedent or subsequent to the behavior, it should be continued for several sessions until the teacher has a picture of the performance under those conditions. The extent of a behavioral change resulting from a modification procedure can be obtained by comparing the baseline response rate with the new response rate.

There may be times, however, when the teacher establishes a baseline, introduces a new condition, and observes no apparent change in the rate of behavior over a period of time. There are at least two things that the teacher should examine at this point. First, has the behavior been precisely defined? If, for example, the behavior is defined as "aggressiveness," any number of separate movement cycles could be involved—hitting, throwing things at other children, biting the teacher, etc. Unless the behavior is defined so that the same behavior will be counted each time, the baseline rate will not be a stable one. Second, have all variables been as carefully controlled as possible? If the teacher reprimands Herman for aggressive behavior in one instance and ignores it in another, the conditions that affect the occurrence of that behavior are not constant and, again, the baseline will not represent a stable rate.

The value of the response rate lies in its sensitivity to changing conditions. Not only does it show the effect of changed conditions on behavior, but, when the rate is examined, it is possible to obtain a pattern of correct and incorrect responses under different conditions. Perhaps what is most important is that the response rate enables the teacher to compare performances made by the same individual at different times regardless of the response period, so long as the responses are comparable. Thus the child's progress is always considered in relation to his own performance rather than to those of other children in this age group or class.

Variables that might be dismissed as having little or no effect, when group comparisons are made, may prove to be extremely powerful when evaluated against a stable individual baseline. Intersubject variability is not a feature of behavioral processes in the individual organism, and when such variability is included in the measurement of presumed individual processes, the resolving power of the measures is inevitably sacrificed. [Sidman 1960, pp. 240–41]

Specifying Terminal Objectives

Effective behavior analysis, leading directly to classroom instruction for the individual child, requires the specification of terminal objectives toward which instruction will proceed. Terminal objectives must be behaviorally defined as observable responses so that they may be counted. They must also be realistic in terms of available instructional materials. Once specified, the objectives will dictate the type of information to be acquired and the responses that will represent criterion performance.

A number of educators have identified sets of terminal objectives for particular levels of skill development (Bereiter and Engelmann 1966; Bloom 1956). In addition, almost every set of well-designed instructional materials identifies specific terminal objectives. Because these objectives specify the type of respones the child will make when he has reached a criterion performance, the teacher can organize materials to determine the child's acquisition of information leading to the objectives. For example, at the preschool level, children should learn to respond to a wide variety of objects: they should be able to recognize opposites, such as big-little; learn a number of cause-effect relationships; distinguish the basic colors; count and enumerate a sequence of items; learn the letter-sound relationships of most of the alphabet; sort pictures from words; and, in some settings, acquire a small sight vocabulary of regular words. The preschool child is also expected to learn to take turns; share objects, activities, and ideas; carry out one or two simple directions; and answer simple questions, using gestures or words.

Terminal objectives which can be taught and assessed at the preschool level require just as much adherence to a systematic program as does the development of any sequence of tasks provided in a textbook. For example, Chalfant, Kirk, and Jensen (1968) suggest five criteria for guiding the selection of language concepts (e.g., "touch," "spoon," "glass") to teach the child as part of his language repertoire. They suggest that the first factor to consider is the importance of the concept to the child. The second factor is the "proximity" of the concept to the child. The third is its placement in a sequence of ideas and its frequency of occurrence. As an illustration, the child should probably understand "Eat your dinner" before he learns to be receptive to "Wash your face." The concreteness of the concept is the fourth factor, and the clarity of auditory discrimination the fifth. With these guidelines, the teacher can sequentially arrange a series of concepts to teach the child. In addition, he can use the guidelines in building procedures for evaluating the child's repertoire of receptive language. In planning cues for the assessment of language concepts, the teacher should avoid using two possibly unknown concepts at the same time. For example, if the concept "touch" is being evaluated, the teacher should not say "Touch the glass" unless he knows that the child understands the meaning of "glass."

Programmed materials provide carefully specified terminal objectives. For example, the Sullivan *Programmed Reading* material (Buchanan 1964) has terminal objectives and successive approximations specified for each of the twenty-one books in the series. The first book is designed for the acquisition of the following information:

1. the letters, m, n, t, p, f, a, and i;
2. *yes* and *no* as sight words;
3. the period and question mark as punctuation;
4. the capital letter at the beginning of sentences.

The Suppes programmed math series, *Sets and Numbers* (Suppes and Suppes 1968), has terminal objectives similarly defined. For example, the information to be acquired at the first level of skill includes—

1. sets;
2. whole numbers and enumeration to 100;
3. order and relation;
4. addition of whole number combinations through 19;
5. subtraction of whole number combinations through 19;
6. recognition of fractions;
7. concepts and vocabulary of measurement;
8. geometric concepts;
9. verbal concepts.

Once he is aware of the terminal objectives of a beginning program, the teacher can determine the prerequisite information to be acquired. With the new Suppes math material, he might decide that the child needs to acquire two items of information: the symbol { }, for an empty set, and the numeral 1.

Some reading programs, other than those which primarily develop word recognition, have less precisely identified terminal objectives. The

Distar reading program (Engelmann and Bruner 1969), developed by Science Research Associates, has designed materials for the following terminal objectives in initial reading skills:

1. symbol-action games;
2. blending (spelling by sounds);
3. rhyming;
4. symbol-sound relationships;
5. reading sounds (blending sounds into words visually displayed).

All these objectives represent information to be acquired. They identify observable responses as well as cues (stimuli) which can be presented to evoke them. Consequently, they can be achieved, and the degree of information the child acquires can be assessed.

The Experimental Education Unit Program

Norris G. Haring and his associates (Haring, in press, 1971; Haring and Hauck 1969a, 1969b; Haring and Hayden 1968; Haring and Kunzelmann 1966; Haring and Lovitt 1967; Nolen, Kunzelmann, and Haring 1967) have developed a systematic form of instruction based on principles of behavior analysis and modification. The system is used at the Experimental Education Unit of the Child Development and Mental Retardation Center at the University of Washington.

The two weeks following a child's entrance into a classroom at the Unit are used to determine his levels of skill development. The teacher undertakes (a) a baseline performance measurement to assess the child's levels of skill in the academic subjects to be included in his curriculum and (b) an evaluation of his response rates with and without a token reinforcement system. The teacher collects sufficient response data to determine reliably the effects of curriculum materials (programmed whenever possible) and reinforcers.

Assessment of the child's levels of skill development is accomplished entirely with commercial and teacher-made placement tests. Rate and accuracy of response are evaluated first under conditions most like those of regular classroom instruction, i.e., where only social reinforcement from the teacher is used to encourage good performance. Then the child's response rates are assessed under conditions where he earns points for correct responses. These points have the same exchange value that they will have when instruction begins under a token reinforcement system.

The information the teacher gains from this initial two-week assessment (baseline measurement of performance) enables him to determine where the child can begin in reading, math, spelling, language, handwriting, science, art, music, and physical education. Most important, he learns what schedules of reinforcement will motivate the child to initiate tasks or respond to them accurately and efficiently. He also learns what schedules will decelerate inappropriate social behavior and prevent satiation from activities available during free time. Reinforcement is scheduled on a ratio (VR, FR) or interval (VI, FI) basis and is determined by the child's response data. Individual performance patterns are the basis for determining the amount of reinforcement awarded, for scheduling the presentation of points, and for specifying when the points can be spent.

Points, each equivalent to one minute of free time, are used primarily to reinforce correct academic responses, although sometimes the teacher may use them systematically as "shaping points"—points given because the pupil maintained appropriate demeanor at his desk.

When it is apparent that the child's response data exhibit some trend (either no change in performance pattern or consistent acceleration or deceleration in response rate), the teacher will make a decision either to maintain the conditions introduced (because he is pleased with the child's performance pattern) or to change one of the instructional conditions. If a change is indicated, more often than not it will be in the conditions used to reinforce performance—either in the type of reinforcer or in the number of points awarded for correct responses. If a child's error rate is too high or his rate of correct response too low, it may be due to conditions which are not reinforcing enough. If the teacher introduces reinforcement conditions which have increased performance in other areas, yet the rate of correct response does not accelerate, the problem may be that the material is too difficult for the child. Only one change at a time can be made in the instructional environment if its effects on the child's behavior are to be evaluated reliably. If the teacher wishes to determine whether it is lack of reinforcement or an overly difficult book which is causing the child to exhibit a low rate of reading response, he cannot change the type of reinforcement and the textbook at the same time. If he does, he will be unable to tell which change is affecting the child's response rate.

Direct measurement of the child's responses is used extensively at the Experimental Education Unit to obtain information on which to base further decisions for instruction. The terminal objectives of the program for each child are the development, within one to two years, of: specific academic skills commensurate with the child's age; self-management skills, including response recording and contingency management; and social skills relevant to the settings in which the child functions.

The procedures of analysis and modification of behavior can be thought of as proceeding in a helical fashion (see Figure 3.1). *Analysis* begins the

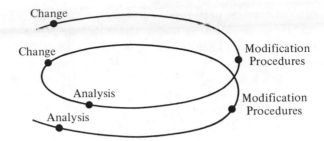

Figure 3.1.   Cycle of analysis, modification, and change

helix by giving the teacher information on the child's current level of achievement. On the basis of this information, the teacher decides on *terminal objectives* for the child, but the achievement of those objectives depends on a number of intermediate steps or approximations. If Phillip can add three-digit numbers and the terminal objective is long division, intermediate steps would include subtraction and multiplication. The teacher introduces conditions to modify the child's behavior, perhaps a programmed text to teach subtraction. Thus, modification succeeds analysis in the helix. The teacher evaluates the success of the modification procedures by analyzing the accumulated data. These data also provide him with the information he will need to decide whether further modification is indicated and when it should be instituted. If the child has a high error rate in subtraction, the teacher may provide a higher ratio of reinforcement for each correct answer. He changes the modification conditions in order to bring the child's behavior closer to the desired end. The procedures of analysis and modification are repeated as each step in the child's progress is measured. At each step the child's behavior has changed, and hopefully he has achieved a higher level of skill on his way to reaching the terminal objectives set for him. Thus, the cycle of analysis, modification, and change in the child's behavior goes on in a spiral toward the terminal objectives.

Because the procedures of behavior analysis involve direct observation, continuous measurement, and systematic changes in instructional conditions, they offer the most functional form of assessment available. This approach is a refined extension of the teacher observation procedures used in a study by Haring and Ridgway (1967) as well as in a number of classrooms.

The teacher who systematically uses procedures of behavior analysis will be precise in his teaching. The guidelines and specific procedures of behavior analysis promote a structured classroom, a more functional assessment of the individual child's skills, more relevant instructional content for developing skills, individualization of instruction based on levels and rates of performance, reliable evaluations of the pupil's progress obtained continually rather than periodically, and dependable information about the child's progress toward terminal objectives. The teacher who avails himself of the information provided by the response rate is in a position to make immediate instructional decisions. And by introducing relevant variables one at a time, he can obtain precise information on which to base his decisions.

The following steps are necessary if a reliable baseline measurement is to be obtained.

1. Plan, set up, and describe the physical environment.
2. Plan, select, and describe the materials to which the child will respond.
3. Describe the child's responses to be measured.
4. Plan and describe responses to be made by the teacher before, during, and after the child's responses. The teacher's responses include—
   a. his instructions to the child;
   b. his locations in the room, particularly his proximity to the child.
5. Hold the conditions constant while responses are being observed and counted, and extend the observation and counting over a number of sessions until a stable rate is exhibited.

Summary

Behavior analysis is a useful procedure for the classroom teacher to employ in the measurement and modification of classroom behavior. As applied in the classroom, the procedure consists essentially of three steps: (a) direct observation, (b) continuous measurement of responses, and (c) systematic changes in the environment.

Observation, the first step in the measurement procedure, will be far more accurate if the behavior to be measured is precisely defined in terms of its movement cycle or basic unit of behavior. Measurement can be carried out in terms of rate or duration of response, depending upon which is more appropriate.

The classroom teacher needs to know the rate of behavior as it is occurring at the beginning of the project. This is called the baseline performance or, in the case of academic subjects, the initial performance. In either case, the beginning of any project should include an accurate measurement of the behavior as it is occurring under constant conditions.

The next step in changing behavior is to determine very carefully, on the basis of observations and any other information available, the procedure for change that will most likely promote the target behavior. Once this procedure has been selected and well defined, it can be introduced, again holding all other conditions constant. The objective for change should be clearly specified and a continuous measurement of performance taken during the change procedure. Often the first step in the procedure will not change the behavior drastically, and a refinement in measurement, or in the controlling environmental conditions, or possibly in the change procedure itself, will be required. In almost all situations where the behavior is specified, the objectives for change clearly outlined, and the classroom conditions held constant—at least as constant as is possible in a classroom—this procedure will bring about behavior change.

Change in behavior occurs in a helical fashion. Essentially, it involves taking a baseline before modification procedures are initiated, instituting the modification procedures, measuring performance, and continually refining the modification procedures on the basis of analyses of performance until the data satisfy the teacher that the objectives have been reached.

References

Bereiter, Carl, and Siegfried Engelmann. *Teaching Disadvantaged Children in the Preschool*. Englewood Cliffs, N. J.: Prentice-Hall, Inc., 1966.

Bloom, Benjamin S., ed. *Taxonomy of Educational Objectives, Handbook 1: Cognitive Domain*. New York: David McKay Co., Inc., 1956.

Buchanan, Cynthia Dee. *Programmed Reading*. St. Louis-New York: Webster Division, McGraw-Hill Book Company, 1964.

Chalfant, James, Girvin Kirk, and Kathleen Jensen. "Systematic Language Instruction: An Approach for Teaching Receptive Language to Young Trainable Children." *Teaching Exceptional Children*, 1 (1968): 1–13.

Engelmann, Siegfried, and Elaine C. Bruner. *Distar Reading: An Instructional System*. Chicago: Science Research Associates, 1969.

Haring, Norris G. "Experimental Education: Application of Experimental Analysis and Principles of Behavior to Classroom Instruction." In *Behavioral Intervention in Human Problems*, edited by H. C. Rickard. London: Pergamon Press Limited, in press, 1970.

Haring, Norris G., and Mary Ann Hauck. "Improved Learning Conditions in the Establishment of Reading Skills with Disabled Readers." *Exceptional Children*, 35 (1969a): 341–52.

Haring, Norris G., and Mary Ann Hauck. *Contingency Management Applied to Classroom Remedial Reading and Math for Disadvantaged Youth*. Proceedings of the 9th Annual Research Meeting cosponsored by the Department of Institutions, Division of Research, State of Washington and the University of Washington, School of Medicine, Department of Psychiatry, 2:2 (1969b). Seattle, Washington: University of Washington Press, 1969. Pp. 41–46.

Haring, Norris G., and Alice H. Hayden. "The Contributions of the Experimental Education Unit to the Expanding Role of Instruction." *The College of Education Record* (University of Washington, Seattle, Wash.), 34 (1968): 31–36.

Haring, Norris G., and Harold Kunzelmann. "The Finer Focus of Therapeutic Behavioral Management." In *Educational Therapy, Volume I*, edited by Jerome Hellmuth, pp. 225–51. Seattle, Wash.: Special Child Publications, Inc., 1966.

Haring, N. G., and Lovitt, T. C. Operant Methodology and Educational Technology in Special Education. In *Methods in Special Education*, edited by N. G. Haring and R. L. Schiefelbusch, pp. 12–48. New York: McGraw-Hill, 1967.

Haring, Norris G., and Robert W. Ridgway. "Early Identification of Children with Learning Disabilities." *Exceptional Children*, **33** (1967): 387–95.

Jastak, J. F., S. W. Bijou, and S. R. Jastak. *Wide Range Achievement Test.* (rev. ed.) Wilmington, Delaware: Guidance Associates, 1965.

Nolen, Patricia A., Harold P. Kunzelmann, and Norris G. Haring. "Behavioral Modification in a Junior High Learning Disabilities Classroom." *Exceptional Children*, **34** (1967): 163–68.

Sidman, Murray. *Tactics of Scientific Research.* New York: Basic Books, 1960.

Suppes, Patrick, and Joanne Suppes. *Sets and Numbers.* New York: The L. W. Singer Company, Inc., A Subsidiary of Random House, 1968.

Behavior Modification in the Classroom

4

The teacher's responsibility is to develop the academic, social, and verbal performances of the children assigned to his class. Despite the children's varied learning or behavior problems, the teacher must ensure that they all learn. In order to accomplish this, he will often have to shape not only academic behaviors, but social behaviors as well. The teacher must determine the responses he wants to develop, the cues which will stimulate the child to make them, the reinforcers needed to establish their predictable recurrence, and the arrangement of contingencies between the responses and their reinforcers (Haring 1968).

Instruction and Intervention

Once a teacher has gathered children together in a classroom, he has intervened in their behavior. Consequently, he might as well apply procedures which will ensure the most effective intervention possible. He should take note of those behaviors that reflect the child's emotional and social disorders, for these are the ones that will need to be modified. Psychiatry and other professional disciplines organized to study behavior have concentrated on the underlying causes of emotional and academic problems, but teachers cannot function effectively if they con-

54

cern themselves only with underlying causes. They cannot play the roles of diagnostician and therapist. In the role of behavior modifier, the teacher must focus on—

1. observable behavior;
2. modification of behavior;
3. instructional procedures and their effects;
4. continuous evaluation of the total process of education.

The teacher is responsible for his program, and he must choose and arrange from a wide selection of instructional media and commercial programs those which are most appropriate for his students as a group, which provide for individualized instruction within a group, and which allow flexibility in the arrangement of instructional cues. In other words, the classroom teacher is the one who determines the instructional materials and the means by which he will change behavior.

Both the physical and social aspects of the classroom environment are sources of the stimuli that affect the child's behavior. The teacher controls the environment through contingency management. He structures the sequences of antecedent and consequent events which cause and reinforce the child's behavior.

The ABCs of Behavior Modification

In order to make a succinct statement about the variables essential to a behavior modification program, we can label them the ABCs of behavior modification: (a) the antecedent conditions, (b) the behaviors to be observed and modified, and (c) the consequences which will reinforce the behaviors. The antecedent conditions are the stimuli that elicit the responses. The behaviors to be observed are those in need of modification. Their pattern of occurrence reflects the influence of conditions introduced to modify them. The consequences are the stimuli introduced to reinforce the desired behavior after its occurrence so as to establish and maintain a particular pattern of response.

Contingency Management. Evaluation of classroom variables in order to determine the extent of their effectiveness in instructing the child is the most important responsibility of the teacher, and measurement and charting procedures are his tools in this process. The procedure by which the teacher manipulates variables of the classroom environment is contingency management—the arrangement of the antecedent and consequent events that are contingent on the child's behaviors and which affect those behaviors.

The teacher's job as a behavior modifier is to manage contingencies between appropriate responses and reinforcers so that for most of the school day the child's responses successively approximate the terminal behaviors identified by the teacher. When the teacher can effectively manage contingencies to shape social, verbal, and academic behaviors, the child's broad repertoire of responses will much more closely approximate the terminal objectives.

The primary requirements of contingency management are that the teacher (a) attend to the *types of reinforcers* in order to bring the child who responds only to extrinsic reinforcement to respond to social reinforcement alone; (b) change *schedules of reinforcement,* first making them appropriate to response acquisition and later to response maintenance; (c) use *measurement procedures* of behavior analysis to obtain data for decision-making; and (d) introduce instructional conditions according to one of a number of *designs* which will make it possible to collect reliable information.

The reversal strategy may be called an A-B-A model research design. After a baseline of out-of-seat behavior is established under certain conditions, step A is introduced. Here, a modification procedure, such as tokens awarded for each five minutes of working-at-seat behavior, is started. In step B, after the terminal objective has been achieved (child remains in seat for specified period of time), the modification procedure is discontinued and the environmental conditions are returned to those of the baseline period. If the behavior (out-of-seat) reverts to the frequency with which it occurred when the baseline was established, the teacher can conclude that the alteration of the behavior noted in step A was the result of the modification procedure. In step C, the token system is reinstated, reestablishing the conditions of step A. Thus, a reversal design enables one to verify the effectiveness of the modification procedure.

In a multiple baseline design, the teacher establishes a baseline for each of several behaviors. Modification procedures can then be introduced, but they should be applied to only one behavior at a time. A complete discussion of multiple baseline design can be found in *Tactics of Scientific Research* (Sidman 1960).

All designs for contingency management share the same basic features and, when carefully analyzed, are really quite simple. They all allow for a period of baseline measurement of performance under well-controlled conditions. In addition, they all allow for some pattern of systematically introducing new conditions—the variables of instruction to be evaluated for their influence on the behavior being measured. The data collected are evaluated according to the pattern of response emitted and charted as rate of response. In several designs, the baseline conditions are reinstituted again and again between experimental treatments. In others, the baseline conditions are never resumed; instead, the response rates obtained under new conditions become the baseline conditions against which successive conditions are evaluated. Designs are of two basic types: reversal and multiple baseline.

Systematic Planning. A major component of modification for children with behavior disorders is individualization of instruction in large groups by means of a systematic plan. The teacher need not acquire new skills. A systematic plan, however, will require some revamping of classroom organization and arrangement as well as precision in identifying, recording, and quantifying those performances of the children that relate to the instructional objectives. This focus on the classroom and on the performances of the children alleviates learning problems which can contribute directly to problems of behavior.

To make effective use of the procedures that directly influence behavior, the teacher must devise a plan. He must determine—

1. the specific objectives of skill and behavior for each child in his class;
2. the specific cues to use to evoke those responses that will lead most directly to the terminal objectives;
3. the responses to be measured;
4. the reinforcers to be used;
5. the reinforcement contingencies to be tried.

When the total environment is properly arranged to present cues to the child in a sequence that restricts him to a minimal number of failures and reinforces his correct responses, changes in behavior can be dramatic. This type of intervention results in successful responses to school work or to chores around the home, thus providing the child with environmental consequences from adults that accelerate these desirable responses.

The Physical Environment
of the Classroom

Physical arrangements involve the placement of desks and chairs; the arrangement of books, supplies, and record-keeping equipment; and the location of work and activity areas, often referred to as low- and high-strength areas (Homme et al. 1963; Haring and Kunzelmann 1966).

The area reserved for academic tasks should be stocked with all the materials the child might need. A child should not have to hunt for a pencil, a book, or paper at a time when he could be making academic responses. This would be an inefficient use of time. Part of readiness-for-task procedures is training students to retrieve and store materials; this ensures that little time is lost in preparation and cleanup.

As children begin a particular program, their location in the room should be considered permanent for the period of time of that program. A change, if made, would be considered a change in conditions which would have a measurable effect on performance and, consequently, affect response information.

High-strength activities may be located in one or several areas in the room, depending on the number of areas available and how many the teacher can manage. The area, or areas, should be arranged for independent use by children. Everything should be accessible to them, including the equipment and supplies necessary for the activities planned. A table for working on projects, a storage place for materials, and the availability of water are essential. Having the high-strength activity area a distance from the work area is desirable but not essential. For most teachers, these arrangements will not necessitate any great changes in the classroom, except possibly the reorganization of some activities and supplies.

With these considerations in mind, a classroom layout can be similar to that diagrammed in Figure 4.1. In the low-strength section, provisions have been made for an academic area; there the child can respond to tasks at his desk as well as at a language and communications center. In the section of the layout containing high-strength activities, provisions have been made for individual activities in science and arts and crafts, and for social activities in which several children can play cooperatively and thus develop appropriate social responses.

For children with inappropriate patterns of behavior, probably the best treatment technique is prevention of the usual response. For example, the child who habitually tips over his desk can have it anchored to a plywood platform. The child who is always out of his seat can have a car seatbelt attached to his desk to be used if his out-of-seat response rate becomes too high. For the child who tries to harm the adult correcting his work, a plexiglass cover can be fastened at an angle over the desk top to enable the teacher to face the child and correct his work without injury. Desks can also be provided with shinguards to protect the teacher as he stands nearby.

Arrangement of the Instructional Environment

The teacher controls the child's learning environment through the use of cues. A cue is anything in the environment that is used to evoke a specific response from the student. Contingency management involves the arrangement of the presentation of cues in order to bring about desired behavior. A child moves toward terminal instructional objectives through a series of successive approximations. The teacher needs to specify the terminal instructional objectives before arranging the cues which will lead to them. For example, consider the terminal objectives often specified for kinder-

High Strength
Activities

Science   Social Activities
Arts & Crafts   Planning
Plastics   Social Occasions
Electricity

— —

Low Strength
Activities

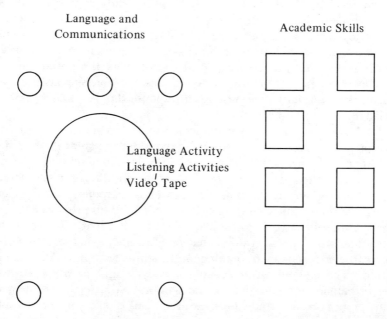

Language and
Communications   Academic Skills

Language Activity
Listening Activities
Video Tape

Figure 4.1.   Classroom design incorporating high and low strength activities

garten—the naming of colors, the mastery of number and size concepts, etc. Cues selected to develop these skills might include: questions from the teacher to identify common objects such as ball, book, pencil, crayons; objects and pictures of animals to illustrate the concepts big-little, up-down, long-short, fat-skinny; items which represent various functions or uses—tools, furniture, vehicles; big and little squares and circles; primary colors as well as white, black, and brown; and groups of ten objects to further illustrate color, shape, and size concepts. Directly relevant cues are necessary to teach the specified terminal objectives.

Academic tasks lend themselves easily to behavior modification. They are complex tasks which can be presented in a programmed format so that even the slightly motivated child can achieve a high rate of success. A programmed text enables the child to compare his own responses with the correct ones without relying on teacher intervention.

Programmed material is especially designed for an effective and sequential arrangement of cues, providing comparable units of textual material and requiring active, observable responses. Other classroom instructional materials are designed to meet these same objectives, but their sequential arrangement does not promote efficient skill development unless the teacher works out an effective arrangement of cues. For example, flashcards can be used to introduce new reading words if the teacher arranges them in the proper sequence of presentation. Most programmed texts that the teacher can use in the classroom are set up in frames of approximately equal length. The child can thus respond at a steady rate. He may, for example, read some sentences where he is required to make a response at the end of each sentence. But what if he is suddenly required to read five sentences each time before he responds? In this situation his rate will certainly decline, simply because he does not have the opportunity to respond as frequently as before. In the interests of precise response measurement, the material which requires a response should come in units of equal length.

To illustrate how to modify commercial materials not necessarily designed for precise response measurement, consider the steps in "framing" basal readers. The plan must include (a) the selection of units of response that are observable and sensitive to changes in conditions for instruction, and (b) the division of the material into equal response requirements. Selecting a response unit according to these specifications presents a unique problem if the objective is to increase the rate of silent reading. Since silent reading is not an observable behavior, it cannot be measured directly. However, the effects of silent reading on the student's performance can be measured. The student, after reading silently, might be asked to read every word aloud, at which time his rates of oral word reading and errors in word pronunciation would be measured. But this is time-consuming.

Alternatively, the teacher could measure the rate of page-turning, the rate of correct responses to comprehension questions, or the rate of words read aloud. But each of these by itself is an inadequate measure of reading behavior. Both the rate of correct responses to comprehension questions and the rate of reading words aloud approach a valid measure, although the former lacks sensitivity to changing conditions since the questions usually occur only at the end of a story. Probably the best way to identify a response unit in basal readers is to divide the text itself into equal units. The basal reader might be framed according to lines of print. For each framed unit of lines of print or each set of framed units, the student would be required to make three types of responses: (a) silent reading, (b) answers to comprehension questions, and (c) oral reading of a randomly selected portion of the total number of lines read silently. A measurement of performance could be obtained by recording the rate of lines of print read per minute, if words per line remain constant, or the rate of words per minute read aloud. For example, the basal reader could be divided into units of three pages, with one comprehension question programmed for each unit. The student's response to the program, then, would consist of silently reading three pages, writing an answer to a comprehension question, and reading aloud. Arrangements could be made to use randomly selected passages for oral reading. For example, for every three pages of silent reading, the child could be required to read a number of lines of print aloud. With this arrangement, several kinds of measurement could be taken: (a) lines of print correctly read per minute, or (b) words correctly read per minute, as well as (c) errors in word pronunciation.

This program allows for the measurement of several types of responses and should provide a reliable measurement of performance sensitive to the changes in classroom conditions introduced for evaluation. Further, the regularly occurring comprehension questions and the routine check on word-recognition skills obtained during oral reading provide continual information about accuracy of performance.

The student's record of errors in word pronunciation during oral reading and his record of lines of print correctly read aloud will be a representative measure of his silent reading response. This kind of response measurement is also sensitive to the effects of changes made in reinforcement conditions while instructional materials are held constant, or vice versa.

Presenting cues through instrumentation is precise—as precise as the "software" developed for the equipment. This form of cue presentation, primarily self-instructional, includes devices as elementary as the Bell & Howell Language Master which provides auditory stimuli, or as complex as the MTA Scholar which provides synchronized visual and auditory display, or computer-assisted instruction which offers an even more individualized presentation.

Teachers must be specialists in curriculum, for instruction is very much dependent on the arrangement of cues designed to facilitate the child's responses. Teachers have relied heavily on commercial publishers for the arrangement of instructional cues, but they have also seen the necessity for providing additional programs to supplement the commercial materials.

Cues must be chosen according to several criteria. First, they must promote performances that are as nearly errorless as possible. The teacher thus avoids the risk of reinforcing incorrect responses. Second, they must stimulate responses that are easy to measure. They must evoke active, observable responses from the child over comparable units of material. Third, their selection and sequential arrangement must be directed toward the terminal objectives and successive approximations of them.

Reinforcing Responses

When provided with an academic task, the teacher's verbal instructions, and directions on the blackboard, most children make a predictable response. They respond to the task. For these children, the task, the teacher's directions, and the written instructions are all controlling stimuli because of the positive reinforcing consequences which have occurred for responding to them. Probably the greatest gains for these normally functioning children will come about through better arrangements of the instructional conditions in effect prior to their responses. For these children, the natural classroom experiences are sufficiently reinforcing.

Some children, however, will not respond predictably. Instead, they may daydream, look out the window, talk to a neighbor, shuffle their feet, or thumb through the book. For these children, the book and the written or verbal directions are conditions which do not promote appropriate behavior. Normal classroom experiences fail as reinforcers of appropriate behavior. Therefore, atypical reinforcing conditions must be used to initiate and temporarily maintain acceptable responses to academic tasks.

All *types* of behavior—verbal, social, and academic—as well as all *patterns* of response, are shaped by environmental conditions which follow their emission. Previous reinforcement has aready established these response patterns. Since behavior is lawfully related to the environment, conditions can be arranged to establish any behavior pattern. Emotional disturbance, social maladjustments, mental retardation, poor performance or learning disabilities, and normal behavior are all behavior patterns which, to a great degree, have become lawfully established as a result of certain reinforcing conditions.

Only recently have social and emotional problems been considered as inappropriately conditioned behaviors rather than as basic, underlying emotional disturbances. Several recent volumes in the educational and psychological literature view childhood emotional problems very broadly, categorizing or labeling a wide variety of behavior as *emotionally disturbed* (Berkowitz and Rothman 1960; Lippman 1962; Long, Morse, and Newman 1965). Although the term "emotional disturbance" has the advantage of being widely recognized by psychiatrists, psychologists, and teachers, it is not descriptive. Labeling a child "emotionally disturbed" tells us nothing about the responses he makes or about the conditions under which he makes them.

Attempts to modify a learning disability have often placed much emphasis on stimuli which precede the child's responses—on programs with built-in color cues, visual perception exercises, auditory perception exercises, and special organization and arrangements. Essentially, this places the responsibility for problems in the classroom directly on the learner—the child (Haring and Ridgway 1967). Programmers, notably Holland (1960), Buchanan (1964), and Suppes and Suppes (1968), have emphasized programmed arrangement as the critical variable in the learning environment and consider only incidentally the importance of events which follow the child's responses.

The regular classroom teacher is usually the modifier of academic performance. The special class teacher is also a modifier of social behaviors, using as his basic modification procedure the reinforcement of academic responses. Behavior modification procedures concentrate on building, strengthening, and molding acceptable and productive behaviors. Inappropriate behavior receives no attention, while desirable and constructive behavior receives reinforcement. One of the most productive techniques of behavior modification is extinguishing an undesirable behavior by strengthening a desirable one that is incompatible with it. For example, sitting at a desk is incompatible with getting out of the seat and roaming around the room. If the former behavior is strengthened, the latter is less likely to occur.

Positive Reinforcement

The presentation of a pleasant event after a response increases the probability that the response will be repeated. This is the principle of positive reinforcement. The teacher may influence the probability of a child's responding to a task, i.e., may affect the accuracy and efficiency of performance, by the presentation of rewarding conditions in the classroom. She may show her pleasure by smiling at Gertrude, who has completed an assignment, or promise a party for good class performance for a week, or offer an afternoon movie for those with all assignments done. The teacher's smile immediately after Gertrude hands in her completed assignment may have a direct influence on the probability of Gertrude's completing an assignment soon again. Similarly, the teacher's kind remark to a child for helping another student may directly influence the probability of help being offered again.

Generally, positive reinforcers can be classified as social reinforcement from teachers, parents, and peers; high-strength activities; token reinforcement; and food. Presented in certain patterns, they have particular effects on performance. Typical pleasant events in the classroom include pleasant interactions with the teacher or with peers or the opportunity for the child to engage in some self-selected activity. For most children, the teacher's smile or compliment serves to increase the rate of the behavior it follows. For some students, good grades are sufficiently reinforcing to maintain or increase the probability of good performance. For students who do not perform well, however, grades will not strengthen performance. And for children with behavior problems who receive little attention from the teacher when they perform well, the teacher's scolding or nagging will act as positive reinforcement for their inappropriate behavior.

For example, when Matilda receives attention at the peak of a crisis (throwing a tantrum, shouting, complaining, fighting), her crisis behavior is reinforced. The adult who intervenes by discussing the upsetting behavior is simply increasing the probability of a recurrence of that behavior. This is "crisis teaching," which unfortunately uses the peak of the crisis as the time to question, probe, listen to, and provide solace to the child (Long, Morse, and Newman 1965). When the child has tantrums, screams, cries, hits out, or complains, the adult often feels encouraged to intervene, empathizing with the child's difficulties and evaluating the causes. All too often, children get attention in class for complaining but never for acceptable behavior. Under these conditions, their rates of complaining, shouting, or pouting accelerate.

Adult attention should be provided, not when the child complains in a disruptive manner, but when he talks about conditions he finds favorable and would like repeated. Complaints should be responded to, but not when the child is being disruptive. When it is made clear to children that any discussion of their interests and ideas is contingent on their accomplishing a certain amount in their school tasks, the teacher ends up with fewer classroom "gripers" and more students with favorable attitudes, and has the opportunity to provide the appropriate kind of attention.

The basic shortcoming of "crisis teaching" is that the child is reinforced for the very behaviors that often make his behavior pattern too extreme for him to remain in the regular class. Teaching should not be conducted on the assumption that the child has inner conflicts causing the crisis and that intervention at the peak of the crisis will uncover basic causes. The child must be listened to only after the crisis has been alleviated for a period of time. Adult and peer attention must be used to reinforce noncrisis behavior.

Effective reinforcement requires the appropriate use of consequences in ways prescribed by the principles of behavior and a continuous check on the effectiveness of the consequences through the measurement of performance. It also demands that the teacher consciously select reinforcers available in the classroom, thus establishing classroom stimuli, especially academic and social stimuli, as reinforcers for the child.

The critical feature of reinforcement is its timing in relation to the occurrence of the response. The event or condition to be used to reinforce performance must be presented immediately following the child's response. Thus, it will be seen as a consequence of the response. If the event is reinforcing or becomes so, there will be a direct effect on performance. Reinforcement too long delayed, however, has a weakened effect on the behavior it was meant to influence. Several kinds of events may serve as consequences to a child for his behavior: teacher attention or contact, peer attention or contact, a new assignment, free activity time, and any number of other work or play activities common to the classroom. These consequences will vary in their neutrality, aversiveness, or positive effect for individual children. Anything can function as a reinforcer, so long as it has the strength to influence directly the acquisition or maintenance of behavior.

Procedures of reinforcement should be as natural to the classroom as possible, both in timing and in *types* of reinforcers used. The most obvious times for reinforcement are the normal breaks in classroom activity. The most natural reinforcers available are academic activities enjoyed by individual children. Next are activities related to academic subjects, such as card games, games of skill or chance, a variety of activities involving manipulative objects, and a selection of arts and craft activities. A number of more extrinsic reinforcers (Bijou and Sturges 1959), such as edibles and trinkets, have proved effective and are becoming more acceptable for temporary use in the classroom when deviant behavior is involved. Classroom conditions can become reinforcers through specific arrangements of the environment. One such arrangement might utilize the process of chaining, a procedure yet to be used systematically in the ordinary classroom. Behavioral research (Kelleher and Gollub 1962) has already demonstrated the conditions necessary for arranging response components in chains to facilitate responses within each component.

In a reading project conducted by Haring and Hauck (1969a), a three-component chained sequence of reading requirements was introduced as the final phase of the program. This sequence required: (a) reading a word list, (b) reading a story from the basal reader, and (c) reading from a basal book or a library book (the choice being up to the student). Silent reading preparation preceding the opportunity to read aloud for points

constituted the basic procedure in each component. Reinforcement for
correct oral reading succeeded silent reading preparation in each of the
three components, and points earned were credited to the student
contingent on his daily completion of all three components.

Establishment of Social Reinforcers

The powerful reinforcing effects of attention from others begins early
in the child's life as he first responds to his environment. The attention
from adults regularly present when he makes these early responses is probably the beginning of his reinforcement history. Mother smiles, nods her
head, and looks with approval, and these responses originally are paired
with primary reinforcers like feeding, changing, and comforting the child.
The mother's smiles and other attending behaviors become generalized
conditioned reinforcers effective under any condition of the child's need
for Mother's attention and capable of producing and maintaining a wide
range of behavior. They can become especially powerful reinforcers for
developing and maintaining verbal and social behaviors.

Parental attention like "Good boy," "Thank you," "Good work," "Right,"
all come to function as conditioned reinforcers. However, they become
powerful generalized reinforcers, effective under any state of deprivation
of the organism, only after they have functioned as conditioned reinforcers
for a very broad behavioral repertoire. Thus, the child who has not developed a repertoire of social skills suffers from a tremendous handicap. As
Ferster (1961) points out:

The normal repertoire of the child consists almost entirely of sequences of
behavior that are maintained, in a chain or sequence, by conditioned and
generalized reinforcers. . . . When the child has achieved a variety of effects
on his environment relative to a range of deprivations and reinforcers, simply
manipulating the physical environment may become a reinforcer. . . . This
[manipulation of the environment] is, of course, the uniquely human reinforcer that makes possible much of verbal behavior, of education in general,
and of self-control. Again, large amounts of behavior—many chains of behavior with many different kinds of conditioned reinforcers—are a necessary
condition for the emergence of a generalized reinforcer. [pp. 448–49]

Where conditioned reinforcers fail to become strong and are not applied
to a wide variety of responses, no generalized reinforcers develop; this
leaves a wide variety of behaviors in varied deprivation states resistant to
effective reinforcement. *This is the state of the socially deficient child.*
His repertoire of social responses is extremely limited. Thus, his environment exerts little control over his behavior. Typical conditioned re-

inforcers, like smiles, approval, and nods, are probably very weak; and because of his limited repertoire of social responses, conditioned reinforcers fail to become generalized reinforcers. A child who does not have a repertoire of social or verbal behaviors can receive only a very low rate of reinforcement from others.

If the environment is ever to exercise control over the child's social responses, he must first acquire a repertoire of such responses through shaping procedures. These involve a program of reinforcement for successive approximations. The sequence of development that is followed must be the same as that which should have occurred earlier and which does so naturally with children who normally exhibit the appropriate responses.

Before the environment can begin to control a specific behavior, the child must first manifest that behavior. After the response is reinforced many times in the presence of a particular stimulus, this antecedent stimulus gains *stimulus control* over the response. The establishment of stimulus control is precisely the same as the development of a conditioned reinforcer.

When the teacher realizes that the child's responses to him are consequences (often reinforcing) of his (the teacher's) own behavior, he will become more aware of the influence that the child's behavior has on him. The responses the teacher makes to a pupil's behavior are a result of the teacher's history of conditioning. A teacher who responds to Igor's talking to Pierre by telling him to "stop talking and go back to work," will respond like that again in a similar situation if Igor actually stops talking and begins to work. However, the behavior that is being maintained is the talking behavior rather than the working behavior, because it is the talking behavior to which the teacher responds. The talking ceases, but only temporarily.

Such interaction between the teacher and child may develop into what Patterson and Reid (1970) refer to as a coercive cycle. Igor, whose inappropriate talking behavior has been reinforced by teacher attention, will emit that inappropriate response again. The teacher, for whom this talking behavior has become a discriminative stimulus, will again emit the response of "stop talking and get back to work." To compound the problem, the teacher's conditioned response to Igor's inappropriate talking generalizes to other children talking out of turn. This is the process of generalization.

The teacher's major objective with reinforcement must be to establish himself as a positive reinforcer for each child. His interactions with children when they exhibit appropriate behavior should strengthen that behavior pattern. If his positive attention has little effect in maintaining the child's appropriate behavior, the environmental conditions must be rearranged so that social behavior becomes a positive reinforcer for the child. If the teacher's attention, positive or negative, to inappropriate behavior maintains the rate of that behavior, the teacher must withhold his attention from the inappropriate behavior and redirect it to other behavior that needs strengthening.

Children who are already learning "normally," i.e., at a rate of accuracy and efficiency which satisfies the teacher, are children who come into the classroom, sit down, and complete their assignments. The classroom stimuli which have shaped this behavior and maintain it are the teacher's social reinforcement together with other stimuli which have gained strength as reinforcers. Effective reinforcers for these children generally are the teacher's "Good for you," his smile, regularly returned assignments, daily grades, and peer respect and interaction. The materials, too, have become strong enough reinforcers to maintain academic and social responses.

Too many children, however, do not respond satisfactorily to these consequences. The stimuli have failed to reinforce them, and, most unfortunately for their learning careers, the teacher has not become a social reinforcer. These children are not reinforced by coming to school or by responding to any academic materials, and, if the teacher continues to apply only natural stimuli as consequences for responding, their skill development will be relatively slow. To strengthen rates of response to instructional cues, the teacher must systematically identify and apply reinforcing consequences and plan the classroom environment to bring each child to the point where he can plan natural consequences to maintain his own desirable academic, social, and verbal behaviors.

Token Reinforcement

Token reinforcement and the use of high-strength activities are two types of positive reinforcement. With token reinforcement, the child is given some small item or mark as a reinforcing consequence for a specific response or pattern of responses. Teachers have used stars, tally marks on the board, strips of colored paper, and other small tokens to signify a job well done or an appropriate response. Token reinforcers have at times been actual tokens or plastic chips. Regardless of what form they take, they are almost always exchangeable for something of greater value. This is their reinforcing strength to the child. Accumulated tokens may have time value, where a number of them will be worth so much time to be spent in some other activity—usually an activity selected by the child from a number of acceptable ones. Tokens have at times been exchangeable for store items, such as candy, trinkets, and toys. Tokens gain their reinforcing strength from the reinforcing consequences they bring. For a number of children, simply collecting the tokens reinforces and maintains desirable responses. Their reinforcement for saving tokens may be attention from others or some other less noticeable gratification. For other children, tokens may be reinforcing only if redeemable for time to engage in some other activity or for a desired object. If the objects or the length of time for which tokens are exchangeable are not reinforcing to the child, the teacher must change her schedule of reinforcement. For example, the worth of a "time token" might be increased from one minute of free time to five minutes.

Token reinforcement may be the most flexible reinforcement plan to adopt in the classroom. It not only allows for the individual needs of all the children but also provides a system whereby satiation and deprivation are best controlled. If the child is given time only for extra gym or extra art after responding appropriately, he will soon be satiated by these reinforcers, even if the events themselves are reinforcing for a time. If token reinforcement is used, however, and diverse opportunities can be paid for with tokens, the child can choose what he would like to do at the moment rather than engage only in a specified event. Thus, tokens always remain strong reinforcers. The teacher would be wise to make a list for himself of all activities, events, and conditions having potential as reinforcers in the classroom. This list will become very extensive as the teacher orients himself to viewing activities in terms of their reinforcing value and as other stimuli become reinforcing through pairing with stimuli already active as reinforcers. The teacher's praise as he presents a token to the child becomes reinforcing in itself because it is paired with the reinforcement of the token.

The following research studies give detailed procedures for the use of token reinforcement in different classroom settings.

Becker and his co-workers (O'Leary and Becker 1967; Kuypers, Becker, and O'Leary 1968) developed an instructional program using token reinforcement and the systematic application of teacher attention. There were two objectives: (a) to apply token reinforcement procedures with one teacher in a classroom of *average* size, and (b) to withdraw the token system gradually, simultaneously replacing token reinforcement with teacher attention, praise, and grades, with no deceleration of performance.

Their token reinforcement system was introduced in an adjustment class of seventeen nine-year-old students, and their project concentrated on the eight most disruptive children. To measure the occurrence of deviant behavior before and during the program, the investigators used two student observers for 100 minutes three times a week, each one observing four of the eight students for a twenty-second interval. Then, for the following ten seconds, the two recorded the deviant behaviors of each child: pushing, answering without raising the hand, chewing gum, eating, making disruptive noises, and talking. These observations were made during the course of three activities: listening to records or stories, doing arithmetic, and group reading. The activities involved group instruction and the children were expected to be in their seats.

The teacher's usual instructional procedures were used for the first four weeks, at which point token reinforcement was instituted. The tokens were in the form of ratings provided by the teacher at the end of each lesson. Ratings from one to ten, recorded in a booklet at the child's desk, were exchangeable as points for store items at a specified time. The children were told that the number (rating) showed how well they had followed directions written on the board; these directions read: (a) In Seat, (b) Face Front, (c) Raise Hand, (d) Work, (e) Pay Attention, and (f) Desk Clear. Where possible, the rating also reflected the accuracy of the child's arithmetic work, since this would be the best indication of how well the child was working.

To prepare the children for responding to tasks under social reinforcement only, the number of points required per prize was increased, as was the interval between earning points and spending them. Items cost from one to twenty-nine cents. Group points, exchangeable for popsicles at the week's end, were given for total class behavior. Token systems in a classroom or in any other setting, as Becker and his associates (Kuypers, Becker, and O'Leary 1968) discovered, must be initiated, guided, and maintained as carefully as any new set of procedures if the results are to be satisfactory.

Several, quite fully developed, instructional programs use tokens as the major reinforcement procedure, basing contingency management on the individual child's response data. Not only do these programs apply the principles of reinforcement generally, but they also apply the specific reinforcement scheduling principles — ratios, intervals, and chains of response.

Wolf and his associates have developed token reinforcement programs for a wide-age range of culturally deprived children: ten- to thirteen-year-old elementary school children with learning disabilities (McKenzie et al. 1968), fifth- and sixth-grade underachievers in an after-school community setting (Wolf, Giles, and Hall 1968), and school dropouts (Clark, Lachowicz, and Wolf 1968).

The program for the children with deficits in academic skills, involving ten children who had been placed in a learning disabilities class (McKenzie et al.), had three important features: (a) programmed and nonprogrammed curriculum materials at the child's level of skills, (b) use of grades as token reinforcement exchangeable for increments of allowance at the end of each week, and (c) measurement of attending behaviors before and during the time the child's allowance was based on grades.

Several systematic procedures and consequences were used:

1. the continuous collection of data on correct and incorrect responses;
2. observer recording of attending behavior;
3. daily recess, permitted if all assignments up to that time had been completed;
4. free-time activities for each student who had completed his work before the work time had elapsed;
5. special opportunities for those whose work had improved;
6. lunch with friends in the cafeteria if all assignments had been completed; otherwise, lunch time spent eating alone in the classroom;
7. attention provided by the teacher to the child when he was working;
8. daily and weekly grades based on the accuracy of completed assignments.

Modification procedures provided that an allowance given by the parents at home be contingent on grades earned in school. This allowance contingency was worked out at monthly group parent conferences with the teacher. To maintain the strength of money as a reinforcer, parents were directed to see that the children bought what they wanted and needed with their allowances and that money given by friends and relatives was banked. For those children who returned to the regular class before the year ended, the grade contingency for allowances was continued, the allowance eventually being paid only every two weeks. "At the end of the school year, all ten students were working successfully one to four levels above their starting levels in all academic areas. Six of the ten students were returned full time to regular classes to one grade higher than the ones they had been in during the previous school year" (p. 751).

The application of token reinforcement in an after-school setting for fifth- and sixth-graders (Wolf, Giles, and Hall 1968) represents a detailed application of contingency management procedures with a group of children. Wolf and his associates established a variety of contingencies on the children's after-school performances, on the teachers and aides in the after-school program, and on the teacher in the regular classroom which the children attended daily. Sixteen children eventually were included in this program for low achievers. They attended the program daily for two and a half hours after school, on Saturday morning during the school year, and for three hours every weekday morning during the summer. The entire program was individualized and standard curriculum materials were used.

The token system was modeled on the trading-stamp plan. Multicolor-paged booklets with squares were marked with points by the teacher after the children had completed their assignments. At first, points were given after the correct completion of one problem, but as the rate of correct responses increased, points were given less frequently and the amount of work required per point was increased. Pages of points were redeemable for various reinforcers—blue pages for weekly field trips, green pages for daily snacks, pink pages for money and store items, and yellow pages for more expensive items, such as clothing, watches, and second-hand bicycles. After a required number of pages were filled, the child was free to redeem them.

Points were given for correct responses to remedial work and homework completed in the after-school setting. Points were also awarded for grades earned in regular classroom assignments: A earned 100 points; B, 75; C, 50; and D, 25. Six-week report card grades given by regular teachers also earned points: for most students, A equaled 1,600 points; B, 800; C, 400; and D, 200. However, three children who had failed almost everything the preceding year now received double this point equivalent for letter grades. Changes in the reinforcement ratio were made periodically to determine the extent of the influence that points had on performance. Response data showed that performance was greatly influenced by point value per correct response.

Contingency management was well designed in this early group application of behavior principles. For example:

1. As the rate of correct responses increased, points earned for a response could not be used for spending, nor could the response data from a particular lesson be graphed, unless at least seventy-five percent of the child's responses in the lesson were correct.
2. Remedial work, placed in a folder on the child's desk, was not specifically assigned by subject but was left for free choice by the child. Choice was later manipulated by varying the point count for different types of responses.
3. The middle hour of the summer program was free-choice time for selecting an academic task to complete. Points were given only for work selected from one of three workbooks, although the child did not have to select this. The workbooks were unavailable at any other time.
4. In the first phase of the program, the number of points given for each correct response was the same for all children; in the second phase, the number of points was adjusted in accordance with each child's first-phase performance.
5. If one academic subject was more reinforcing than others, work in it was made contingent on the completion of some less reinforcing academic task.
6. Completion of a less favored academic task, with errors of less than five percent, earned the child the opportunity to select his next activity.
7. If the student asked for work beyond that which was allotted for the two and a half hours, he could take home other academic assignments, provided his school performance had been satisfactory.
8. Each teacher in the after-school program was reinforced with a bonus of ten dollars at the end of a six-week period for each child whose six-

week report card average improved over his previous six-week report.
9. Perfect attendance in any one month earned the child a 100-point bonus.
10. In-seat behavior was reinforced on a variable interval—the less the child was out of his seat, the higher his reward. Each student was ranked and awarded points from zero to sixty accordingly.
11. Each student whose six-week grade average improved or who maintained a B average could attend a party after report cards had been received.
12. Regular classroom teachers could award the child points which could be spent in the after-school sessions. These teachers could also take away the "store" privilege established in the after-school setting.
13. To use the points earned, children had to use their math and reading skills at the store.
14. Group cooperation was developed in several academic games where team members in competing groups could earn points for their team.
15. Groups of five or six students competed with one another in accumulating "A" papers completed in the regular classroom.

This program demonstrated that reinforcement conditions in an instructional program can produce improved performance.

The other program developed by Wolf and his associates (Clark, Lachowicz, and Wolf 1968) was designed for females from sixteen to twenty-one years of age who had dropped out of school. This project, developed in association with the Neighborhood Youth Corps program, used control and experimental groups to determine which of two conditions was more effective for developing basic academic skills.

The experimental group attended a school setting every morning, working at academic tasks and earning two cents for each correct response. The control group continued at their jobs or were placed in jobs by the Neighborhood Youth Corps. The girls in each group earned the same monthly salary, but the salary of the classroom group was contingent on academic performance. Results showed that the classroom group made significantly greater gains in reading and arithmetic. Both groups made similar gains in language skills.

High-Strength Reinforcement. Token reinforcement usually incorporates the use of high-strength activities, a second form of reinforcement management. Premack (1959) and Homme and his associates (Homme 1966; Homme et al. 1963) have demonstrated the effectiveness of arranging classroom activities so that the opportunity to engage in a high probability activity is programmed to follow the completion of a low probability one. For each child in any classroom, a number of activities will be pleasurable and a number of others unpleasurable. For instance, one child may derive a great deal of pleasure from arithmetic, gym, and art, but none at all from reading and spelling. Activities which are pleasant to the child are high probability activities; that is, there is a high probability that, given the option, the child will choose to engage in them.

High-strength areas should contain a wide variety of activities. Thus, as academic performance rates are acquired and maintained at a high level over a period of time, types of available reinforcers can be gradually changed from play activities to activities of an instructional nature. For example, children could move from the sandbox to games of naming such things as pail, shovel, and sand castle.

Each child's preferences must be considered in light of his repertoire of responses. Some children should be allowed to earn time in the high-strength area for very little work initially, but the amount of time earned should be brief. The typical behavior of these children, when they find they can earn time to do something of their own choosing, is to spend small amounts of time in the activity area as soon as it is earned in the work area. Although the child who uses the high-strength area more often and for shorter periods must be attended to more often by the teacher, the immediate reinforcement is effective in accelerating a response rate. The child may then be able to work for longer, albeit more infrequent, periods in the high-strength area. This condition of variable interval reinforcement serves to maintain his response rate.

The teacher will need to keep a record of the amount of time earned, the number of minutes spent in the high-strength area, and the number of minutes remaining to be spent. The number of minutes due the child is important. The Event Record used at the Experimental Education Unit (Haring and Kunzelmann 1966) provides for recording all data, including the types of activities consequent to responses (see appendix).

In brief, the teacher has several specific tasks to accomplish if he is to reinforce behavior in the classroom. He must—

1. select those conditions and events available in the classroom that can serve to strengthen patterns of behavior;
2. arrange classroom conditions so that they can become reinforcing consequences of behavior;
3. make himself a social reinforcer for each child;
4. adjust schedules of reinforcement as behavior patterns become acquired;
5. direct the child from teacher-managed reinforcement toward self-management of contingencies;
6. establish academic stimuli as reinforcers.

There is much evidence that the systematic use of positive reinforcement will accelerate and maintain a high rate of response, but further investigation is needed to establish techniques for stabilizing the rate. And to avoid the effects of satiation, further research is also needed to determine effective numbers and strength of reinforcers, and effective alternatives in timing of presentation, proximity of reinforcers, and increments in scheduling.

Negative Reinforcement

The withdrawal of an aversive event after a particular response will increase the probability of the recurrence of that response when the aversive event is again presented. This is the principle of negative reinforcement. Scolding, nagging, and prodding are usually aversive stimuli. When such events are presented to stimulate the child's response to something, they usually cause the child to respond in a particular way. If, during arithmetic, the teacher walks swiftly to Albert's desk and says, "Get to work on that assignment," Albert will probably begin to work. Albert's response has removed the scolding and prodding. Negative reinforcement of this sort should not be confused with the withholding of positive reinforcement. If the teacher does not allow Eve to go to art class because she refused to share her apple with Adam during lunch, the teacher is withholding an event that he considers positively reinforcing for Eve.

According to the principle of punishment, withholding a pleasant event or presenting an aversive one after a response temporarily decreases the rate of that response. Eve will probably not refuse to share her apple soon again, because she has been punished for that response.

Extinction

If a behavior that has been conditioned by positive reinforcement is no longer reinforced, its rate of occurrence will decrease. This is the principle of extinction. For example, to decrease the frequency of crying in a child who has received much attention for this behavior, the teacher should ignore it, thus withholding the positive reinforcement of her attention. Applying any principle of behavior modification requires consistency, but extinction procedures also demand an extraordinary amount of persistence and self-control, as any mother who has tried to ignore a child's persistent demands for a cookie knows. Most behavior pinpointed for extinction has been strongly conditioned and is maintained by very infrequent reinforcement. Consequently, it is extremely difficult to extinguish. Once the teacher ceases to reinforce an inappropriate behavior, she must be careful to ignore it completely. She can then anticipate two lawful effects. The first is that the behavior will initially accelerate in frequency. For example, when the teacher ignores Anthony's crying behavior, Anthony will at first cry more. But if nothing else maintains his crying behavior, the rate of its occurrence will soon begin to fall rapidly, especially if the teacher positively reinforces acceptable responses at the same time. If Anthony is ignored for crying and praised for doing arithmetic, he will soon discover that the latter is a much "better" response than the former. This initial acceleration of a behavior identified for extinction is a typical transitional pattern to which the teacher must respond correctly. If he succumbs to attending to the inappropriate behavior during this period of acceleration, he will only reinforce a behavior pattern that is occurring at a high rate and thereby strengthen it.

The second effect is that the particular behavior may recur spontaneously after it appears to have been extinguished. Here again, the teacher must be prepared not to respond. With both effects of extinction procedures, the teacher must have confidence that he is witnessing a natural behavioral effect rather than a failure on his part.

Management

Management incorporates direct observation, continuous response measurement, and the systematic application of reinforcers. Management primarily involves selecting and implementing the time, amount, and kind of reinforcement. For example, frequent reinforcement for appropriate responses in the initial stage efficiently increases the response rate. Too much or too little reinforcement will also affect the rate. Too much reinforcement presented each time it is due will decelerate a rate that has begun to strengthen; praise, time, and candy all lose their strength as reinforcers if overused. Similarly, too little reinforcement presented each time it is due will not strengthen the response rate, even though the same reinforcer in a larger amount is successful.

Research efforts have provided us with the following guidelines for effective contingency management.

1. To accelerate a rate of performance, reinforce the performance frequently in the beginning stages.
2. To maintain the high rate that has been achieved, reinforce the pattern only intermittently.
3. To secure and maintain the most stable pattern of response, reinforce the *number of responses* made rather than the number of minutes worked and use intermittent reinforcement after the initial stages.

Instruction is a procedure that demands an infinite number of decisions by the teacher. These decisions, especially with children who have learning or behavior problems, depend on the child's rate of response. This rate, graphed over a number of days, will exhibit a pattern of acceleration, deceleration, or no change. An acceleration of the response rate may be positive or negative; a deceleration, too, may be positive or negative. Whatever the case, or if the rate is constant, it is due to the effects of a particular set of conditions. With the response data guides, the teacher can introduce a new condition to attempt to accelerate positively the rate of response.

Relative changes in rate, rather than discrete or numerical changes, are the important data. Specific conditions may have the same relative effects on a group of children but different quantitative effects for individual children. It is not important to know that under a particular set of conditions one child's response rate changes from three to four responses per minute over several days and then from four to eight per minute, while another child's changes from eight to ten and then from ten to fifteen. What is important to know is that the prevailing conditions had a positively accelerating effect on both children's performances.

From daily performance graphs showing rates of correct and incorrect responses, the teacher can determine the effectiveness of the cues and the strength of reinforcers. The child's pattern of errors, of correct responses, of points earned, spent, and saved, and of activities engaged in during the use of earned time all reveal the effectiveness of the learning conditions. With this information, the teacher can plan changes in instructional programming for the child, and he can evaluate the effectiveness of the new instructional decisions by examining the new response data.

The counting of most classroom responses is a simple procedure. Before beginning to count, the teacher determines the length of time during which the response is to be counted. The period selected may be fifteen minutes every other hour of the school day; or it may be ten minutes twice a day, once in the morning and again in the afternoon; or the teacher may decide to observe and count the child's responses continuously for an entire morning.

An Event Sheet (see appendix) is used to collect data in classrooms of the Experimental Education Unit (Haring and Kunzelmann 1966). However, no special equipment is needed to count responses, and a small pad serves the purpose quite well. There should be a space at the top for the child's name, the date, and the length of the observation period. Below, there should be space for two columns, one labeled Correct Responses and the other Incorrect Responses. If the child's responses are emitted frequently, the teacher may want to use a counter. There are several on the market. Perhaps the simplest is the counter that knitters use on the tip of a knitting needle. If the observation time is to be of short duration—fifteen or twenty seconds—a stopwatch can be used. When the observation session is over, the responses should be totaled (if a counter is used, the total is, of course, automatically registered).

Although teachers are interested in the amount of responding a child does, that information is much more useful if the rate of the child's responses is determined. Two children may display the same inappropriate behavior in class, but there is an obvious difference between Mario, who emits the behavior ten times in ten minutes, and Luigi, who does so once every ten minutes. To obtain the response rate, the total number of responses is divided by the time (usually in minutes) during which the behavior is observed. The response rate indicates the effectiveness of the independent variables used to encourage performance.

The teacher should attempt to have the children take over some of the responsibilities of response measurement as soon as possible. Even children in the very early grades can learn to count and record their own correct and incorrect responses, provided the procedures used are not complicated. At the end of the session, the teacher has only to total the response data, and this, too, can eventually be done by the children. Older children can be taught how to calculate response rates, and some can be taught to plot their rates on six-cycle log paper. Teachers find that students are often reinforced merely by plotting their own response rates.

The final step in response recording is the charting of the response rate on six-cycle log paper, a graph paper designed by Dr. Ogden Lindsley.* Six-cycle log paper has a number of advantages over the commonly used arithmetic graph paper. For example, it allows recordings to be made of response rates that are as infrequent as .001 responses per minute or as frequent as 1,000 responses per minute. (See appendix.)

The goal of behavior modification in a special class is to give the child those self-management skills that will enable him to function in a regular school setting. His reentry into the regular classroom begins when he first enters the special class. For a child who is unable to function in a regular classroom, the successive approximations to terminal objectives in the special class are the sequential steps needed for reentry into the regular class.

The ultimate objectives of the teacher in applying contingency management for skill building are to use the type of consequence for responding that is a reinforcer for the child; to build other stimuli, like academic events and teacher and peer attention, as reinforcers; and to bring the child to the point where he responds to contingencies that he has set up for himself. The child is taken along a reinforcement continuum, from continuous reinforcement, planned and presented by the teacher, to accurate and efficient performance maintained entirely under his own contingencies. The teacher's most critical task may be to arrange the reinforcement program in such a way as to bring the child gradually to

* Behavioral Research Company, Box 3351, Kansas City, Kansas 66103.

take over his own scheduling of reinforcement (Lovitt and Curtiss 1969). As the child becomes effective in self-management in the special class, he is close to readiness for reentry into the regular class, so long as the regular teacher has the skills necessary to maintain his progress.

The return of the child from a setting in which contingencies have been precisely controlled and predictable responses readily established to the regular class, where sporadic contingencies often obtain, is not easy. If contingencies are not systematically provided in the regular class, successful reentry is hardly probable, and the child's performance rate most likely will not be maintained. The procedures for returning a child to his regular class need to be planned as meticulously as was the program for changing his behavior. Hewett (1967) has made a general reference to the need to attend to reentry problems, but no educator has succeeded in devising procedures to ensure the smooth maintenance of behavior from one setting to another, dissimilar one.

In brief, the teacher's own repertoire of responses must include some skill in—

1. sequentially arranging instruction materials;
2. establishing terminal objectives which specify the development of certain skills;
3. developing successive approximations of terminal objectives;
4. providing immediate feedback to the child about his progress and accuracy of performance;
5. recording instructional data daily;
6. attending to the child's appropriate responses;
7. making decisions based on performance data.

If the teacher in the new setting fails to apply these skills, the child's new behavior will eventually be extinguished.

Contingency Management in the Regular Class

The teacher's role, as he manages contingencies for a group, is exemplified in a study describing a reading program conducted for twenty-four students in an ungraded regular classroom (Haring and Hauck 1969a). Grade levels ranged from four through six. Basal reading levels ranged from two through five. The teacher established procedures for obtaining direct response measurement of performance in order to evaluate precisely her contingency management program for each child.

Each thirty-minute session began with silent study of an individualized list of words not known the previous session. Words the child missed were listed with other words having similar word parts in order to promote discrimination. When the student felt he knew his list of words, he reported to his assigned monitor to read the words aloud. After reading the words aloud, he silently read three pages in the basal reader, wrote an answer to a comprehension question, and orally read eight lines of print to the monitor. The student could proceed through this series of requirements as many times as he was able to in the half-hour period. During silent reading, he raised his hand if he needed the teacher's help with unfamiliar words.

The children were assigned to pupil-monitors, who had read at least several of the stories in advance. Each pupil-monitor had several responsibilities at his station in the room, and his thorough training was an important feature of the program. He was responsible for his students' folders, which were kept in a master folder. He distributed comprehension questions and corrected the answers, used a stopwatch to time the oral reading of lines of print, and recorded response data on the student's reading record sheet. For direct response measurement of oral reading, the pupil-monitor randomly selected eight lines of print from the three pages silently read. He used a stopwatch to time the rate of oral reading and marked each mispronounced word. On the student's reading record form, the pupil-monitor recorded the number of lines of print read correctly, the time spent, and the specific words mispronounced. Pupil-monitors were changed each week, and, interestingly enough, response data consistently showed marked acceleration in their own reading performances after holding this job.

At the end of thirty minutes a timer rang and all students closed their books. Each student totaled the number of lines of print he had correctly read aloud and the number of seconds he had taken to read them. Then, using a rate chart, he determined his reading rate and plotted this new response data on his graph on the wall.

The classroom teacher in this program provided information on unknown words when requested during silent reading, checked the pupil-monitors' accuracy in conducting their responsibilities, and reviewed the performance data after each session in order to make decisions about the effectiveness of the contingencies for each child.

After determining the pupil's average performance at the end of each week, the teacher established two easy-to-manage contingencies for the following week: (a) average performance earned five minutes additional recess or physical education time, and (b) better-than-average performance earned ten minutes of either activity. For most of the children, this condition was reinforcing. Consequently, it effectively maintained rates that were high, accelerated rates that were low, and stabilized rates that were variable. Thus, three different response patterns were managed with one type of manipulation.

Results. The teacher felt that these procedures of contingency management provided her with a reading class where students could hardly wait for reading, where discipline problems were nonexistent for thirty minutes, where no student ever handed in an incomplete assignment, and where students performed their tasks so efficiently that they read themselves right out of material.

Summary

Instruction and intervention are similar in that, to be effective, they both require that behavior change take place. The primary responsibility for such change rests with the teacher; it is he who must manage any program designed to increase the child's repertoire of responses in academic and social performance and in fine and gross motor skills. His main concern must be the ways in which the environment—the specific cues for evoking responses and the conditions under which reinforcement is scheduled—can best be arranged to increase the rate and accuracy of response.

As a behavior modifier, the teacher must learn to measure behavior accurately and to make use of measurement data in arranging the environment so that it provides the most effective instructional conditions.

Designs for establishing behavioral control in the classroom are quite straightforward. They require that a baseline measurement be taken over a period of time, under well-controlled conditions, before any instructional change is introduced. In addition, they require that measurement continue throughout the period of change. A return to baseline conditions is usually not necessary; more likely, the next change will be a refinement of the earlier treatment, and additional refinements will be made throughout the intervention project. The teacher, whose aim is to increase the level of precision in classroom instruction, makes his decisions on the basis of continuously gathered data.

Programmed materials are especially suited to a systematic plan for changing behavior because their frames (cues for response) can be arranged in a sequence to produce gradual approximations of the desired terminal behavior. Instructional programs can be used to great advantage in bringing about changes in academic response, particularly if they require active responses. These responses can serve as a record of the behavior being shaped and thus provide the teacher with information on correct and incorrect response rates.

All types of behavior—verbal, social, and academic—are shaped by environmental events which occur both before and after the child has responded. In education, a great deal of attention has been given to the range of activities and conditions (amount of group stimulation and number of instructional cues) which occur before the child makes a response. However, the events which ocur after a response has been made are probably as important for changing behavior as those that take place before, and it is therefore necessary to consider the principles of reinforcement. Reinforcing events, among them tokens, trinkets, food, and high-strength or high probability activities, have been used successfully to strengthen behavior. Making high-interest or high probability activities contingent on responses in low-interest activities (e.g., academic work) provides a practical way of applying reinforcement in the classroom, since activities of great interest to children are known to be reinforcing. Time earned by responding to academic tasks can be used for pleasureable classroom activities, thus making use of natural conditions in the classroom.

Negative reinforcement and punishment are used much less frequently. While teachers sometimes apply them in dealing with inappropriate behavior, far more research is needed to determine whether their widespread use in the classroom is advisable.

The goal of behavior modification is to provide conditions which will allow the child to manage his own contingencies effectively. The success of any intervention project is achieved when appropriate behavior can be maintained by the individual himself without the need for outside manipulation of reinforcement contingencies.

References

Berkowitz, Pearl H., and Esther P. Rothman. *The Disturbed Child: Recognition and Psychoeducational Therapy in the Classroom.* New York: New York University Press, 1960.

Bijou, Sidney W., and Persis T. Sturges. "Positive Reinforcers for Experimental Studies with Children—Consumables and Manipulatables." *Child Development,* **30** (1959): 151–70.

Buchanan, Cynthia Dee. *Programmed Reading.* St. Louis-New York: Webster Division, McGraw-Hill Book Company, 1964.

Clark, Marilyn, Joe Lachowicz, and Montrose Wolf. "A Pilot Basic Education Program for School Dropouts Incorporating a Token Reinforcement System." *Behaviour Research and Therapy,* **6** (1968): 183–88.

Ferster, C. B. "Positive Reinforcement and Behavioral Deficits of Autistic Children." *Child Development,* **32** (1961): 437–56.

Haring, Norris G. *Attending and Responding.* San Rafael, Calif.: Dimensions Publishing Co., 1968.

Haring, Norris G., and Mary Ann Hauck. "Improved Learning Conditions in the Establishment of Reading Skills with Disabled Readers." *Exceptional Children*, **35** (1969a): 341–52.

Haring, Norris G., and Harold Kunzelmann. "The Finer Focus of Therapeutic Behavioral Management." In *Educational Therapy, Volume I*, edited by Jerome Hellmuth. Seattle, Wash.: Special Child Publications, Inc., 1966.

Haring, Norris G., and Robert W. Ridgway. "Early Identification of Children with Learning Disabilities." *Exceptional Children*, **33** (1967): 387–95.

Hewett, Frank M. "Educational Engineering with Emotionally Disturbed Children." *Exceptional Children*, **33** (1967): 459–67.

Holland, James G. "Teaching Machines: An Application of Principles from the Laboratory." *Journal of the Experimental Analysis of Behavior*, **3** (1960): 275–87.

Homme, Lloyd E. "Human Motivation and Environment." In *The Learning Environment: Relationship to Behavior Modification and Implications for Special Education*, Norris G. Haring and Richard J. Whelan, coordinators. Symposium sponsored by the School of Education, University of Kansas, 1965. *Kansas Studies in Education*, **16**:2 (1966), pp. 30–39.

Homme, L. E., P. C. deBaca, J. V. Devine, R. Steinhorst, and E. J. Rickert. "Use of the Premack Principle in Controlling the Behavior of Nursery School Children," *Journal of the Experimental Analysis of Behavior*, **6** (1963): 544.

Kelleher, Roger T., and Lewis R. Gollub. "A Review of Positive Conditioned Reinforcement." *Journal of the Experimental Analysis of Behavior*, **5** (Suppl., 1962): 543–97.

Kuypers, David S., Wesley C. Becker, and K. Daniel O'Leary. "How to Make a Token System Fail." *Exceptional Children*, **35** (1968): 101–9.

Lippman, Hyman S. *Treatment of the Child in Emotional Conflict*, 2nd ed. New York: McGraw-Hill Book Company, Inc., 1962.

Long, Nicholas James, William C. Morse, and Ruth G. Newman, eds. *Conflict in the Classroom: The Education of Emotionally Disturbed Children*. Belmont, Calif.: Wadsworth Publishing Company, 1965.

Lovitt, Thomas C., and Karen A. Curtiss. "Academic Response Rate as a Function of Teacher- and Self-imposed Contingencies." *Journal of Applied Behavior Analysis*, **2** (1969): 49–53.

McKenzie, Hugh S., Marilyn Clark, Montrose M. Wolf, Richard Kothera, and Cedric Benson. "Behavior Modification of Children with Learning Disabilities Using Grades as Tokens and Allowances as Back Up Reinforcers." *Exceptional Children*, **34** (1968): 745–52.

O'Leary, K. Daniel, and Wesley C. Becker. "Behavior Modification of an Adjustment Class: A Token Reinforcement Program." *Exceptional Children*, **33** (1967): 627–42.

Patterson, G. R., and J. B. Reid. "Reciprocity and Coercion: Two Facets of Social Systems." In *Behavior Modification in Clinical Psychology*, edited by C. Neuringer and J. L. Michael. New York: Appleton-Century-Crofts, 1970.

Premack, David. "Toward Empirical Behavior Laws: 1. Positive Reinforcement." *Psychological Review*, **66** (1959): 219–33.

Sidman, Murray. *Tactics of Scientific Research*. New York: Basic Books, 1960.

Suppes, Patrick, and Joanne Suppes. *Sets and Numbers.* New York: The L. W. Singer Company, Inc., A Subsidiary of Random House, 1968.

Wolf, Montrose M., David K. Giles, and R. Vance Hall. "Experiments with Token Reinforcement in a Remedial Classroom." *Behaviour Research and Therapy,* **6** (1968): 51–64.

Programmed Instruction and Behavioral Control

5

Learning objectives vary, depending considerably on the individual involved. But no matter who the individual is or what his capabilities are, learning for him means that he must, at least to the limit of his capabilities, broaden his knowledge and acquire competency in those skills necessary for survival in a modern world, whether these entail decision-making, problem-solving, or coping with the environment. One of the most efficient ways to accomplish these objectives is to use programmed instruction.

Characteristics of Programmed Instruction

The characteristics of programmed instruction that promote effective learning can be summarized as follows.

The material to be learned is presented in a way that *requires active responding* by the student. By "active responding," we mean that the student has to respond to a question in some way (e.g., answer "yes" or "no," write out an equation, spell a word, give a name or date, select a key word from a passage, or compose a response). The question usually follows the presentation of a small segment of material called a *frame*. An underlined space, either beneath or to the right or left of the question half of the frame, is reserved for the student's response. Generally, the programmed format is so arranged that the left side of the page contains the frames while the right side is reserved for the responses.

> **Frame:** George Washington, 1732–1799, served as the first president of the United States of America.
>
> **Question:** The first president of the United States was G._____ W._____.

In the example above, *George Washington* is the correct answer to the question half of the frame. The reader is helped somewhat by being given a cue to the answer: a *G* before the first blank and a *W* before the second blank. The frame could have been written without the cue. Here is another example:

> **Frame:** Books on battles of the Civil War are found in the nonfiction section of a library.
>
> **Question:** Books about war battles are found in what section of a library? _____.

An even simpler example, perhaps more readily applicable to a handicapped learner at the elementary school level, would be the one shown in the following frame.

> **Frame:**

> **Question:** Now look at this man and name (or draw) the important part that is missing. ____

Figure 5.1. Frame for programmed instruction

After the child has drawn in the missing head, or has named the word "head," the teacher might say, "Yes, you're right—the head is missing." But the child must *respond;* he must write, draw, or name the missing part. The teacher, using the programmed format, does not credit the child with knowing the right response unless it is evident. The teacher does not say, "Sure, you know what is missing—why, the head, of course," and then expect the child to nod or smile in agreement. The teacher must wait for the appropriate active response.

A second characteristic of programmed instruction is the step-by-step presentation of the material. To the experienced or knowledgeable person, these steps sometimes seem overexplicit and boring, and well they may be if the program is below the level of the learner. But the small-step progression is important and helps to ensure that the learner works through a series of steps which, as a whole, contribute to the mastery of some subject matter, however limited.

For example, a teacher who wishes to improve the body-image concept of a handicapped learner might present successive drawings of a man with various parts missing. One drawing might have the head missing; another, the arms missing; still another, the legs missing; and so on, through perhaps five or ten steps that successively integrate the child's identifications of the missing parts. Whether the child responds verbally or in writing will depend on the nature and extent of his handicap.

An introduction to American History at about the third-grade level may also proceed step by step, as in the following example:

> **Frame:** Today our country is called the United States of America. It is a big country, but many years ago it did not have many people. Some of the first people to come to our land were called Pilgrims
> a. Our country today is called: _____ _____
> b. Some early settlers were called: _____
> c. Is our country bigger today than it was when people first came here? (Yes or No) _____

Here is another example, using a current social studies topic:

> **Frame:** Most people in our country ride in or drive cars each day. Many people use cars for their work, and others use cars for pleasure.
> **Question:** People drive or ride in cars because they need cars in their _____, or because they like to ride in them for _____.

> **Frame:** Many millions of cars are sold in the world each year. More cars are made and sold in the United States than in any other country.
> **Question:** The country that makes and sells the most cars in the world is _____.

Frame: Cars range in size from very small to very large. The smallest car is about 5 feet long, but the largest cars may be 22 feet long.

Question: The shortest cars are very short—about _____ feet; but the longest cars may be as long as _____ feet.

In this manner, information is gradually presented in a succession of frames. Each step or frame contributes in some material way to the topic under study. Each frame should contain some important item of information which the student, by his answer, reveals that he understands or differentiates.

The third characteristic of programmed instruction is immediate knowledge of results. Immediately after the student responds, he can check on whether he is right or wrong. If he is correct, he proceeds to the next frame. If he is wrong, he should read the frame again and correct his answer, if he can. If the student misses too many frames in succession, it may mean that he has failed to master some earlier frames or that the whole series is too difficult for him. A simpler or different series is then indicated.

Many studies of learning reveal that immediate knowledge of results—immediate feedback, or the reinforcement of knowing that one is correct—greatly enhances learning. If knowledge of results is long delayed, as with a test that is not returned to the student for days or weeks—its tenuous temporal connection with the performance will weaken, or even obviate, the relationship between the two. It is even more important for the handicapped learner with a limited behavioral repertoire to be informed continually of his progress by receiving feedback of results as soon as he has responded. Frequent verbal remarks, such as "Good" and "That's fine, Jim," and marks from the teacher that signal success ("100"), all contribute to greater motivation and to a higher level of success.

Studies also indicate that if the learning conditions are well constructed, a single trial learning session that is immediately reinforced may result in optimal behavior. In most cases, however, complex learning takes many steps, each of which is more effective if there is an immediate feedback of results (immediate reinforcement).

"Self-pacing," where the student can proceed at his own pace, is a fourth characteristic of programmed instruction. The student can do as few, or as many, frames per learning session (or per day) as he desires; he can go as rapidly or as slowly as his capabilities allow. In this way, students at the high school level have been known to cover a whole year of beginning algebra in less than one semester, or a semester of trigonometry in just a few weeks' time. On the other hand, for the handicapped or very slow learner, no penalty is attached to a performance that may take him twice or three times as long as the "average" learner. It is true that learning problems for the former may necessitate his exposure and re-exposure many times to the same programmed material that a nonhandi-capped learner may master in one session.

Even though the self-pacing feature of programmed instruction is not pressured, it is important to realize that the learner's cycle of response—reading the frame, reading the question, responding, receiving feedback, progressing to the next frame—is a tight chain and that slowness per se does not mean that the child is not paying attention or is lazy. The learner working at his own pace—slow or fast—is, in a sense, "locked in" to the cycle of activity; this tends to enhance his learning and, correspondingly, his memory or ability to use what he has learned (Margulies and Eigen 1962).

Since the student proceeds at his own pace, a good share of the teacher's time, which under other circumstances would be used to present material, can now be devoted to keeping track of the learner's progress and to individualizing instruction to a considerable degree. Children working at different rates and at different places in the Sullivan Programmed Reading Series (Buchanan 1964), or in one of the programmed arithmetic series, are able, on completion of a unit of work, to hand in their written responses to the teacher. However, even though a child who has completed a programmed reading series by writing in key words or short phrases may have an errorless record, he may need additional help from the teacher: his printing may be too large, say, or his writing illegible. The teacher might say, "You have done an excellent job on this unit, Ralph, and your answers are all correct; I hope that with the next unit your handwriting will be easier for me to read." Ralph is thus reinforced for his good performance, and the qualitative and extra-programmed nature of the teacher's comments and guidance serve a useful purpose; Ralph can build his next performance on the accuracy of his past work and at the same time enhance his communicative powers by producing a more legible script.

As programs become longer and require more complex or lengthy responses, the teacher can further enhance his own role by adding other qualitative help to the cues provided by the program. For example, the student using programmed instruction in history or in foreign languages may be technically accurate in his responses but err in spelling or in sentence structure. There is no problem with his basic knowledge, but he will need the teacher's help in polishing and extending his skills in spelling and grammar. Placing the extra help from the teacher in these qualitative dimensions can simultaneously increase the student's knowledge and help him achieve better communication skills.

It is possible in a classroom of either normal or handicapped learners to have each student work under his own self-pacing routine and still be helped by the teacher's observations and guidance. And once children who are using programmed materials set their own paces and move along at predictable rates, the teacher can learn more about them, explore their activities, and sample their responses more fully, and keep a number of individually occupied children working gainfully for sustained periods of time.

The student who proceeds from one step to the next at his own pace, and who is given immediate reinforcement, will usually show a low rate of error. This is the fifth characteristic of programmed instruction. If the student's rate of error on programmed material is high—more than ten percent in such subjects as spelling, arithmetic, history, geography, and social studies—this may be a signal to the teacher that the level of the material is too difficult. A simpler program is probably indicated. However, the technique of putting the student through the same programmed reading or arithmetic series on two or more successive occasions in order to decrease the rate of error has also been recommended and used. For example, if a child goes through fifty pages of basic skill problems in arithmetic (addition, subtraction, multiplication, and division) and has to repeat the assignment, his rate of error will decrease and he will not be bored if conditions continue to be reinforcing for him. His rate of response will usually increase under such conditions, though a higher rate of response is less important than a higher percentage of accurate responses.

In conventional teaching, the student is too often carried along by the pressure of time and by the teacher's urging to cover a given number of pages within the span of a grading period (six to nine weeks). Students taught by older methods are "paced," then, not by their own learning rates and reinforcement schedules, but by external pressures. As a result, students in the intermediate and secondary grades frequently will not know how to add, subtract, multiply, or divide, and their spelling may be full of errors. The problem here is not the inability of the learner, but the pacing and the error rate which characterize the learning that does take place. In addition, teachers using the older methods probably do not employ feedback and reinforcement as conditionally or as accurately as they should.

Levels of Instruction and Response

Programmed material can be pitched at a very simple level. Most of the examples cited earlier require single-item (word, number) types of responses. As the learner's comprehension and the subject matter increase in complexity, the programmed format incorporates more qualitative responses.

One distinction regarding levels of instruction concerns the matter of selecting a response (as with multiple choice items) versus originating or composing the answer. An arithmetic problem may be presented in multiple choice format:

```
Add: 6              Answers: a) 29
      8                      b) 32
      9                      c) 30
      6                      d) 27          _____
     ──
```

Here the student selects a, b, c, or d, inserts his choice in the blank to the right of the frame, and then compares his answer with the correct one. Or, the problem may be presented without multiple choices, so that it is the student who must construct the answer:

```
Add:  7             Answer: _____
     15
      4
      9
     ──
```

One may ask what the difference is. The student doing the first problem may guess at the answer and guess inaccurately at that. In the second example, he is more likely to be careful and accurate, since he has no guide to follow. As items become more complex, ingenuity and answer-constructing ability are called for. The constructed answer may reflect more maturity and thoughtfulness; also, originality is more likely to emerge. Here is an example from reading material at the elementary level:

> **Frame:** *The Story of Jack and the Beanstalk* has been read by most of the children of the world. Jack found great treasures at the top of the beanstalk, ran into many dangers, but finally escaped from harm. He returned to his mother's side safely, and together they overcame their poor living conditions.
>
> **Question:** Why did Jack climb the beanstalk? (Some possible answers: "Because he wanted to explore new things"; "He wanted to see if he could help his mother"; "They were poor and he wanted to help his mother get food for them"; "Jack thought he might find something up there.")

These answers, suitable at the elementary level, all signify the carrying out of some thought process by the responding child. The question does not call for a single-item response; rather, it gives free rein to the child's imagination. Many equivalent responses would be acceptable in this learning situation.

Even at the middle elementary level, the child, whether handicapped or normal in his learning potential, is able to construct answers to questions. Many frames on nature study, for example, can be constructed in programmed format, leaving open the construction of accurate, but inventive, responses (Pearce 1968).

Designing a Program

There is an extensive literature on ways to develop programmed instruction. Our purpose here is not to try to cover all the complexities involved in actually writing programs, but to highlight some of the necessary preconditions.

Terminal Objectives

The first and most important step in planning programmed instruction, or in utilizing available programmed instruction, is to have some *terminal objectives* in mind. These are the behaviors the student should display when he has completed the program. Terminal objectives should be clear and precise; they cannot be vague or general. "Being able to read" is not a suitable terminal objective in programmed instruction. The questions that arise immediately are: "Read what?" "At what level?" "With what vocabulary competence?" "At what speed and accuracy?" And so on.

A more suitable terminal objective might be to have the student read at a third-grade level. This would require a fairly good mastery of vocabulary, the ability to answer questions about what is read, and the ability to discuss the topic orally (if not in written form). As an example, the following oral résumé was given by a ten-year-old handicapped reader who had worked intermittently on *Jack and the Beanstalk* for one month.

> "Well, you see Jack was climbing up this beanstalk. His mother didn't know about it. He went up to the top and a bad man got after him up there. He got scared and came down as fast as he can. I guess he ran away from the bad man; and he got kill't when he fell down the beanstalk."
>
> Question: "Did Jack grow the beanstalk?"
> Answer: "Yes—in his own back yard."
> Question: "How did Jack get the beanstalk?"
> Answer: "He had a seed and planted it."
> Question: "Was Jack's mother pleased at first when Jack planted the seed?"
> Answer: "No."

Question: "Why not?"

Answer: "Because they were hungry and needed food."

It is apparent that this handicapped learner has handled the story moderately well. Yet six months before reading *Jack and the Beanstalk*, he was unable to read beyond first-grade level, as measured by several word-recognition tests. With oral and written responses to short sentences, brief stories, and brief question-and-answer sessions following his reading, all in programmed format, the youngster gradually mastered a third-grade vocabulary. His independent reading increased from short snatches of a minute or two at a time, several times each week, to a high of twenty-three to twenty-five minutes a day, usually divided into three or four reading periods. In addition, he increased his silent reading to the point where it covered about ninety percent of his total reading time.

Different degrees of mastery must be identified in order to decide on terminal objectives. For example, a child learning to handle simple and common tools may be able to identify each tool—hammer, pliers, saw—but not know how to use it. At a more complex level, he may work as helper to a carpenter, supplying the tools upon request or using the tools himself under supervision. And at an even more sophisticated level, he may select several tools from a tool kit and proceed to make a birdhouse, shoeshine box, or mailbox.

Each area of subject matter and each important topic or concept within that area has a specific role in the defining of a terminal objective. Where motor skills are involved the terminal objectives and their levels of complexity are quite easily specified. When the learning objectives are verbal, abstract, and based on several independent skills—reading for instance—the various levels of competence are harder to specify.

Program Evaluation

The development of a program requires some basis for testing and extending (revising) it. The teacher has to have some feedback for himself in order to know whether the program is meeting its objectives. There are several ways of increasing the likelihood that the instructional program and its terminal objectives will indeed be valid and useful. One way is to compare the effectiveness of the programmed teaching with traditional (essentially nonsystematic) teaching. When a child, or even a class, is given an arithmetic or a reading book to work with, some learning of arithmetic or reading will take place. The less systematic ways of teaching result in some learning, *but* they are less efficient.

In the case of handicapped learners, another way to test the effectiveness of the programmed approach is to examine the rate of progress. In mathematics, for example, this rate can be determined by dividing the number of math problems correctly solved by the period of time spent in doing them. The rate can then be graphed. It is very likely that, under properly reinforcing conditions, the learner with a higher response rate will know more about arithmetic and be able to score better in novel arithmetic situations than the learner with a lower rate. The students can also be tested by the teacher at the end of a period of time. For example, scores on a standard arithmetic or reading test can be used to compare results of programmed instruction with those of less systematic methods.

A final consideration in this brief discussion on designing programs for informal classroom use is to recognize that a programmed format for instruction can be—indeed, has to be—highly flexible. One-frame-at-a-time procedures have their advantages, but programs for handicapped learners can take many different forms.

Broadening the programmed format is a "must" with most deficient learners. To supplement the programmed sequence in reading, for example, the words to be learned can be presented on flash cards. Arithmetic problems can be presented in this manner also, as teachers have traditionally done. Tape recorders can also be used to present brief individualized instructions for each child to follow before reporting to the teacher. Maps can serve as the basis for semiprogrammed stimuli and response requirements, using the identification of cities or countries, the learning of directions, and the more subtle identification of lakes, plains, and mountains on the terrain as the terminal objectives. Often geography or history lessons can be semiprogrammed in this manner and presented to the class as a game. Teachers often fail to consider games, but they are an ingenious application of at least some of the ingredients of programmed instruction: the sequential presentation of stimuli, individual pacing, and immediate knowledge of results. Further, games may offer the extra reinforcement that is provided by support from one's social peers.

Programmed materials have the advantages of specifying learning objectives and arranging sequential steps leading successively toward those objectives. Since the child is continuously making active responses, progress throughout the learning sessions can be seen by both the teacher and the child. Areas where the program is inadequate become readily apparent, and the teacher can rearrange, add, or delete frames to provide additional information and more practice.

Programmed material also provides a way of comparing the child's progress from day to day. His total of correct responses and errors can be computed at the end of each session. Where programs provide for equal response units, i.e., where each response is comparable to all others in the length of time necessary for its emission, the child's rate from session to session can be charted by the teacher. By using response rate as a basic measurement, each child's learning progress can be charted, the median for the week can be established, and trends can be seen. With this information, the teacher can establish a precise instructional program.

Teaching Machines and the Cybernetic Influence in Instruction

There are areas where programmed instruction and more complex teaching systems are complementary. This is especially true in content areas where the information is relatively easy to program and can, with computer assistance, be offered to many students simultaneously. The computer can record the progress of each student continuously, thus ensuring that data on the current progress of individual students and the class as a whole are always available to the teacher. The computer extends the capability of the simpler programmed format in order to meet the simultaneous demands of many different learners. Just how much the computer-assisted instructional systems can be used with behaviorally deficient learners is yet to be determined, but each year educators become more confident that the computer will eventually help us solve many problems in teaching and learning which today are necessarily handled at a less precise level.

Educational technology approaches human behavior according to the cybernetic view of human development. In order to understand the applicability of a general systems or cybernetic approach to instruction, one must review its particular features and its application to the development of human behavior (Silvern 1968).

What Is Cybernetics?

Cybernetics, derived from the Greek *kybernetes*, means, roughly, steersman. It refers to the observation that the behavior of an organism depends on the feedback information that is available, not unlike the behavior of a bird soaring in for a landing, a pilot steering a ship into port, or a person coordinating his eyes and hands to thread a needle. Some behavior is under the control of available information which, in turn, enables the behaving organism to steer, direct, or guide his actions. It is interesting that the learning concept of *reinforcement* is so similar to the cybernetic notion of *feedback*. The use of knowledge of the consequences of an action to guide the person or to direct the action is important in both cases (Dechert 1967).

Learning can be viewed as a "flow chart," i.e., as a model or a picture of how things flow from some beginning point to a terminal one. The stimulus (in programmed instruction, the frame that presents the information) is the first point in this "flow." Then there follows some reaction to the stimulus (making a mark, selecting from alternatives, saying "yes" or "no," or producing more complicated responses). Following this there is some stamp of approval or disapproval, some feedback of information, some knowledge of consequences—such as when the learner is told to move ahead since he is on the right track, or when he is told that some change is needed.

A simple feedback system is like a direct communication with another person. One person says, "Please come here." The second person moves toward the first person. There is a stimulus (the words spoken); there is a response (the movement of the second person); and there is a consequence or reinforcement because the message results in the desired, or approved, action. The first person may complicate the message and say, "Please come here and sit by me on the piano bench." Or, he may complicate it far more: "Please come and sit on the piano bench and play this four-hand selection with me. You play the treble." The reinforcement involved in the last message might not be fully forthcoming for many minutes—not till after the piano duet has been completed—but when it does come it might take the form of thunderous applause, which would be a powerful reinforcer indeed.

Consider for a moment that most human interactions are made up of just this kind of communication flow. Some differentially understandable stimulus complex (usually multiple stimuli) is presented. This, in turn, invites responses of varying degrees of complexity, followed by some signs of approval, or disapproval, or both. This cycle continues ad infinitum (Rath 1968).

To capitalize on these observations from the standpoint of teaching and learning—especially for the defective or handicapped learner—we must (a) recognize the pattern or flow of events, (b) recognize the cycle, (c) break down the events into manageable units, and (d) reinforce the outcome so that the whole pattern or flow is encouraged and eventually improved (Silverman 1968).

These events are said to "flow" because they take place in time; they are identified as "patterns" because of their predictability and similarity when repeated. The flow and pattern of events are considered when a programmed instruction manual is written, when a computer is used to assist learning, and when the behavior of a person is regarded within a behavioral framework.

How the Computer Can Help

The computer is simply a convenient tool for organizing the flow and pattern of events that lead to learning. It houses the significant events that have to be controlled if the learner is to progress. The computer is a "package" that can unfold to produce a large number of stimuli and reinforcers designed to affect the learner in some desired way.

In order to have learning take place, the environment must be organized. There must be a stimulus, followed by some events in the form of responses from the learner. There must also be some consequence (feedback-reinforcement) associated with this series. All this is contained in the organization of the environment. All school rooms, all words printed in books, all words spoken by other people, constitute some special organization of the environment. The computer takes up at this point and provides, on the basis of what is known about learning, a special and efficient organization of some important part of the environment designed to influence the learner's behavior in some specific way.

Feedback: The Most Important Concept in Cybernetics

As previously indicated, the most important single concept in the cybernetic application of computers is *feedback*, a notion which is strikingly similar to the concept of reinforcement in learning theory. Feedback enables a person to regulate his own behavior by adapting to the inflow of information. The notion of feedback can be illustrated by a person trying to thread a needle. As he guides the hand holding the needle, he also guides the hand holding the thread. If the hand guiding the thread should drift away from the target, i.e., the eye of the needle, the thread will not go through. Through visual information, the individual receives "feedback" concerning his accuracy or the changes in direction that must be made for correction. In addition, he is reinforced for some incremental progress toward threading the needle. There is, then, a continual interplay between vision and motor coordination as each sensory channel feeds back information. Feedback information comes through one or more channels (sensory organs) which, in turn, serve to guide action and correct error. A complex activity can be viewed as comprising many feedback junctures—many points where reinforcement might occur; as the whole process smooths out, the many junctures are integrated into one continuous procedure.

There are countless other examples of feedback. A person parking a car or bringing a boat into dock is using very explicit and minute pieces of evidence from his senses (vision, hearing, feeling) to control his movements in order to position the car or boat properly. In the development and practice of high-level skills such as playing a violin, painting, putting together an apparatus, or cooking a meal, there are many avenues through which the individual receives information to guide his further decisions and thus arrive at the final product (a properly pitched tone, the desired balance between color and form, a functioning piece of equipment, or the right flavor for a food).

An interesting feature about many feedback processes is that they are often difficult to translate into words. It is hard to tell another person how to drive a car, how to tie a tie, how to cook a meal; and certainly words may fail us completely if we try to tell him how to do something as complex as tuning a violin. The feedback process—the process of receiving information through our senses—seems highly specific and often impossible to put into words. This observation will be important later when we discuss ways of improving instruction in the classroom and controlling the behavior of children, especially children who have behavior and learning difficulties.

There is probably no instance of communication between people (or between people and animals, or between people and machines) that does not involve feedback. Sometimes this feedback is very simple, as when a master calls his dog, but it can be very complex when one is regulating the many processes involved in teaching children such skills as reading or long division.

Feedback in Learning. Feedback is also basic to learning and is involved in learning in several ways. First, the individual must learn to be alert to the particular cues from which feedback emanates. When we learn to read music, we learn to respond in highly complex ways to the printed notes, to the time value of notes, to the position of the notes on the staff, and to the relationship between notes and pitch. A simpler instance of the same learning of cues which feed back information to us is when we learn that the green light at the traffic intersection signals "go" and the red light "stop." Perhaps the simplest illustrations of feedback are what the information specialists call "go" or "no go," meaning that the signal or cue is either "off" or "on," like a light switch.

Feedback is also an important factor in learning how to correct or regulate the responses that have already been made. Through feedback, the child learns how to overcome his tendency to press the wrong key on the typewriter or to confuse the letter *b* with the letter *d*. If we could not correct our responses through the use of feedback, we would be welded to our errors and rigidly unadaptive.

Through feedback, the stimulus materials gain control over behavior. The establishment of environmental and behavioral control is essential in all learning, but it is even more critical in the teaching of children with behavior or learning difficulties or with handicaps of a different nature. Control of environmental variables, i.e., the stimuli and the responses, is essential for attaining more complex levels of skill. Anyone can press three keys correctly, in sequence, in order to type the simple article *t-h-e*. Think, then, of the additional control needed to type *T-h-e b-o-y i-s t-y-p-i-n-g* and so on, through additional levels of integrated complexity until fifty words or more can be typed per minute with few or no errors.

Control through the use of feedback results in highly integrated behavior. The child who first learns to walk, then to run, then to jump, and finally to skate or dance, is an example. The child learning his new song on the piano to the point where he can engage in a recital with peers is another example. In the past, learning theory too often emphasized a specific response and gave insufficient attention to the integration of series or patterns of response, the type of behavior that truly characterizes high-level performance and the optimal use of human skills (Thomson 1968).

Feedback in the Evaluation of Behavior. Feedback is important in yet another way. It allows a person to know the outcome of his action. That is, information fed back tells the individual if he has done the job correctly and whether he is entitled to reward or reinforcement. If the individual has no information on the adequacy of his performance as compared to the desired goal, he has no way of assessing his behavior. If a blindfolded individual were taken into a room, given a dart gun, and told to shoot at a target somewhere in the room, but then provided with no information about whether he hit the target, he could fire forever without any appreciable results. He would have no cues to go on and no information about how he might be missing the mark—a perfect situation if one's purpose is to deter learning. Correct all these points, and the person would have perfect (or nearly perfect) conditions for improving his learning.

The reader is already familiar with the concept of *reinforcement*, which is integral to the study of learning. Reinforcement is, in a sense, the knowledge of results, a stamp of approval or correctness placed on performance. The use of reinforcement increases the likelihood that later, given a similar situation, the new performance will resemble the previous one. Many psychologists (Ferster and Skinner 1957; Keller and Schoenfeld 1950) believe that learning depends on reinforcement; that is, if there is no reinforcement, then no direction is provided for the organism's activities, and if there is no direction, learning does not take place. Reinforcement has the effect of shaping or regulating the very behavior that was reinforced. There are, of course, preferred ways of reinforcing behavior. Further, the timing of reinforcement is of great importance.

Some psychologists think that the phenomenon of reinforcement should be subsumed under the concept of feedback. For these psychologists, feedback is the broader concept and reinforcement a particular instance of it. They point to balanced and spatially oriented behavior (e.g., walking) as being based on feedback information, in that feedback enables the organism to maintain an erect posture and locomote in various directions. The purpose here, however, is not to discuss the primacy of feedback over reinforcement, or vice versa, but to make use of both concepts in order to deal effectively with disturbed children.

The Loop: The Second Most Important Concept in Cybernetics

After feedback, the next most important concept offered by cybernetics is the *loop*. If behavior is controlled by feedback, the flow of information from the control center through various media and various points, and finally back to the control center, is viewed as a loop. Returning to the example of a person threading a needle, the eyes feed back information on the location of the thread and the needle, this information is processed in the brain, the messages are returned to the controlling fingers, corrective responses are made, and, ultimately, through successive approximitions and corrective efforts, the individual succeeds in threading the needle.

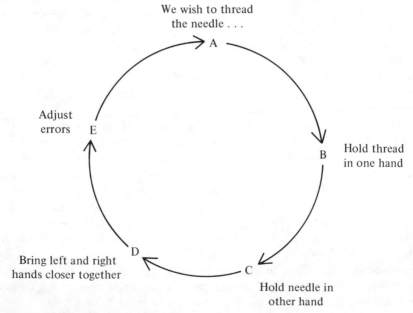

Figure 5.2. Threading a needle

The feedback system involved in threading a needle (Fig. 5.2) can be further illustrated through another step or two. Suppose the person threading a needle is doing so as a preliminary step to darning a hole in a garment. First comes the threading of the needle; then comes the use of the threaded needle by passing it through the edges of the hole to be repaired. As the individual guides the needle back and forth through the garment, the hole is gradually made smaller (information fed back to the individual) and in time it is filled in. This process might be described as a loop in the following way:

Hole in garment . . . thread needle . . . pass needle through garment to opposite edge of hole area . . . draw thread through garment . . . return thread to beginning side by inserting needle alongside first thread . . . continue from one side to the other until a series of threads (the warp) is built up . . . insert needle at right angle to warp threads, place needle over first strand, under second, over third . . . continue until row is completed . . . return by inserting needle under first strand and over second, etc., until second row is completed . . . continue this procedure until the hole is filled in. (See Fig. 5.3.)

There may be many steps in such a feedback loop. However, the number of steps is not as important as the way in which one step leads to another and the fact that these steps control the whole process that results in the accomplishment of the desired goal (the repair of the hole in the

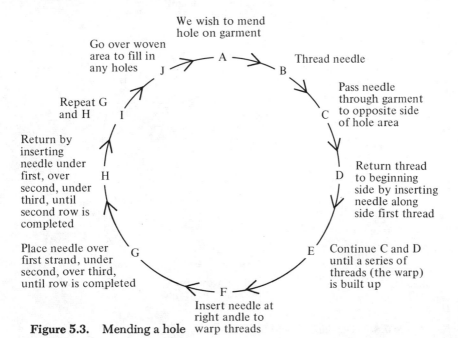

Figure 5.3. Mending a hole

garment). Generally speaking, the fewer the steps or junctures, the simpler the instructions and the more easily the feedback process is regulated.

Any activity can be broken down into a *feedback loop*. The loop is similar to the step-by-step progression in programmed instruction. A feedback loop has the advantage of explicating the steps needed to accomplish some objective. By making the steps clearer, improved control is introduced, and the probability of arriving at the desired end is enhanced. In other words, reinforcement is made more likely and more effective.

Educators are confronted with many examples of feedback loops. The following section illustrates how feedback loops may apply to a variety of situations in which the objective is to influence the behavior or learning of disturbed children.

Examples of Feedback Loops in Education

The examples of threading a needle and using the threaded needle to mend a garment can serve as prototypes. However, let us take a more typical education problem, that of a child learning to write the capital letter *A* (Fig. 5.4).

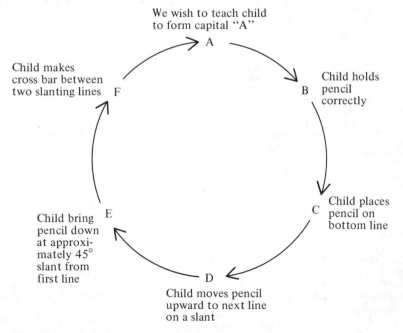

Figure 5.4. Teaching a child to form letters

Child, holding pencil at about a 45-degree angle, starts mark at bottom of line . . . moves pencil upward to next line at a slant of about 45 degrees . . . brings pencil down at approximately a 45-degree slant from first line . . . places crossline midway between the two slanting lines.

As the teacher or parent well knows, the letter A formed by the novice is usually very awkward. It is only with the practice that follows feedback that the child perfects, or makes more functional, his printing. A similar procedure, delineating various steps in the loop, could be illustrated for the formation of any letter.

Another important point about the feedback loop is that the identification of the beginning point also identifies what the goal is. In the example of needle-threading (Fig. 5.2), the goal was to insert the thread through the eye of the needle; in using the threaded needle to repair the garment (Fig. 5.3), the goal was the closing of the hole in the garment; and in the illustration of the child learning to print (Fig. 5.4), it was the formation of the letter A. Each example serves to illustrate a loop: Note that in each of the figures, the beginning point (e.g., "We wish to thread the needle") and the ending point (the threaded needle) are the same in that the identification of the problem also identifies the reinforced product, the terminal objective. In the case of mending the garment, the hole in the garment is the beginning point in the series, and the mended garment, resulting from the delineated steps or junctures in the loop, is the objective or terminal behavior. It is not difficult to see the formation of the letter A in this way also. After one has stated as the beginning point, "We wish to accomplish this goal," and has delineated the steps, feedback is obtained from each step or juncture along the way to the achievement of the goal.

If a particular step proves to be a problem in the applied situation, the loop may be further broken down. There is no fixed or *a priori* number of steps or junctures in a loop; some loops would be very long if all the steps were detailed. If the number of steps seems inappropriate to accomplishing the objective, it may be necessary to add or subtract some of them. For the handicapped learner, this usually requires introducing additional, smaller, steps.

Delineation of a feedback loop in this way defines the learning process more explicitly and affords the teacher or parent an appreciation of what, specifically, the child is being asked to accomplish. Too often the adult merely presents the learning task to the child, saying, in effect, "Get busy and do it," without realizing the problems the child may face. Research on learning has shown that a sequential presentation is an effective one. If there are too many steps, they can be telescoped, and if there are too few, they can be broken down. The process of teaching and learning in this way demands a setting down of the steps, a delineation of the beginning and end points, and a flexible position regarding the number of intermediate steps (Charp and Wye 1968).

**Using Feedback Loops to Describe
and Change Behavioral Goals**

As the reader has probably realized, there is no need to confine the analysis of feedback loops to academic learning. Presumably, all learning follows a loop sequence, including old learning that has been in effect for a long time. What we are especially concerned with here is undesirable learned behavior that should be changed. All such behavior can be presented advantageously in loop terms. It may sometimes be more difficult to specify the junctures in the loop which describe social behavior or the interaction of one person with others, but it is possible and it offers an interesting and rewarding challenge to the teacher or adult concerned.

The child who behaves in a disorderly fashion and never completes his work is fairly common in the classroom. He may be described as dawdling, inattentive, and easily distracted. Having made this description, the teacher can determine both the sequence of steps that must be taken to improve some particular unwanted behavior of the child and the relevant events associated with these steps, as illustrated in the following feedback loop analysis.

We wish to improve the child's concentration in working arithmetic problems . . . set a small limited task (say, one problem in arithmetic) . . . have child show work . . . reward correct answer, correct incorrect answer . . . give an additional problem . . . assess results again, etc.

This loop is deceptively simple, for it merely states an important, but often overlooked, feature—namely, that small, consistent, closely adjacent steps are necessary. However, like all feedback loops, it fails to specify the conditions that should obtain or may have to be held constant when the *sequence of steps* is supposed to occur. For example, in many practical situations the handicapped child may be unable to screen out distractions. Consequently, he may have to be placed in a separate room (or in a small cubicle, or faced to the wall, away from others) in order to minimize distractions. This tactic is necessary to the orderliness or overall structure required before instruction is presented on the step-by-step basis already described.

The feedback loop, based on small increments of one, two, or three arithmetic problems at a time, can be extended so that the child will concentrate on perhaps a dozen or more problems before checking is necessary and will show increasing accuracy in responding to the task. If the teacher fails with a child in the beginning, it is usually because he has expected too high a level of performance. The child has to be encouraged first by simple steps, each of which gives him the feedback necessary for the next small step. This same feedback informs the teacher of the child's progress.

Like the other feedback loops, the present example begins with a desired objective, "We wish to improve the child's concentration (and success) in working arithmetic problems," and goes on through other steps or junctures to help bring about this objective. Here again, if a breakdown in the sequence occurs somewhere, it is the teacher's responsibility to locate the point where the behavior does not flow smoothly toward the desired end or where distractions interfere with progress. It may be that even simpler problems will have to be inserted at some point in the loop. For example, short division problems may have to be mastered before long division can be performed. Further, the steps may have to be more detailed. The steps in the loop are, after all, empirical matters and cannot be set up rigidly in advance. The format must be tailored to the individual student and must begin at a level commensurate with his skills.

A behavior problem—for example, picking fights or verbally abusing others—can also be described in terms of a loop (Fig. 5.5). Social control or other preventive measures can be delineated as steps in the loop. These measures can be established by separating the child physically and socially from other children, with the teacher acting as intermediary in all

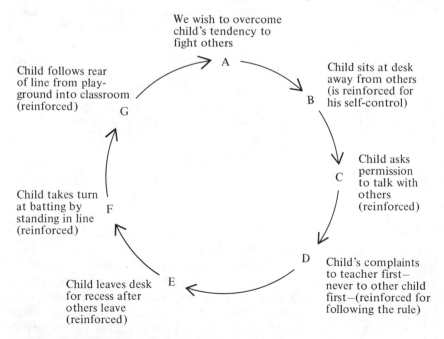

Figure 5.5.   Overcoming a child's tendency to fight

disputes. The teacher does not deny the child the right to feel a certain way, but she does provide an avenue through which he can respond appropriately to other children.

Modifications made at various junctures in the loop are dictated by empirical considerations and must be adjusted to the individual situation. The loop in Figure 5.5 may be telescoped as the child's behavior improves and self-control is reinforced. What is important in the feedback loop, as has already been pointed out, is the overlap between the problem that is delineated and the desired objective. The steps in the loop show how the various features of the situation can be brought under control.

The following list of problems presented by children in the classroom might be used by the reader to formulate loops that could be adapted to similar situations or used in future classroom instruction and management.

1. "Sassing" the teacher
2. Continual tardiness for work or play
3. Unwillingness to participate in athletics or sports
4. Unwillingness to participate in group discussions
5. Trying to monopolize the group
6. Noisiness and offensiveness

In all these examples, and others the reader may think of, the stated problem is used as both the beginning and end points, with the first statement in the loop being on the order of: "We wish to overcome the child's 'sassing.'" The junctures which may be expected to occur in order to change the behavior in the desired direction are then described. This analysis in loop terms should not be viewed as an emphasis on the negative aspects of behavior. Rather, it is a mechanism for clarifying *positive* alternatives, keeping in mind the gradual, sequential solution to problems and the need for reliable consequences (reinforcement).

Some Other Features of Cybernetic Control

The preceding section of this chapter concentrated primarily on the remediation of skills and behavior. The present section is more concerned with the prevention of learning problems, although remedial considerations are still of interest. Computer centers over the past few years have developed a considerable amount of teaching and communication system hardware, much of which has proved useful in educational settings. These systems for presenting material to the learner are examined in this section in an effort to understand how the learning activities of the student can be affected (Carter 1968).

Cybernetic and informational systems tend to be very efficient in the transmittal of information. There is a high degree of correspondence between the message sent and the message received. In the ordinary interchange of social and verbal communication, the message often gets lost or distorted. One might say, "The message sent was not the message received," or,.in less technical language, "I didn't intend to say that."

When the points in a feedback loop are closely linked, and when the loop is well defined and economical, the message can be transmitted more efficiently, and the response of the receiver or the goal to be achieved can be readily discerned and progress assessed. Since we know that ordinary human communciation is vulnerable to misinterpretation or breakdown, it is helpful to understand how to increase the efficiency and effectiveness of communication through informational or cybernetic systems and how to apply this knowledge to teaching children with behavior and learning deficiencies.

Perhaps the simplest teaching system is one that uses the direct request or command requiring a single response or action. For example, if you say to the dog, "Down, Rover," and the dog lies down (and is reinforced for his behavior), the communication system has considerable specificity, efficiency, and reliability. If you say to a child at his desk, "Please close your arithmetic book and look at this geography map on the wall," it is not too difficult to determine if the message is received and acted upon. Any simple, direct communication which sets a very finite goal that can be observed and judged easily can be called a simple communication system, even though it is based on verbal communication and the use of abstract symbols (Burns 1968).

Both teaching machines and textbooks utilizing programmed material are cybernetic or communication systems. This is true because in each case, the message to be sent or the material to be learned is specifically stated (the terminal objective is specified) and because a fairly specific and delimited response is required. This response is reinforced if the person is correct, as he should be a good deal of the time if he is attending and working at a suitable level. If he is in error, a correction can be made. The junctures are those already specified: reading the presented problem (or frame); reacting in some specific way in order to answer the frame (writing down a letter, word, or phrase, writing numbers in a math problem, selecting from among multiple choice answers); verifying the accuracy of the response; and then either proceeding to the next frame or reworking the present one. In longer chains of response, there may be a number of steps before the final answer is reached. For example, steps in a long-division problem suitable to the fourth- or fifth-grade level might number from five to ten in the case of a problem involving no more than three or four digits in both the divisor and the dividend. Almost any elementary-level arithmetic book delineates the steps for solving long division and other arithmetic problems. These steps can be seen as comprising a communication system which enables the student to communicate with the program and with the teacher as he learns how to do the problem, with each step a feed-in to the next step as well as a feedback from the previous one.

Programmed textbooks in English, mathematics, history, and other fields all show these sequential characteristics. The student is ushered through a series of steps in order to arrive at some goal, such as learning the materials programmed, preparing for a test, or earning credit for a course. The degree to which the goal is achieved is judged by the quality of the performance. The type of programmed textbook most commonly used takes the student through one frame at a time but interposes tests at certain intervals to provide periodic feedback. Thus, the student does not have to respond too long before his general knowledge is assessed. Tests for periodic assessment can be written into a feedback loop.

Our examples are derived from what is often termed *software* or from actual textbook (or workbook) materials. The content of a program is referred to as software. The *hardware* is the machine used to house and present the software. For example, if an electric typewriter is rigged in a way that precludes the child from making typing mistakes, and the child is also given a frame to study and respond to, the typewriter is called the hardware and the instructional content the software.

Electronic gear and computer-assisted learning devices have become very popular in recent years. In fact, learning or teaching instruments (hardware) have been developed at such a rapid pace that only an engineer specializing in the field can keep up with all the advances. Our purpose here is not to study the electronic hardware used for instruction but to understand how the hardware operates as a cybernetic or communication system relevant to the discussions in this chapter.

In the simplest sense, the information presented by the hardware or electronic instrument acts as a stimulus to the child, just as a spoken or printed word or a frame in programmed instruction does. The child responds to the stimulus in some specific way—punches a key, draws a line, pushes a button, makes a mark on paper—after which the machine either brings up another problem if the child is correct, informs the child that he is incorrect so that he can review the problem and try to answer it correctly, or otherwise instructs him about how to proceed. Figure 5.6 provides a schematic representation of this system.

The electronic machine as a cybernetic or communication system differs from verbal instruction or programmed textbooks as cybernetic systems

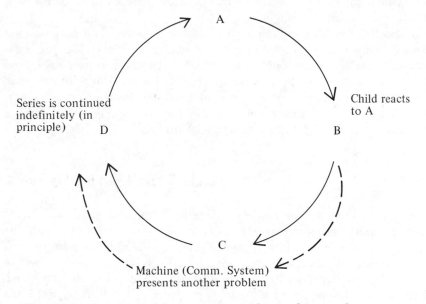

We want to schematize how an
electronic teaching system
operates by presenting a
problem (or frame of instruction)

A

Child reacts
to A

Series is continued
indefinitely (in
principle)   D   B

C

Machine (Comm. System)
presents another problem

Figure 5.6.   Loop design for instruction with a teaching machine

in several major ways. The electronic machine can (a) present problems
or frames indefinitely, (b) reverse itself to review previously known or
studied materials, (c) accelerate or skip over materials which the student
need not study, (d) present different programs at different rates to several individuals simultaneously, and (e) interpose tests and checks and
then handle them in the various ways dictated by the educational objectives. The teacher is thereby freed to do other work, such as supplementing
the cues presented by the computer for students needing help unavailable
from the computer or other machine, and attending in other ways to
problems of individual students. Thus, the teacher is free to cope with
idiosyncratic and unusual problems while the machine or communication
system proceeds to handle the basic learning sequences (the loops) of
importance in well-defined situations.

If learning were to take place in this modular way, perhaps very few
learning problems would develop in children—a speculative point, but
a logical one. If learning problems of children are due to faulty presentation, poorly differentiated steps, and a failure to reinforce differentially

the desired responses, it is no wonder that learning becomes inaccurate and inefficient. Nor is it any wonder that learning problems mounting day after day and year after year result in faulty learning methods, a lack of acquired information or the accumulation of misinformation, and a tendency to aggravate many of the unfortunate emotional responses which the learning problems themselves brought on.

If effective teaching—whether by a teacher, a textbook, a programmed manual, a machine, or a computer system—is based on the clear presentation of materials at the right level, followed by the learner's self-paced progress through the material, with appropriate feedback or reinforcement, then any system so regulated and calibrated can function as a teacher. Such a system will prevent or remedy the development of untoward emotional, behavioral, and learning problems.

Teaching and Learning Systems

One important aim of modern educational technology should be to carry programmed instruction to higher levels of generality with the assistance of the computer and other devices. Although the term *systems* has a variety of meanings, it generally refers to any method whose presentation of materials to be learned (stimuli) is relatively organized, provides for sequential and self-pacing progress by the learner, and leads to some discernible consequence (reinforcement, feedback). This teaching and learning *system* is characterized by several features. It has definite beginning and ending points, clear-cut objectives, and a flexible mode of operation that takes the learner's skill or behavioral repertoire into consideration. These attributes can be found in computer-assisted instruction, in some noncomputerized but systematic attempts at teaching, in programmed textbooks and machines, and even in some more crudely fashioned procedures of instruction.

Anyone can construct a teaching and learning system if he adheres to a fairly set format which, in turn, is based on a number of questions that have to be answered. These questions concern the activities of the learner. How they are answered determines whether one has a "teaching and learning system." In addition, the answers to these questions often lead to the selection of one or another procedure for solving the learning problems at hand (Carter 1968; Charp and Wye 1968).

The basic questions to be answered for implementing a system include:

1. What behavior is to be learned? This is a statement of the terminal objectives.
2. Does the learner's repertoire already include any behavior related to the

behavior specified in the answer to question 1? If so, how can it be increased or generalized to help meet objectives? If not, how can it be learned most economically?

3. How can the behavior to be learned be presented most efficiently? This is especially important in the case of handicapped learners, for it concerns the development of procedures to adapt common stimuli so that they impinge upon the learner efficiently and effectively (e.g., braille type for the blind). The subject of the handicapped learner brings up the problem of developing interfaces—that is, prostheticlike devices—to enable him to make responses to existing stimuli through modes adapted to his handicap.

4. What existing instruments and procedures are there for reaching the objectives stated in questions 1 and 3?

5. What defects or excesses (or competing responses) in the learner's present repertoire will hamper the acquisition of new skills? Significant modification in the learning situation may be necessary when teaching extremely handicapped learners (e.g., paralyzed persons who have to learn how to handle equipment, the blind or deaf who must learn new behaviors to overcome their limitations).

6. What reinforcers exist to help overcome any of the above limitations on the learner's capabilities (e.g., the selective use of money, free time, engagement in high-strength activities)?

7. Can answers to the foregoing questions be found by using any existing instruments (typewriters, tape recorders, mechanical dispensers of reinforcement) or can they be found only by modifying these instruments? The answer to this question, which is related to number 4 above, may involve some modification of equipment (e.g., painting the keys of a typewriter to facilitate learning for "brain-damaged" children), or some extension of existing programs, or some adaptation of instruments already available.

8. Can the answers to the questions above lead either to improved learning systems for individuals or to more efficient learning systems for groups of people? If the answers are "yes," then to some extent we have an advanced teaching and learning technology and perhaps have increased our knowledge of how people learn most effectively in a variety of practical situations.

The Functions of the Teaching and Learning Systems

Once educators learn to think in terms of teaching and learning systems, the development of these systems can become an important and challenging aspect of educational technology. Basic to this systematic approach to teaching and learning is, of course, the phenomenon of reinforcement and the related concepts described in this chapter, such as the emphasis on small steps, individual rates of learning, and reinforcement contingencies. Once these learning conditions are supplied, it is possible to extend the technology of learning to more general levels (Silverman 1968).

The rationale for adhering to teaching and learning systems or to the cybernetic enhancement and extension of learning is based on the belief that the details of learning are fairly well understood and only require extension, just as any technology extends basic scientific knowledge. How, then, does this extension take place, and what does it accomplish? Perhaps several answers can be provided at this point.

The details of learning do stand on their own, just as instruments in the orchestra are entities in their own right. But just as an orchestra makes possible the realization of musical effects not available to the individual instruments, so must the separate details of learning be "orchestrated" to produce a more general system that will make the achievement of new ends possible.

One attribute of teaching and learning systems is that they can be based on learning principles. Once the rudiments of learning are known, it is the task of the systems-maker to incorporate them into a system that functions smoothly with little or no human intervention, much as an automatic transmission does in contrast to the clutch-and-shift method. Also, the enhancement of learning through reinforcement techniques enables the systems-maker to look for new reinforcement contingencies inherent in the use of the system. That is, the system's gadgets themselves may arouse interest, thus providing new ways of reinforcing the learner.

The use of systematic teaching and learning technology accommodates the goals of many individuals. The system would be worth little if all learning had to proceed by lock-step method, where all children begin and end at the same point. The computer can adapt to the slow as well as to the fast learner, programming each according to his strengths and idiosyncrasies.

The computer can keep data in the form of response rates for all the students involved in the program. These rates provide immediate information on the progress of each student with regard to particular objectives—say, in high school algebra. The information is available to the student as well as to the teacher. In addition, exams can be added at various points in the system, with examination results noted and reinforced. With this information, decisions on whether a student should proceed or go back to review essential materials will have relevance to his overall progress. Once the general system built into the computer is made to emulate the ideal classroom teacher who adheres to the essential features of programmed instruction, the computer can do anything the teacher can do and more.

Once the system is in operation, it is possible to envision ways in which other subject matter areas can be organized to fit into it. The more objective and quantitative fields, such as math and physics, have lent themselves well to programmed and computer-assisted instruction. This application points to the value of organizing less rigorous subject matter areas so that they may be incorporated into a systems framework. Even in teaching English composition, it may be possible to computerize limited instructional goals and to parlay these into broader goals. For example, paragraph-writing might be an immediate objective, followed by learning to organize several paragraphs under suitable topics to form a section of a composition. Such a systems approach may not produce accomplished original writers, but this need not be our objective. Rather, it can efficiently teach elements of writing to those who cannot write, and it can measurably enhance communication for verbally deficient students who must be educated. Again, it is a matter of goals; with specific goals, computer-assisted instruction can certainly play an important part in teaching even the less structured subject matter areas.

The invention of the typewriter made the secretary more competent and more productive. The more versatile the machine, the more tasks it can do, and the accomplishment of additional tasks can conceivably reinforce the user. Therefore, better instruments—such as the teaching machine— can increase the repertoire of the learner or performer and extend his behavioral competence at the same time.

In this connection it is important to realize that the use of teaching and learning systems is not limited simply to the *presentation* of stimuli or learning tasks. It is not like a visual aid that is viewed more or less passively, requiring little more than cursory attention from the learner. The carefully conceived teaching and learning system requires more of the learner and, in so doing, offers him the opportunity to enlarge his behavioral capabilities.

An often repeated phrase having considerable validity is that if one can teach a subject under nonsystematic conditions, he can teach it better (more efficiently) under systematic ones. The role of the systems-maker, the user of computers or instruments, is to enhance the process of learning, not to impede it with extraneous or fancy gadgets. The computer, or any other such instrument, is designed only to facilitate instruction through a more efficient and precise presentation of instructional cues and measurement of performance.

A teaching and learning system can reinforce more systematically, can make for better use of intermittent schedules, than a teacher can. A teacher cannot easily keep track of a simple reinforcement schedule for one child, and still less a complicated schedule involving many students. Since the reinforcement schedule is built into the teaching and learning system, and since it proceeds in small increments, many of the personal frustrations that attend a nonsystems approach are inevitably reduced for students and teacher alike. This use of the cybernetic system provides an excellent illustration of the extension of learning principles far beyond the teacher's capability.

Particularly in the case of handicapped learners, the low tolerances for frustration that must be contended with often lead to social conflicts between students, which occupy a good deal of the teacher's time. The identification of the learning objectives by means of instrumentation will channel student interest and activity toward the educational or behavioral objectives and thereby decrease distracting social conflicts and unproductive competition among students.

People often remark that instrumentation cannot build student incentive or motivation. They say that the student has to "want to learn" or "be motivated" in order for a system to operate effectively. This attitude fails to acknowledge the influence of reinforcement—and what the well-constructed program provides is reinforcement, the instructional feature essential to motivation. The successful student builds on his success, and motivation is derived from the feedback that follows success. Thus, if a teaching and learning system is properly scheduled and programmed, the student will receive many educational, social, and personal benefits—in short, he will be reinforced. If anything, the machine system increases motivation and reinforcement by promoting effective and efficient interaction between the subject matter and the student, rather than deterring progress. Because the system can reinforce immediately with no distractions, considerable control over the reinforcement contingencies (and hence over motivation) is provided. The instrumentation can be "set" for various reinforcement schedules. Furthermore, the sheer fun and enjoyment of making a machine work effectively is often reinforcement in itself.

Summary

Programmed instruction has several basic features. First, it requires active responses from the student; second, the material to be learned is presented in a step-by-step sequence; third, the student can work through the material at his own rate; fourth, the program specifies terminal objectives; and fifth, immediate feedback of results is provided to both student and teacher.

Programmed materials have the advantage of specifying learning objectives and arranging sequential steps leading successively toward these objectives. Since the child actively responds throughout the learning session, progress or lack of it is immediately evident to both teacher and child. In addition, areas where the program is inadequate are easily determined, and the teacher can arrange for supplementary frames to provide the student with additional information and more practice.

Instructional programs form the basic content for teaching machines and computer-assisted instruction. The computer can extend the capability of the simpler programmed format by providing an automatic display of each frame, scoring the child's response, informing the child as to whether or not the response is correct, and instructing him either to proceed to the next frame or to rework the current one. The computer also contains an accurate record of the child's correct and incorrect responses.

Cybernetics refers to the observation that the behavior of an organism depends on the feedback information available. Some behavior is under the control of available information which, in turn, enables the behaving organism to steer, direct, or guide his behavior. Feedback, the most important concept in cybernetics, is similar to the learning theory concept of reinforcement. Because he can depend on the inflow of information, a person can, with feedback, adjust his own behavior. For this reason, feedback is an important part of learning. Immediate information regarding performance helps the learner pick his next response and gradually produce ever more correct responses to the material to be learned or the skill to be developed.

The second most important concept offered by cybernetics is the loop. If behavior is regulated or controlled by feedback, the flow of information from the control center to various media and points, and thence back to the control center, is viewed as forming a loop. When a person threads a needle, his eyes feed back information on the location of the thread and the needle. This information is processed in the brain, and the messages are returned to the controlling fingers, allowing for correction. Ultimately, through successive approximations and corrective efforts, the individual succeeds in the task. The whole process is known as the feedback loop. The application of cybernetics to behavior offers a conceptualization that provides for better understanding of many complex human behaviors.

References

Buchanan, Cynthia Dee. *Programmed Reading.* St. Louis-New York: Webster Division, McGraw-Hill Book Company, 1964.

Burns, Richard W. "Measuring Objectives and Grading." *Educational Technology,* **8:18** (1968), pp. 13–14.

Carter, Joseph B. "Learning Laboratories in North Carolina." *Educational Technology,* **8:18** (1968), pp. 5–10.

Charp, Sylvia, and Roger E. Wye. "Philadelphia Tries Computer Assisted Instruction." *Educational Technology,* **8:9** (1968), pp. 13–15.

Dechert, Charles R., ed. *The Social Impact of Cybernetics.* New York: Simon & Schuster, Inc., 1967.

Ferster, C. B., and B. F. Skinner. *Schedules of Reinforcement.* New York: Appleton-Century-Crofts, 1957.

Keller, Fred S., and William N. Schoenfeld. *Principles of Psychology.* New York: Appleton-Century-Crofts, 1950.

Margulies, Stuart, and Lewis D. Eigen. *Applied Programed Instruction.* New York: John Wiley & Sons, Inc., 1962.

Pearce, Lucia. "Environmental Structure: A Third Partner in Education." *Educational Technology,* **8:17** (1968), pp. 11–14.

Rath, Gustave J. "Non-CAI Instruction Using Computers and Non-instructional Uses of CAI Computers." *Educational Technology,* **8:3** (1968), p. 13.

Silverman, Robert E. "Using the S-R Reinforcement Model." *Educational Technology,* **8:5** (1968), pp. 3–12.

Silvern, Leonard C. "A Cybernetic System Model for Occupational Education." *Educational Technology,* **8:2** (1968), pp. 3–9.

Thomson, James C., Jr. "From Reason to Technology." *Educational Technology,* **8:6** (1968), pp. 3–8.

Roles of School Personnel

6

In the classroom, the teacher teaches Clifford to read and write and spell, but if he wants to know the child's I.Q., he sends him to the school psychologist. If Clifford has a fight with another student, the teacher may send him to the principal's office; if the child sprains his wrist on the playground, the teacher will send him to the school nurse. Classes in art and physical education conducted by other teachers may be part of Clifford's curriculum. Thus, the child may come in contact with a number of school personnel during the day. A good many of them—administrators, the school psychologist, the nurse, the social worker, and resource teachers—are agents in the behavior modification team and contribute to the success or failure of the behavior modification program. Therefore, it is essential that they understand the procedures of behavior modification and contingency management. In some instances, this requirement may alter their traditional roles. For instance, the school psychologist must be able to offer more than a descriptive analysis of the child's difficulties. He must know educational theory and be able to apply behavior principles in individual and group instructional settings. He should be able to determine the child's instructional levels, arrange and implement a teaching program, and clearly describe the procedures used so that others can follow them. He is often required to assume a liaison role between teacher and parents, supporting the behavior modification program and ensuring cooperation from all personnel. In some modification programs, other school personnel may be required to serve as change agents (those who influence changes in the child's behavior). Before discussing the particular duties each of them will be required to assume, let us clarify some clinical terms.

The child whose behavior is to be changed is generally referred to as the *change object*. Ordinarily, he is regarded as "wanting to change" or as being "motivated" to change to some degree. We are often admonished that a person will change "only if he wants to change," which is another way of saying that the child, or change object, is his own *change agent*.

It is not always true that a child will behave differently just because he wants to. George may be unhappy, petulant, and ineffectual in his work and social relations, but he may not know the cause of his difficulty or what goals to work toward. While an adult may behave in a specific way in order to achieve some goal, George has no goals and therefore does not know how to change. A behavior modification program is designed to change his environment—to provide him with goals—and to encourage him to change in that environment. The child may be his own change agent, but it is more likely that this role will be filled by the teacher, a parent, a boy scout leader, or any person acting in a way which controls or alters the environment in which the child operates. It is the responsibility of the *change architect* to design a *change plan* to apply to the child's behavior. The change architect may be someone involved in supervising special education, a behavioral psychologist, or a staff member of the school. It is his responsibility to design a program of behavior modification for each child that will structure the environmental conditions. The change agent then carries out the plan. The plan may specify a simple command or set of teacher activities affecting a particular child at a given time, or it may be a very complex program to change group behavior (as in a classroom for disturbed children) as well as individual behavior within that group.

To illustrate the integration of these elements of change—object, agent, plan, and architect—we shall present several examples of the functions of various school personnel.

The Resource Teacher

The classroom teacher working with children who have learning and behavior problems can be helped enormously by a resource teacher who has a broad knowledge of instructional programs and procedures and of such materials and equipment as The Language Master and multisensory devices. The resource teacher can show regular teachers how to pinpoint behaviors, how to count them, how to graph the data, how to change the behaviors by changing the environment, and how to evaluate the effects of the environmental changes (Lovitt 1968). The resource teacher can guide teachers in the assessment of skills and in the selection of instructional materials. She may also be in charge of a resource room, where she works with individual children or small groups in need of special help.

The resource room (Fig. 6.1) offers a special setting for the effective shaping of behaviors in children who exhibit such severe deficits that they are unable to function even in the special classroom. In addition, it provides a place for the precise assessment of entering behaviors and the rapid shaping of specific behavior of those children who are already able to function part-time in a regular classroom. Finally, the resource room setting offers a situation for more precise cue presentation and more refined reinforcement scheduling.

In some schools, the resource teacher is the person who deals with particular behaviors which the regular classroom teacher may want to change. The resource teacher may also design plans for the modification of these behaviors. If the classroom teacher observes that Carlos cries too much, the resource teacher may assume direct responsibility for managing Carlos whenever he cries. However, the sooner the classroom teacher learns the special procedures used by the resource teacher, the sooner he will be able to apply them in his classroom. Following is an illustration of how the resource teacher might function in a school.

John would cry about twelve to fifteen times a day, according to a baseline measure taken by the teacher. It was decided that the resource teacher should handle this problem for a period of one week to see what could be done to help John. Many children had commiserated with John when he cried, and too much of the teacher's time had been spent in coping with John's upsets. The change plan specified that the resource teacher would spend three twenty-minute periods each day alone with John. If John cried during this time, the resource teacher was to ignore him unless he was hurt, but she was to respond warmly to the child's efforts in academic work or in play. At a general staff meeting one week later, the resource teacher reported her data on John's crying behavior. The data showed that the behavior had decreased in frequency. Consequently, the staff decided to continue the plan until John's crying episodes were reduced to two or less per week. Three other teachers reported that they had children with similar problems and needed the resource teacher's help. One child spit at other children when angry or frustrated, another always cried when assigned to use the typewriter as part of his reading and spelling work, and a third tried to run out of the schoolroom and into the halls or outside if not watched constantly.

The resource teacher became an effective change agent. His activity was directed toward solving problems that the regular classroom teacher was unable to handle, and the classroom teacher learned procedures

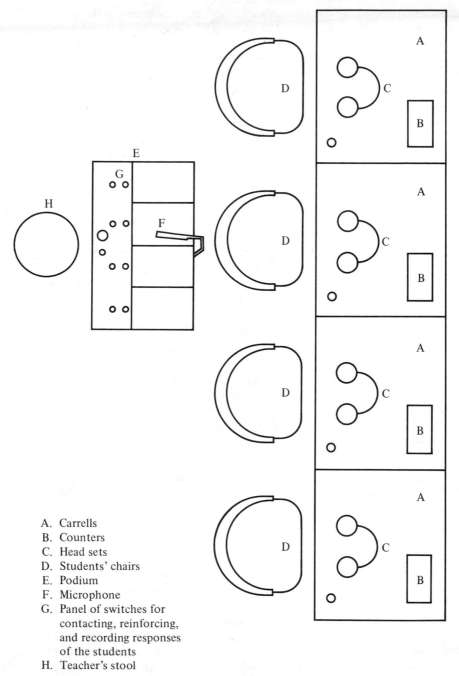

A. Carrells
B. Counters
C. Head sets
D. Students' chairs
E. Podium
F. Microphone
G. Panel of switches for
   contacting, reinforcing,
   and recording responses
   of the students
H. Teacher's stool

Figure 6.1.   Design layout for a resource room

from the resource teacher which enabled her eventually to manage such problems herself.

Special teachers in physical education, music, or art can act as resources in a different sense. The activities they handle can serve as powerful reinforcers for children. For example, the teacher may say, "If you do all of your arithmetic, you may go to art class this afternoon." Since these special teachers are part of the child's total educational environment, their management procedures must be in accord with those used by the regular classroom teacher and the resource teacher.

The School Psychologist

The school psychologist is another member of the school's behavior modification team. Traditionally, school psychologists have been responsible primarily for the psychological testing and the occasional interviewing of parents. However, the increased interest in and application of behavioral methods in the school have markedly changed this role. The school psychologist now assumes several functions: first, he takes data directly on the child and the teacher in the classroom; second, he interviews the child to determine what conditions may be rewarding or motivating to him; and, third, he interprets the observation data on the teacher-child relationship and classroom behavior to the principal, supervisors, parents, and any others interested in the child or in the program of behavior modification.

Direct observation and data recording are important procedures for the school psychologist. Through these techniques, he is able to interpret the child's repertoire and the conditions influencing his behavior and performance.

For instance, Dr. Z., the school psychologist, was called into Miss J.'s classroom to observe a threatening ten-year-old boy. Aloysius taunted others, would not study or hand in his work, and often would try to talk the teacher out of giving him assignments, saying he had already done "that stuff," or that he had lost it, or that it was too hard for him. As the data taken by the psychologist showed, Miss J. gave Aloysius attention when he misbehaved but tended to ignore him when he was productive. "I took it for granted that when he worked, that was what he was *supposed to do,* and so I failed to reinforce him to keep him going in the desired direction."

The psychologist plotted a baseline of Aloysius's disturbed and disturbing behaviors for two weeks. A second observer, working simultaneously with Dr. Z., observed and recorded the teacher's behavior. By comparing their data for the same time period, Dr. Z. and the observer were able to relate the teacher's behavior to that of Aloysius. Their efforts demonstrated that the teacher actually shaped and maintained Aloysius's behavior in the very direction she wished to reverse.

The school psychologist and his observer then met with the teacher to discuss the results of their observations. They all agreed that Miss J. should not respond to Aloysius when he misbehaved or was stubborn, but should reinforce him with attention, a smile, a touch on the shoulder, or a statement of how well he was doing when his efforts were appropriate to the task. She was taught to acknowledge his work efforts when they were desirable, to ignore his occasional recalcitrant behavior, to turn her attention away from him when he threatened, but to be ready to return him to his task if he actually tried to get up and leave the room. Miss J. was afraid that Aloysius would actually leave the room if she did not listen to his threats, but when she realized that her ignoring and reinforcing tactics were actually instrumental in changing his behavior, she no longer hesitated either to praise or ignore him when the occasion warranted.

Part of the school psychologist's role should be to interview the child to obtain more information on his behavioral repertoire and identify potential sources of effective reinforcement for him. The classroom teacher may insist that "nothing gets to that boy," implying that the situation is beyond her control. But the school psychologist may discover things that do get to him. For example, our school psychologist, Dr. Z., was able to bring to the classroom teacher's attention some information that proved useful in motivating children. One child was given the opportunity to go to the library to read about motors when he had successfully completed his arithmetic assignment. The child had never read about motors in his school work, not even in his science class (the unit on motors and gasoline engines came late in the year). But the school psychologist had noted his enthusiasm for motors while interviewing him. When reading about motors at the library was made contingent on finishing his arithmetic and other assignments (including homework) according to the teacher's criterion of excellence, the boy's work improved noticeably within one six-week grading period and remained high throughout the rest of the school year. As the boy progressed, the librarian agreed to buy several other books on motors for him to read, provided he attended to his regular studies. The librarian also allowed him to check out a few books to take home when he had done very well on a six-weeks test.

In another case, one girl's motivation for school work improved when a contingency was arranged between her academic performance and the opportunity to go to the nursing station and help the nurse. The performance of another child improved when his work earned him the opportunity to help the science teacher set up labs in biology and to fix malfunctioning electrical equipment around the school.

The school psychologist must have the ability to define a problem, measure it (or describe it with adequate data), and suggest and implement a remedy (or help the teacher implement it). Too often in the past, the school psychologist provided a description of the child's behavior that only confirmed what the teacher already knew, and he failed to prescribe effective action for changing that behavior. If the school psychologist defines the child's problems in environmental terms, he can then proceed to explain how the environment can be changed.

The Social Worker or Visiting Nurse

The school social worker or visiting nurse is often a vital member of the team. He interprets the child's behavior at school to the parents and designs a plan involving parental cooperation. Normally, he does not work directly with the child in the classroom but acts as a go-between, linking home and school in effective action. Patterson and Reid (1970) have developed a systematic procedure for working with parents in the home.

The social worker or visiting nurse may have to go to the home to talk to parents and help them work out a behavioral plan similar to the one used at school. She can teach the parents how to observe behavior and record data. The following report illustrates the role of the social worker.

A staff discussion of Robert, a nine-year-old boy labeled autistic, resulted in the assignment of the social worker to a specific role vis-à-vis the parents. Since both parents worked, it was decided that the social worker would visit Robert's home (once a week) after school for a one-hour period, dividing this time between direct attention to Robert, with the parents observing, and a discussion with the parents of what he, the social worker, had done with Robert. He would also visit once a week at mealtime—either breakfast or dinner—in order to help the parents develop better ways of coping with Robert's voracious appetite and his exceedingly sloppy eating habits. The social worker took data on the one-hour meetings after school for a two-week period. He then reviewed the data with the teaching staff, and it was decided that he and the classroom teacher should begin simultaneous programs—one at home and one at school. In addition, several of Robert's school lunchtime behaviors were pinpointed so that the social worker could specify them to the parents as behaviors to concentrate on at home during the evening meal. As a result of the school and home programs, Robert's eating habits improved considerably and he was put on a diet under medical supervision. He lost weight, his activity increased, and his social participation at school and in the neighborhood improved. The improvement in his out-of-school behavior was demonstrated by the data kept by his parents.

In a different school-based project, another social worker was able to go into a particular neighborhood during the day and hold group discussion and training sessions with the children's mothers. The social worker used a manual on behavior modification in her work with the mothers, kept data on specific behaviors of the children, and set up teams of mothers where one would focus on training a child to respond to a specific task and the other would take data on both the mother and the child. Parents who were particularly successful in handling mealtime problems would monitor the work of other parents who were less successful. Similarly, those who were better at managing eating, reading, sports, or teaching arithmetic would monitor the work of those who were less effective. The crossing over of functions (with a mother acting as monitor of one activity but manager of another) and the general weighing of these experiences by the parents with the social worker became an exceedingly productive venture. It developed expertise in the mothers where it had not existed before and helped shape the behavior of the children in the classroom.

Some investigators have considered it important to introduce additional monetary reinforcers to influence parental behavior in these training sessions. In most cases, however, the parents' satisfaction with their children's progress, with data to prove it, appeared to preclude the need for monetary reinforcement. There are times when the added reinforcing value of money can be productive, but in most instances parents who have disturbed children are powerfully reinforced by the gain in control over the unwanted behavior and the relief from frustration provided by the child's progress.

The Administrative Staff

The principal and the special-education supervisor participate in classroom behavior modification programs. Since their administrative abilities influence the success or failure of these programs, they must understand behavior principles and participate in setting up special classes, staffing them, and using the skills of the school psychologist, the resource teacher, the social worker, and all other personnel involved in working directly with the children.

The principal and the supervisor usually have only indirect contact with the children in special classes. Consequently, they must rely on feedback from the professionals who are directly involved. Both of them should participate in the staff decisions which bring a child into the special education program, and both should be involved in the review of the data used to

initiate any change plan. Parents and teachers alike are keenly affected
by the ways in which these administrators handle their roles: The cooperation of the parents increases if the principal and supervisor strongly support programs in special education. And the principal's dominant position
in the structure and organization of the school gives to him the ultimate
responsibility for reinforcing teachers to provide good instruction, effective behavior management, and careful measurement of the children's
performances.

When the principal and the supervisor see special classes progress, when
they see children who have had problems begin to mature behaviorally
and academically, and when they see their teachers and their classroom
efforts supported and rewarded in practical ways by other personnel working with the children, they cannot help but be strongly reinforced themselves.

Three major considerations dictate the roles, responsibilities, and specific
behaviors of the administrative staff and the specialists working to improve
classroom instruction. First, all plans for the child must be individualized,
objective, and continually reviewed until the desired change takes place
and the classroom teacher has the child and the procedures under control.
Second, the instructional procedures used in the classroom must be
systematic. Here, the personnel who assist in the educational process must
be receptive to the use of behavior modification procedures. Third, the
specialists involved in this team effort must work toward mutual objectives.
They must plan together for the achievement of these objectives and, above
all, collect and examine accurate measures of performance.

Summary

A large proportion of school personnel are engaged in changing the
behaviors of children. The child should not be considered a "patient,"
but a change object, often capable of engaging in his own efforts to improve
learning or to overcome problems. Teachers are the primary change agents
in the school setting, but other personnel play important roles, too. For
a comprehensive change effort to be systematic and effective, change
plans must be drawn up by all those who are significant to the child's
school setting—the teacher, the school nurse, the school psychologist, etc.
This is environmental planning for the benefit of the child, and it may
require overall "architectural" planning.

The resource teacher may be called upon for special curricular help
or to help the classroom teacher carry out a contingency management
program. The school psychologist, in addition to making his usual edu-

cational evaluations of children, can perform an important service by describing the children's educational or social behaviors and by obtaining "baseline" data on them. He can also help by suggesting ways to change behavior in terms of reasonable objectives and by evaluating the overall programs for change. Social workers or visiting nurses can coordinate home and school influences by preparing parents to assist in (or at least not hamper) the change plans developed at school. They can also furnish information basic to the decisions that school personnel may have to make. And, not least in importance, administrative personnel can support and extend the efforts of other personnel to achieve behavioral objectives, thus broadening the functions of the school.

Reference

Lovitt, Tom C. "Classroom Management: An Empirical Approach." Unpublished manuscript; copyright, Tom C. Lovitt, Experimental Educational Unit, Child Development and Mental Retardation Center, University of Washington, Seattle, Wash., 1968.

Working with Parents

7

Whoever interacts often with the child, whoever arranges the environment in which the child interacts, and whoever is present when the child interacts with others will strongly influence the development of the child's behavior patterns. In infancy and early childhood, this role is usually assumed by the parents or by surrogate-parents. During the early school years, the teacher shares this influence with the parents.

Despite the importance of their influence on the child's life, parents have traditionally been relegated to a minor role in educational systems. The parent raises a child to the age of six and then turns him over to a school. This is a particularly unfortunate situation for those parents who have a child with behavior problems. All too often, when they have sought concrete help in handling their child, they have been treated as though *they* were the cause of the problem and could do little to help the child. However, when teachers, psychologists, and other professionals in behavior management have worked with parents, they have found the experience gratifying and helpful.

Parents need to be informed about what they can do to help instead of being told the numerous ways in which they may be "going wrong." Too frequently, at child guidance centers and clinics, parents seem to display guilt rather than a desire to help themselves and their children.

Most parents occasionally feel that their methods of child rearing have failed, but parents of children with severe behavior problems may rarely, if ever, experience success. These problems have sometimes been attributed to hereditary conditions or to some particular fault in the child's personality. Today, however, we think that no matter how abnormal a child's behavior is, or how handicapped he is because of his heredity, there are a number of guidelines that parents can follow to improve their child's behavior and avoid undesirable social results.

When motivated and correctly guided, parents very frequently can act in therapeutic ways with and for their children (Haring and Phillips 1962; Ferster and DeMyer 1962; Patterson and Gullion 1968; Williams 1959). This does not mean that they are therapists in the clinical sense of the term, but that they can learn to act more therapeutically.

A program for helping parents to modify the behavior of their children needs to be systematic. First, it requires that a behavior manager work with the parents to modify their behaviors toward their children. The behavior manager must have procedures to cue the parents' responses to specific behaviors of the child, for measuring the parents' responses, and for providing reinforcement to the parents contingent on their responses.

The important features of a behavior modification program involving parents include changing the patterns of the parents' responses to the child's responses and changing the patterns of the child's responses to those of the parents. Eventually, the parents will initiate their own plans for modifying the child's other behaviors. The ultimate objective is achieved when the parents bring the child to the point where he exhibits consistently "self-managed" behavior—i.e., where he can manage his own contingencies.

Contingencies on the parents' behavior are as important for effective modification here as are contingencies of the child's. Parents must be reinforced systematically for maintaining contingencies on the child.

In the beginning, all contingency management must be controlled by the behavior manager. There are three reasons for this. First, almost all behavior modifications in the home require behavioral change on the part of parents. Second, the initial changes in the child's behavior in relation to the parents' new behavior are not strong enough to reinforce the parents. Third, the parents' new task of keeping a record of the child's behavior—a task which, when accomplished, provides the first evidence of behavioral change—is not reinforcing at first and is often considered objectionable because of the systematic effort required. Consequently, the behavior manager must institute contingencies on record-keeping and parental reinforcing behavior until the data show that the child's behavior is in itself changing sufficiently to reinforce the parents.

The behavior manager can provide the parents with various rewards. One is the home instruction he gives them on how to manage the child. A second is the opportunity to share information and problems with other parents who have similar difficulties. A third involves the contingencies the manager promotes among various family members—for instance, contingencies where the mother reinforces both the problem child and the sibling who responds appropriately to him; where the father reinforces the mother for her success with the child; and where the mother reinforces the father for his initiation of a reinforcing contact with the problem child. When the last type of reinforcer succeeds in maintaining desirable parental behavior, the manager can tally up another successful case of behavior modification.

To make one reward—visiting the home—contingent on the parents' behavior, the manager should tell the parents at the outset that he is interested in periodic home visits. As his program develops, he can determine what parental responses should be required before a home visit is made. The requirement may simply be that they produce five days of data on their own and the child's behavior. Or when modification has begun, the requirement might be a specified approximation of the terminal objective.

Parent meetings can also be rewarding. They should be regularly occurring events designed to accomplish specific objectives. In addition, they should follow specific procedures, with attendance and assistance contingent on data brought from home.

Parents should be taught specific procedures for pinpointing behavior for modification, for collecting reliable baseline information, for continuously recording specific behavior, for instituting and maintaining modification procedures, and for using the data to make further modification decisions. Evaluation procedures should be applied to the behavioral data on the parent and the child.

The manager may use examinations as a contingency on parents. Parents are assigned a set of readings in a standard work on behavior modification and then they are tested. If they pass by a certain criterion (say, nine out of ten questions answered correctly), they can progress to another level of interaction with the behavior manager and with other parents. Each new and more advanced—and hence, more helpful—step is contingent on having passed the earlier step.

There are various ways to conduct parent meetings. All the usual paraphernalia of education—tests, written assignments, behavioral records and on-the-spot observations—can be employed, and all the usual auditory and visual aid devices—tape recordings, video tape records—can be used to display data. Parent meetings, beginning with the presentation of parent and child response data furnished by the parents, are most effective when they move toward specified terminal objectives. The data presented at the beginning of the meeting should be used in discussions and to guide further decisions on the training of parents and the modification of the child's behavior.

The contingencies the manager establishes between parent and child are of two types: social or token reinforcement in some pattern related to the child's responses, or a contract between the child and parent specifying the response's requirements and its consequences. Contracts are best when they specify the type of response expected, the duration of the contract, and the reinforcement earned by meeting the contract.

The overall objective of parent management is to enable the child to manage his own contingencies and eventually to set his own objectives. A child who can do this is instrinsically motivated and well adjusted.

A behavior modification program in the home begins with the parents' statement of their expectations for the child. These are the terminal objectives toward which the modification program is aimed. The statements below, taken from first interviews with parents in a behaviorally oriented special education program, are typical examples.

I want him to learn to talk to people. He rarely says anything unless spoken to directly, and even then he may not respond.

He has a great deal of trouble concentrating. If I can hold him to a task, such as reading or arithmetic, he will do fairly well, but if I leave him for a few seconds he wanders off and forgets entirely about the task.

She cries all the time—maybe thirty to forty times a day. Even if she isn't crying, she is giving out high-pitched sounds which just unnerve me something awful. I would like to see her crying stop and those awful sounds, too.

My child has never progressed educationally. He is brain-damaged, I know, but I have been told that this does not keep him from learning *something*. He's been in school four years and we have absolutely nothing concrete to show for it.

Although we know the autism diagnosis for our child, we do not think this precludes her getting down some speech patterns in relation to her daily life and trying to learn to socialize some with other children. She seems so aloof that we often become very discouraged. She is thirteen; we need to know what we can teach her to do and how we can provide for her security in the future, whether she can ever learn any skills, and lots of problems like these.

We have been told that Robert *can* learn, that he is not retarded but has some kind of "learning disability" which is not well understood. Tutors and other special programs have not reached him at all. We want to see some educational benefits from our efforts and also to see him mature more socially.

While these statements do not contain the detailed information needed for developing modification plans, they are a beginning. Gradually, with the help of teachers and others skilled in shaping new behavior, parents can make these broad statements more specific.

Williams (1959) demonstrated the effectiveness of systematic procedures for behavioral change in the home. In this program, parents were taught to apply extinction procedures to their child's bedtime crying and tantrums. The child's behavior was observed first, in order to plan an effective procedure. Both the crying and the events associated with it were revealed to usurp an inordinate amount of parental attention. The child managed to keep one of the parents at his bedside for thirty minutes to two hours every night merely by crying whenever the parent attempted to leave or even tried to read while sitting in the room.

To modify the child's behavior, the parents were directed to put him to bed in a relaxed manner, sharing some pleasantries with him while he was settling down, and then to leave the room and close the door. They were specifically directed *not* to return to his room when he began crying and screaming. The stimulus event (parental attention) which had maintained crying was withheld, with a consequent decrease in the crying. The data showed that the crying lasted more than forty-five minutes on the first night but rapidly dropped to zero over the next few nights. Data also showed the effect of reinforcement on crying: when attention to the bedtime crying was inadvertently provided by an aunt one week after the parents had started extinction procedures, the child's crying behavior returned at a high rate and took longer to extinguish than before.

Procedures followed by Wolf, Risley, and Mees (1964) to change the behavior of an autistic child in a ward setting provide more than sufficient evidence that inappropriate behavior, regardless of its severity, can be changed by effective modification of the stimulus events influencing it. The child in this case exhibited a severe lack of appropriate verbal and social behavior. His eating and sleeping habits were very poor, and he had tantrums during which he banged his head, scratched and slapped his face, and pulled his hair. Further, he refused to wear the glasses that were prescribed for his cataract condition. By direct intervention, and by training ward personnel and the parents in the home to modify systematically the stimulus events which followed these deviant responses, the investigators were successful in changing the child's behavior.

When the child had a temper tantrum, he was immediately taken to his room and the door was closed. The child was thus removed from all events which might have strengthened this behavior. When the tantrum ceased, the door was opened immediately. Through instruction and actual practice on the ward, the parents were taught how to make these responses at the *appropriate time.*

To get the boy to wear his glasses—which was necessary if he was to retain his sight—a program was designed to provide him with reinforcing stimuli after each response which approximated his putting the glasses on. Since the child's typical response was to throw his glasses, initial reinforcement was given to him simply for picking up and holding pairs of empty frames. As this response accelerated, reinforcement was switched to responses which gradually approximated putting the glasses on. Two kinds of reinforcers were used. When the program began, the attendant, who provided the reinforcement for responding, presented small bites of candy and fruit immediately following the click of a toy noisemaker, regardless of what responses the child was making. The clicking sound became the stimulus event which signaled reinforcement time and subsequently became a reinforcing stimulus itself. When the child responded to the click by coming for candy or fruit, the click began to be used only when the child made responses that approximated putting the glasses on. Eventually, reinforcement was presented only for wearing the glasses. Throwing the glasses resulted in the child's prompt removal to his room for ten minutes. As a result of these two procedures, the boy was soon wearing his glasses regularly.

The verbal behavior of the child was shaped first by providing the child with statements to mimic and later by setting the occasion for an unmodeled response. When the response was appropriate, the attendant reinforced the child with bites of his breakfast or lunch. The presentation of food as a reinforcer seemed to be the most powerful stimulus event available for strengthening verbal behavior.

During meals, the boy was very disruptive and stole and threw food. These behaviors were changed by training the attendant to remove the child's plate when he threw food, to direct the child to use his spoon, to remove the child from the dining room if he stole food, and to remind him of the possible removal of the plate or himself from the dining room. These stimulus events rapidly decreased the occurrence of the unwanted behavior. By determining what behaviors to increase or decrease, by using selected stimulus events to strengthen or weaken them, and by training ward attendants and parents to carry out these procedures, the social and verbal behaviors of this child were remarkably and permanently changed.

When the parent is given explicit instructions on what procedures to use, and when the procedures are systematically followed, the results can be dramatic. But instruction must include details about *when* and *how* to interact with the child (Hawkins et al. 1966) and must emanate from information obtained through direct observation of the child's behavior and the events occurring in the environment at that time. In the home, this usually entails observing and recording both the child's responses and the parents' responses to the child. Hawkins and his associates trained a mother to change her own behavior toward her child, whose repertoire of objectionable behaviors was extensive. The child's typical responses included biting his shirt or arm; sticking out his tongue; kicking or hitting himself, others, or objects; calling someone or something a derogatory name; removing his clothing or threatening to remove it; saying "no!" loudly and vigorously; threatening to damage objects or persons; throwing objects; and pushing his sister.

This mother was cued at home, with the observer signaling which of three responses she was to make to her child's behavior. For unacceptable behavior, she was directed to tell the child to stop. If he did not, she was to remove him to his room and lock the door for five minutes. For appropriate behavior, she was directed to give attention, praise, and physical contact. In other words, she was to react aversively to the child's inappropriate behavior by telling him to stop, to impose "time out" from a pleasant event by removing the child to his room for not stopping the unacceptable behavior, and to react very pleasantly to strengthen all acceptable behaviors when they occurred.

These instructions and the cue sessions in the home were very successful in changing the mother's pattern of response to the child's behavior. Rather than attend to the child's unacceptable responses and ignore the acceptable ones, she reversed the emphasis of her attention. Consequently, the child's behavior became much more appropriate.

Terminal objectives must be specified before contingencies can be established, because behavior modification procedures are determined by the specific objectives involved. These objectives are usually such ordinary activities as finishing homework each day, doing chores, avoiding squabbles, going to bed on time, and not eating between meals except under prescribed conditions. It is simply a matter of stating the objectives precisely and motivating the child toward achieving them. The following case study demonstrates how parents modified the behavior of a fifteen-year-old girl.

Case of Elsie

Elsie's parents sought help when the school reported to them that Elsie was skipping classes, failing in her work, and sassing teachers. In the past, Elsie had been a good B-level student, commensurate with her 120–125 tested I.Q., and she had generally been a cooperative child, producing only minor and brief problems at home and at school.

Reports from the parents on their management practices indicated that although they frequently admonished Elsie, they failed to exercise control when undesirable incidents occurred. They were concerned that Elsie stayed out too late on Friday nights when she went with her friends to basketball games. She failed to keep her room picked up. She often sassed her father and occasionally her mother. She spent her allowance and then proceeded to use her mother's credit card to buy additional items without permission. She refused to eat many foods served at the family dinner table, choosing instead to have cookies, pretzels, soft drinks, and other foods between meals whenever possible.

Contingency management was definitely indicated. The rewards were easily selected, for there were many privileges and activities that Elsie desired. Up to now, she had retained these privileges, even when this was contrary to the parents' wishes, because the parents had always acted too late to be effective. The parents' failure to establish clear objectives for themselves and for Elsie had resulted in the girl's presumptuous behavior and flaunting independence and in their own continual frustration.

In the behavior modification program set up, Elsie was allowed her privileges contingent on certain performances. At the beginning, the parents listed the privileges that Elsie desired and the corresponding objectives they desired.

Parents' Contingencies	Elsie's Privileges
1. Elsie must clean her bedroom each day during the week.	To attend the Friday night school functions.

Other contingencies were added to this privilege to strengthen certain behavior patterns. Before Elsie could attend the Friday night school function, each day before school she had to—

2. hang up her pajamas in the closet;
3. clean out the washbowl;
4. make the bed, changing the sheets on Thursday morning;
5. close the window and raise the blinds.

The parents monitored this behavior from each Friday to the Thursday of the following week, and, depending on her performance, Elsie was either given or denied the privilege of attending the Friday evening function.

The parents made a chart covering these before-school duties, placed it on the kitchen bulletin board, and had Elsie check off the duties each day before leaving for school. The mother checked the chores each morning, initialing Elsie's checks for each chore satisfactorily completed but not initialing anything improperly done or incomplete. There were other privileges that Elsie desired:

Parents' Contingencies	Elsie's Privileges
1. Elsie must help her mother clean two bedrooms and the dining and living rooms on Saturday morning.	To go to a movie with a friend on Saturday afternoon.
2. Elsie must exhibit good eating habits.	To have a Sunday afternoon driving lesson with her father in the school parking lot.
3. Elsie must not charge articles to her mother's credit account.	To spend up to $2.00 a week on herself as she wished but not retain the charging privilege.

The last privilege resulted in a compromise between Elsie and her parents: Elsie was permitted a once-a-month charge not to exceed $10.00, provided she paid half the bill from her baby-sitting fees.

Actually, the contingencies for the first and second privileges were more explicit. To meet the contingencies for the first privilege, Elsie was to help her mother clean four rooms of the house each Saturday morning from 10:00 A.M. to 12:00 noon. During this time she was not to have phone calls, visitors, or other distractions, and she was to follow her mother's directions. The contingency for the second privilege was that Elsie eat small portions of all foods served at family meals, with between-meal snacks limited to a glass of milk and a piece of fruit twice a day. In addition, Elsie was further limited to one ten-cent candy bar and one other ten-cent item (a soft drink, popcorn) at the Friday evening school function. These contingencies were difficult to monitor, but the parents hoped that Elsie would develop self-control in order to keep her privileges. A Thursday night "accounting time" was agreed to, since it was a good break-off time before weekend privileges and gave the parents time to curtail the privileges if the week's data showed that Elsie had not met the contingency requirements.

Behavioral objectives and the means to achieve them are usually worked out during consultations between the parents and the behavior management consultant. For the project to be effective, parents must keep response data on the child that are pertinent to the objectives specified and the procedures used.

A behavior management program cannot be expected to work wonders. There are bound to be snags. Sometimes it is necessary to revise, extend, or perhaps even drop some objectives or procedures. In addition, new objectives may emerge as a result of successes or failures, and these new objectives will change the course of the program.

For example, after two weeks Elsie began to spend too much time on the telephone talking to her peers and, consequently, sometimes neglected her homework. This made it necessary to set a new goal which had been implicit before but not specified by the parents. The decision was made to limit Elsie's time on the telephone to a period from 6:30 to 7:30 P.M. daily, with homework to follow. The parents risked losing a contingent hold on Elsie by allowing her the telephone privilege *before* she had completed her homework, but the program succeeded and it was not necessary to change the temporal arrangement. This is a fortunate example of a child's satisfying a less stringent contingency in the realization that her not doing so would result in the imposition of a stricter one. Elsie knew that if she did not agree to the first contingency her parents could rearrange the temporal order of the telephone-homework arrangement.

The success of contingency management with Elsie came from determining the privileges she wanted and using them as reinforcers for specific types of behavior. Elsie enjoyed driving lessons with her father on Sunday, going to a movie with a friend on Saturday afternoon, and school functions on Friday nights. These activities served as reinforcers contingent on appropriate behavior.

Reciprocal Relationships

Patterson and Reid (1970) describe the social interaction between a parent and a child as one of reciprocity or coercion, depending on whether the interaction is pleasant or aversive. Their observations on the interactions between two members of a family, a child and a parent or two children, demonstrate that a family can be described in terms of the interactions of groups of two people. In their research, which shows how to change these interrelationships to bring about a change in the behaviors of two or more members of a family, the procedures introduced led directly to the development of reciprocal relationships.

The two authors describe reciprocity as observable when two people "reinforce each other at an equitable rate," that is, when they are equally pleasant to each other. This is positive reinforcement, which strengthens the behavior it follows. The parent and child who respond to each other with smiles, compliments, and a good deal of spontaneous cooperation exhibit a pattern of reciprocal social interaction. The term coercion describes the pattern of interaction in which one person uses aversive action to control the behavior of the other and is strengthened in this tendency by the responses of the victim. The parent who always attends to the child when he makes an inappropriate response but rarely or never attends to him when his behavior is appropriate is responding aversively, i.e., being coercive.

The authors stress that in order for a child to develop normal reciprocal relationships at home, at school, and in the neighborhood, all relevant people in his early environment must become social reinforcers for him. Their research suggests that, for social interaction to occur, the two who are to interact reciprocally must have some common social skills in their repertoires.

Patterson and Reid clearly define patterns of parent-child response and give procedures for modifying even well-established ones. Two conditions are necessary for such modification: the modification must take place within the child's social environment, and the dispenser of the child's reinforcement (the adult in this environment) must also be programmed for specific behavioral change.

Patterson and Reid have carried out a study whose procedures were designed specifically to reduce the output of deviant behavior and establish reciprocally pleasant relationships between dyads of parents and children within one family. After two weeks of observing the parent-child responses in the home, they initiated a specific program of behavior modification. This program was designed to: (a) increase the number of pleasant reactions the children received from their parents; (b) change the parents' passive "pleasant reactions" (listening or attention) to more active approval, such as praising, smiling, or laughing; (c) decrease the amount of attention the children received for unacceptable behavior; and (d) increase parent-child and child-child reciprocity.

Summary

Parents can help or hinder a school's efforts to improve instruction, increase learning, or change social behavior. School personnel, therefore, must learn to work effectively with parents. Otherwise, they may expend a great deal of energy, only to find that the parents are working at cross-purposes to the objectives of the school.

Parents can contribute to constructive efforts to achieve behavioral goals for their children if school personnel will take the time to help them. But if parents are to be truly helpful, they need to be taught the techniques of positive and negative reinforcement and contingency management, and to tone down their (often characteristic) aversive control methods. Home visits by school personnel, classroom observations, and structured parent discussion groups are ways, singly or in combination, in which school-home cooperation can be strengthened and behavior management improved. School personnel must decide how much they can or must do to enlist full and enlightened parental participation.

The setting of behavioral objectives with parents is important at the outset. The parents may state their goals only vaguely at first, but, with the help of school personnel, specific objectives can be established. Data on behavior can be taken by parents as well as by school personnel.

Perhaps the core problem in working with parents on behavioral objectives for their children is to teach the parents the importance of contingency management. Under a contingency management system, the parents' objectives for their child and the child's own objectives can be effectively interwoven. Parents are often too aversive in their efforts to control their child's behavior, but, if some practical help is given them, contingency management can usually solve both their problems and the child's problems in one concerted, economical effort.

References

Ferster, C. B., and Marian K. DeMyer. "A Method for the Experimental Analysis of the Behavior of Autistic Children." *American Journal of Orthopsychiatry,* **32** (1962): 89–98.

Haring, Norris G., and E. Lakin Phillips. *Educating Emotionally Disturbed Children.* New York: McGraw-Hill Book Company, 1962.

Hawkins, Robert P., Robert F. Peterson, Edda Schweid, and Sidney W. Bijou. "Behavior Therapy in the Home: Amelioration of Problem Parent-Child Relations with the Parent in a Therapeutic Role." *Journal of Experimental Child Psychology,* **4** (1966): 99–107.

Patterson, Gerald R., and M. Elizabeth Gullion. *Living with Children: New Methods for Parents and Teachers.* Champaign, Ill.: Research Press, 1968.

Patterson, G. R., and J. B. Reid. "Reciprocity and Coercion: Two Facets of Social Systems." In *Behavior Modification in Clinical Psychology,* edited by C. Neuringer and J. L. Michael. New York: Appleton-Century-Crofts, 1970.

Williams, Carl D. "The Elimination of Tantrum Behavior by Extinction Procedures." *The Journal of Abnormal and Social Psychology,* **59** (1959): 269.

Wolf, Montrose, Todd Risley, and Hayden Mees. "Application of Operant Conditioning Procedures to the Behaviour Problems of an Autistic Child." *Behaviour Research and Therapy,* **1** (1964): 305–12.

Case
Studies
of
Behavior
Modification

8

There are several reasons for gathering accurate case studies. A good case study may serve as a model for future treatments; it may be a record of a procedure, incorporating data and information from all involved personnel into an easily readable report; or it may be used in a publication to describe an unusual problem or unique treatment procedure.

Medical case histories have traditionally served as valuable records of change in individuals or groups under prescribed programs or treatments. They have emphasized relevant background information about the subject, describing the treatment prescribed for him and explaining the changes in his condition resulting from that treatment. In programs of behavior modification, case studies assume a different dimension. The historical perspective is altered, so that the focus is on the subject's present behavior—what he does and under what conditions he does it. The causal factors are deemphasized, while the analysis of behavior is highlighted. Thus, a case study in behavior modification features—

1. a description of the behavior problem, the conditions under which it occurs, and the consequences it evokes;
2. a brief description of previous treatment (if any);
3. a description of the modification program designed on the

basis of baseline measurement, accompanied by a description of how the program was implemented in the classroom;

4. a description of the results of the program.

This chapter will serve as a guide for writing a case study in behavior modification. Four case studies illustrate the application of behavior modification procedures to individual problem management.

Case studies, written in a clear narrative style, may be anecdotal, but they must also include data which support the modification procedures. We emphasize that not all data compiled during the behavior analysis should be incorporated into the final report. Only those figures which are the bases for the behavior modification program, or for the alterations made in it, or which reflect behavioral changes, should be included in the final case study. Therefore, the researcher will need to review all the data, all the histories, and all the reports from participating personnel and select from this material that information which is most pertinent to a final report.

The first step in writing up the case study is to describe clearly the behavior problem. It may involve social behavior or learning disability. For example:

Freddie refused to take his turn on the playground. He always wanted to be first, said it was due him because he took charge of the balls, bats, and other sports equipment. He wanted to be captain of his team and assign the other children the positions they were to play. If the teacher was unaware of his manipulations, Freddie would organize the whole ball game according to his own desires before anyone else realized what was going on. Moreover, he refused to budge on any point, feeling that yielding would be a humiliation. If opposed, he often became angry, walked off the field muttering to himself, and later complained to anyone who would listen that others were not fair to him. This disgruntled attitude carried over to his classroom and study activities, greatly diminishing his effectiveness.

Becky was very withdrawn. She seldom spoke to another child unless that child spoke first. She did not continue a conversation, but let it die away with weak "yes" or "no" replies. In class, she did not volunteer for discussion and slumped down in her seat as if to avoid the teacher's view. When Becky was called on, she replied as briefly as possible in a weak and halting voice. Sometimes she was teary-eyed when she arrived at class in the morning. Some students reported that other children teased her and asked her if she had left her tongue at home. In class or in school social activities, Becky kept to her retiring ways, remaining on the periphery of any social encounter.

Notice that the examples above describe the problems but do not state their causes. The concern is not with causes, but with accurate descriptions of behavior on which the procedures for change were based.

Furthermore, these descriptions do not include all the dimensions of the child's behavior, nor do they give an exhaustive survey of all of the child's problems. It was probably neither possible nor necessary for the researchers to know all facets of the problems, nor was it necessary to postpone taking action because they did not know them. A description of a learning disability follows.

> Thirteen-year-old Jeff was scheduled to enter the seventh grade in the fall of 1967. Then it was discovered he could not read.
>
> His mother explained: "That spring I had noticed that Jeff didn't seem to have any enthusiasm. He didn't want to go any place or do anything. One weekend, because one of Jeff's older brothers was in a hospital in Alaska, I suggested to Jeff that he write a letter to his brother. Hours passed and still he hadn't written the letter, so I began to insist. That's when I learned Jeff couldn't even write the word 'the.' He could copy words, but he simply couldn't write the letter by himself."
>
> When Jeff's academic abilities were evaluated, the data showed that he read at a primer level. He had no sound-symbol relationship. At the same time, he had a very mature attitude, consistent with his age. He could discuss current events, for example, from what he saw on television news. [Norman 1969]

A clear statement of the behavior problem indicates the direction which the modification program should take—whether it should be designed to accelerate an academic behavior, decelerate inappropriate social behaviors, or shape appropriate behaviors.

The second step in a case study of behavior modification is to state what, if anything, had previously been done about the problem. This section should include medical information if the child is receiving special treatment, a brief record of past psychological help, and accounts of previous techniques used in classrooms to alleviate the child's problem. This information should be concise, for the emphasis in behavior modification is to determine where the child is at the present and not to repeat past investigations. It is also important to make special note if no professional attention had previously been given the problem. We continue now with the case of Jeff.

Concerned about Jeff, his mother contacted the family doctor, who recommended a psychologist. The psychologist suggested that Jeff come to the University's Adolescent Clinic to find out what was wrong. The doctors there determined that Jeff was neither mentally retarded nor suffering from brain damage or disease. They advised that Jeff attend the University's Experimental Education Unit, where new ways of teaching children were being developed. During the period when Jeff's behaviors were being evaluated, baseline data were accumulated on his rates of response. In the classroom, Jeff was put on a program of contingency management.

During Jeff's first year at the school he earned free time as he increased his number of correct responses—in reading, arithmetic, geography, or whatever subject he was studying. For example, twenty-five correct responses a minute might earn him one free minute. He could choose what he wanted to do with his free time. Sometimes he played billiards, but more often he played basketball.

The amount of free time a student earned was worked out between him and his teacher. At first, Jeff received one minute of free time for fifteen correct answers. After a while he asked that this be changed to a ratio of 1:25, explaining that the first ratio was too easy. Later he received one free minute for fifty correct answers.

Gradually Jeff's program was changed to teach him more self-sufficiency. First he began correcting his own papers. Then he started doing his own graphing, and, finally, he made his own decisions. His teacher said "We try something new, and if it doesn't work, we pull back and evaluate the data."

The chart [reproduced in Figure 8.1] depicts such a situation. During the first week shown, Jeff was receiving one free minute for ten correct number responses. He and his teacher talked about his forthcoming return to public school and how his program might be changed to make it more comparable to the public school routine. She suggested that the free-time reward be discontinued in one subject, but Jeff decided to go whole hog and discontinue the free-time system for all subjects.

The chart shows that during the five-week period, Jeff's rate of response (covering both correct and incorrect responses) dropped from a median of eight responses per minute to three and one-half per minute. With this evidence to think about, he and the teacher decided to establish a contract system of the sort commonly used in public schools, whereby they would mutually agree upon a goal for achievement and, if Jeff reached the goal with time to spare, make that extra time his. The chart shows that Jeff's median rate of response increased to eleven responses per minute when this new system was in effect.

Today, two years later, Jeff reads at the fifth- or sixth-grade level. His last year's teacher says, "Jeff can sound out words and make sense of them. He never tried to read things at home before, but now he does. He's not a fluent reader, but he can get along."

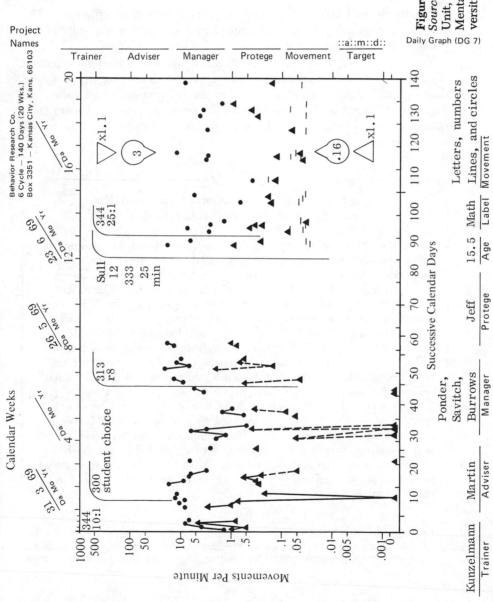

Figure 8.1. Math responses. *Source*: Experimental Education Unit, Child Development and Mental Retardation Center, University of Washington

Jeff's math ability, now that he can read the problems, has progressed even more. He has finished decimals, percentages, and plane geometry and is studying algebra and trigonometry this summer. When he enters junior high school he will be well up to the level of his classmates in mathematics. [Norman 1969]

The fourth and final step is to describe the results of the program. The last two paragraphs of the case study above describe the results of the program that was set up for Jeff.

The case studies which follow illustrate the individualized management of children, whether in groups or alone. The effectiveness of the programs they describe can be attributed to the careful planning and control of procedures, for it was this that enabled the researchers to implement their management techniques as planned and as modified after analysis of response data.

Behavioral Case Study One:
Modification of Autistic Behaviors*

Kevin was a thin, fair-haired boy, just turned ten. At our first meeting, he was bundled up in a long coat buttoned down the front. His hands were tied behind his back, his legs tied together at his knees, and a fur cap was tied to his head, with a cord across his mouth. He had asked to be immobilized in this way, and any efforts to change the bindings brought on head-banging, self-biting and scratching, and biting or kicking his would-be "liberator." At no time could we allow his hands to be untied, since they had become severely bruised and swollen due to his biting. On other visits to the school, we often observed that he would wear either a large cardboard box, cut to resemble a television set, over his head, or a paper mask over his face.

There were no requirements made of him at school, and he would spend most of the time sitting by himself, staring and making very few movements. He seldom had any interactions with his peers and was never observed in any verbal interaction with them, nor did he, except in one instance, exhibit any cooperative behavior or participate in any cooperative efforts. This was when one of the older girls was making a mask for him.

* For this first case study, we are indebted to David L. Williams, member of the Psychological Clinic at The George Washington University, Washington, D. C., and Director of Research, School for Contemporary Education, McLean, Virginia.

Kevin refused to eat either at home or at school. The staff had used aversive control procedures to get him to eat in school, one teacher holding him while another tried to feed him. When he refused to eat, he was threatened and occasionally pricked with a paper clip until he would say "Big boy" and take a bite of food. This procedure was not too effective and resulted in increased kicking and biting.

Although he emitted sounds quite frequently, usually in response to the teacher's questions, they were not distinguishable as words. For example he would often say "po-po" which everyone interpreted as meaning "No." Kevin's mother reported that the boy did not speak until he was five years old, making his desires known only by pointing to various objects.

Kevin had a high rate of self-biting behavior. Over the fifty-nine days during which he was observed by the school staff prior to the study, he bit himself 281 times. His self-biting behavior varied from days with no episodes to one day when he bit himself twenty-eight times. Records indicate that his biting drew blood on several occasions. Head-banging occurred 217 times, ranging from zero to thirty-five times per day. Hitting, biting, or kicking others, or attempting to do so, occurred 176 times, with a daily range from zero to thirty-eight times. These data are merely descriptive and should not be considered baseline measurements of the child's behavior.

Procedures

Teacher training. One of the major features of the project was training the individuals who interacted with Kevin to use procedures of behavior modification. At first the teacher was observed. The consequences and the methods that the teacher used dependent on the child's behaviors were noted. These observations made it apparent that the teacher was already somewhat familiar with behavior principles, so that feedback from the data with brief discussions of their implications probably produced some effect. The teacher was required to read Holland and Skinner's programmed text, *The Analysis of Behavior* (1961), and there were weekly discussions of this material as well as of the behaviors of various children in the school. The teacher's admission ticket to these sessions was her written answers to the programmed text. She would then lecture on the material covered, and the experimenter would ask leading questions to fill in gaps that were missed; the experimenter would also try to relate the material to examples in the school. During these discussions, the experimenter tried to refrain from directly answering most of the teacher's questions on the material. Following this, behavioral vignettes were presented to the teacher. These required written answers, to be brought to the next session. Questions that were answered incorrectly were discussed with the experimenter. Social praise was used extensively to reward appropriate comments. An observer was also present at all sessions to provide feedback to the experimenter.

The actual sessions with Kevin were an important part of the training. At the first session, the manager remained in the room with the teacher. The teacher was instructed to present questions to the boy every ten seconds. When he responded incorrectly, the experimenter turned his head away. This cued the teacher to provide a time-out. For the remaining sessions, the experimenter remained behind the observation screen. After each session, the experimenter met with the teacher for a few minutes to provide feedback, to deliver praise for appropriate behavior, and to answer any questions. In addition, he frequently brought candy or fruit for the teacher and Kevin to eat after the session was finished.

Individual treatment sessions. Instead of trying to deal with Kevin's behavior over the entire day, the experimenter decided to begin by structuring a small portion of time in order to establish limited social control and then gradually to expand it. Consequently, fifteen-minute sessions were instituted, during which the teacher would teach Kevin phonetics, spelling, and writing, concentrating on increasing the clarity of his speech. Praise, such as "Good," "Excellent," "Terrific," "Bravo," smiling, and patting him on the back, were used as social reinforcers. During the first session, the reinforcer was followed by a sip of milk-shake. For the second through the tenth sessions, M & Ms were paired with praise, and during the remaining sessions, praise alone was used. Any disruptive behavior was followed by a time-out, which consisted of the teacher's turning away from the child and picking up a book to read for one minute. Disruptive behavior was defined as getting out of the chair and leaving the session area, exhibiting any negative physical act, and making any disruptive noise, such as crying, shouting, or asking for some object not included in the session. Correct responses were defined by the teacher, who was gradually to increase the requirement for the clarity of pronunciation.

The procedure required the teacher to ask a question approximately every ten seconds, wait for a response, and, when it was correct, to deliver social reinforcement. If the child failed to respond after the third time, the teacher would prompt him by saying, "Say . . . ," and giving the correct answer. Correct pronunciation was shaped by successive approximations, and sentences were occasionally developed by chaining words together.

As the rate of Kevin's correct responses increased, the teacher was instructed to increase the ratio of social reinforcement to correct responses. Instead of receiving reinforcement every time he made a correct response, Kevin now had to give two, and later, three correct responses before he received social reinforcement.

Certain requirements were made for participation in the session. After the first session, Kevin was not allowed to wear a box on his head. Later on, his coat was removed, his legs were untied, his hands were tied in front, and he was allowed to wear either a cap or a mask but not both. During the last few sessions, his hands were completely untied for increasing portions of the session until, on the last day, they were untied for the entire time. The mask that he wore was diminished by gradually increasing the open space in it. First the eyes and mouth were cut out, then the cheeks, and finally, on the last day, only a small portion of the mask remained around Kevin's eyes.

Kevin had been a problem eater, and his loss of weight was a concern. It was suggested that instead of using aversive control techniques, his place be set at the table with the other children, lunch be announced, and, if he sat down to eat, he be praised. If he refused to eat, he was not to be forced, but his lunch would be thrown away at the end of the lunch period. The staff was advised to recommend that the same procedure be used in the home.

Early in the intervention and several weeks before actual sessions began, it was suggested that attention might be the reinforcer maintaining the negative physical behaviors; therefore, it was decided to ignore them. No other specific procedures were initiated in a controlled manner, however.

Parent training. About a week before the termination of the program, it was learned that Kevin and his family would be moving to California. Consequently, the mother was asked to participate in a crash training course so that there would be some continuity of the behavior modification program. The mother was seen once by the experimenter, who gave her a general introduction to the procedures used. The next day she observed a session through the one-way observation screen while the experimenter indicated the important variables in the procedure. Following this, the mother herself conducted a session with Kevin; during this session the experimenter and the teacher provided feedback and social praise to her when she correctly reinforced her son.

This session is indicated as session nineteen in figures 8.2 through 8.10. The figures show that the mother presented social praise contingent on correct responses sixty-five percent of the time. Kevin worked the entire fifteen minutes without any disruptive behavior. Consequently, the mother had no need to administer time-outs or to give commands.

As the session progressed, the mother became more enthusiastic and self-assured, her voice became louder and clearer, and she delivered the social reinforcers in a crisper manner. She was very positive in her statements about conducting the sessions and expressed her eagerness to show her husband what Kevin could do.

On the following day, the mother administered another session, this time with only Kevin in the room. On the last day, she brought along Kevin's twelve-year-old brother, who also conducted part of the session. Although no data were kept on the brother's behavior, observers noted that he used a few social rewards. He seemed to participate with enjoyment and interest, asking Kevin about nearly every object in the room, even as they were leaving.

Because of the shortage of time, only the basic concepts of reinforcement and time-out were emphasized. Several other suggestions, however, were given the mother, one of them being to have as many people as possible spend time with Kevin.

Data collection. During the fifteen-minute individual sessions, data were recorded by one or two observers behind a one-way observation screen. The data were broken down into units, the first consisting of the antecedent stimuli presented by the teacher, such as a question like "What is . . . ?" The second unit of data covered Kevin's behavior, and the third those instances in which his behavior was followed by a reinforcing stimulus provided by the teacher. The antecedent behaviors, or stimuli, were tallied in columns on an event sheet marked: (a) questions (including requests made by the teacher within the context of the session, such as, "Give me the green crayon"); (b) commands (tallied only when the subject was not performing properly and was requested to return to his work with some phrase like, "Sit down"); (c) prompts (referring to situations in which the teacher would give the correct response for the subject to imitate, e.g., "What does this word spell? It spells boy."); and (d) fades (referring to situations in which the teacher would force a physical response and then gradually reduce his guidance of the response). The last category was never used for this subject.

The behavior of the subject was scored as either a correct or an incorrect response. It was separately scored when the subject corrected himself without the teacher's aid or when he emitted no response at all. Disruptive behaviors, such as leaving the chair, negative physical acts, and verbal behavior incompatible with the tasks of the lesson, were also recorded.

Another measurement of the degree of control was secured by using a stopwatch during those times when the subject was seated facing the teacher and responding to her questions. This was defined as the "working time." More than half the sessions were recorded on tape. The consequences provided were categorized as verbal praise alone, verbal praise paired with a food reinforcer, or time-outs, and each of these occurrences was noted in the appropriate column. If no reinforcers were provided, the last column was left blank.

Observations of Kevin began approximately one month before starting the individual sessions and were continued until the sessions were terminated. A time-sampling technique was used with observations for fifteen-second intervals followed by fifteen seconds for the recording of the observations. Data were collected for twenty-minute periods, with the days and the times of day randomly selected. Observations were made of Kevin's behavior and of the social consequences provided for it by teachers or peers.

Results

Observer agreement on data from individual sessions. Agreement between observers was computed for ten of the twenty sessions. Percentage agreement was computed by dividing the total number of disagreements by the average of the total number of behavioral events. Since totals only were used in analyzing the data, disagreement was simply the difference in the total number of events scored for each category. Thus, if one recorder scored eighty questions and another eighty-six for the fifteen-minute period, the disagreement would be six for the category, and this number would be divided by eighty-three (average of eighty and eighty-six) to find the percentage disagreement. Data for percentage of observer agreement are presented in Figure 8.2.

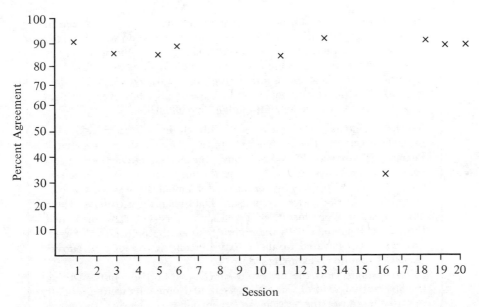

Figure 8.2. Percent observer agreement for individual sessions

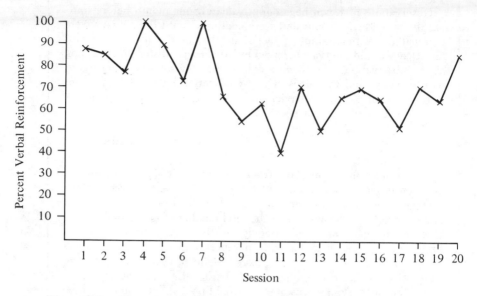

Figure 8.3.   Percent verbal reinforcement by teacher contingent on correct responses from Kevin

For nine of the ten sessions, agreement fell in a restricted range of between eighty-five and ninety-five percent. One session was unusually low—thirty-four percent. Observers attributed this to the speed of the session, with questions being asked every two or three seconds. Also, the regular data sheets were forgotten on this particular day. The data were used despite their low reliability. Generally, however, the data appear to be of satisfactory interjudge agreement.

Teacher behavior. One purpose of this study was to develop the teacher into an effective behavior modifier. The data show a very satisfactory performance. Figure 8.3 shows the percentage of times that a correct response was followed by social reinforcement. The early sessions were characterized by verbal reinforcement after seventy-five to 100 percent of the correct responses. Data from the two days where 100 percent reinforcement was given show very low rates of correct responses. Beginning with the eighth session, the percentage of reinforcement was lowered to about sixty percent as the ratio of correct responses required was increased.

The sessions show the increased effectiveness of time-outs. During the first session, control was rather weak and time-outs were used only toward the end of the session, and then not very clearly. Too much

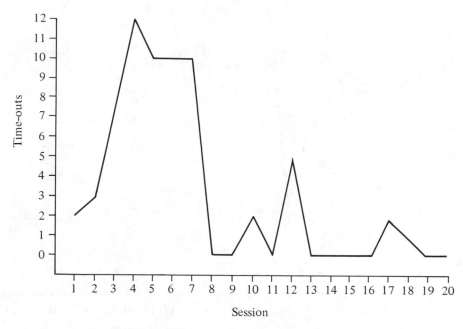

Figure 8.4. Number of time-outs given by teacher

verbal control was attempted by using various if-then statements. As the sessions progressed, time-outs were used more frequently (fig. 8.4). This procedure continued through session seven, after which there were few occasions when time-outs were needed. The effectiveness of the teacher's use of time-outs was perhaps most clearly demonstrated during session six, when Kevin's hands were tied in front for the first time. This was an occasion for much disruptive behavior. Kevin bit himself severely, attacked the teacher, scratching her and pulling her hair, and threw materials about the room. All this behavior was effectively ignored, and control was restored. From this session on, there were no instances in which disruptive behavior was reinforced by the teacher's attention. It appears, then, that—at least during the training sessions—the teacher functioned as an effective behavior modifier, and that the teacher-training procedures produced this improvement.

The influence of social reinforcement. As sessions progressed, Kevin's behavior was increasingly controlled by the social reinforcement provided by the teacher. There were many indirect indications that social reinforcement was maintaining Kevin's behavior, although it was impossible to test this hypothesis through a reversal procedure. Figure

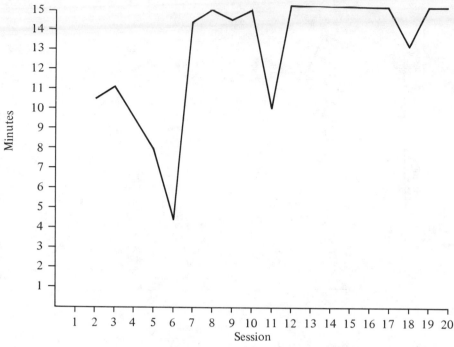

Figure 8.5   Number of minutes that Kevin was 'working' during the fifteen-minute sessions

8.5 shows the amount of time Kevin actually worked during the fifteen-minute session. By the ninth session, he worked 100 percent of the time. Ten of the last thirteen sessions are characterized by Kevin's sitting in the chair for a full fifteen minutes, facing the teacher or the material, responding readily, appearing interested, and working diligently.

This measurement was not taken during the first session. In that session he knelt on the floor away from the table with a box over his head, emitting a great deal of extraneous noise most of the time. An observer noted that he answered questions only when he wanted to. Also, there was some difficulty at first in getting him into the room, and he spent time running around the basement, picking up and chewing small specks of lint.

Another indication of the establishment of control was the decrease in disruptive behavior. In eleven of the last fourteen sessions, there was no disruptive behavior at all (fig. 8.6). An indirect indication of this is that the number of time-outs was greatly reduced (fig. 8.4), as was the number of commands given (fig. 8.7). Commands were pro-

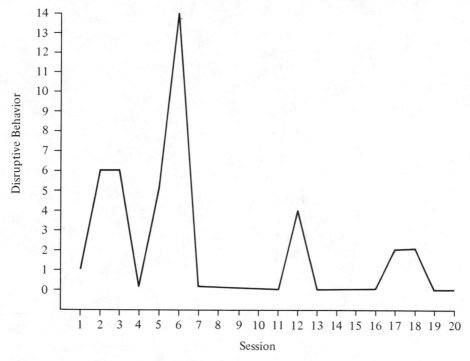

Figure 8.6.   Number of times Kevin emitted disruptive behavior during the fifteen-minute sessions

vided only when the subject was not cooperating. That Kevin's disruptive, self-destructive behavior was socially motivated was clearly demonstrated in the sixth session, the worst one according to a number of measurements. During this session, when Kevin's hands were tied in front of him rather than behind his back for the first time, there was the least amount of working time, the highest amount of disruptive behavior, the highest frequency of commands given, and the second highest frequency of time-outs (which, although less frequent than those of another session, tended to last for a longer period of time). In addition, the observers and the participating teacher all agreed that it was the most difficult session to handle. Kevin bit himself on the arms very frequently. The bites were severe, drawing blood, and observers could hear the sound of ripping flesh. When a time-out was used because of this behavior, Kevin ran in front of the teacher in an attempt to display his self-inflicted wounds. When this produced no effect, he tried to scratch the teacher's face and pull her hair. As the teacher slowly stood up and walked away, Kevin threw the materials from the

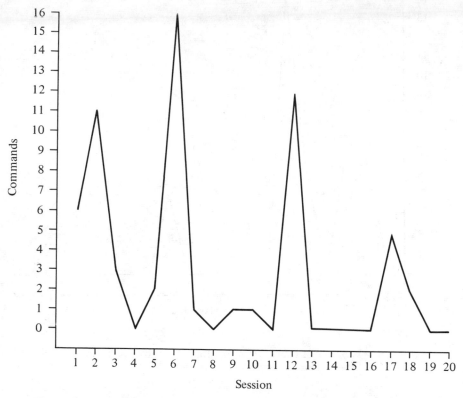

Figure 8.7. Number of commands given by teacher

table onto the floor. When he had exhausted the repertoire of behaviors that had probably brought his social environment under aversive control in the past, the behaviors began to be extinguished and Kevin quietly picked up the materials and resumed the lesson. The remainder of the session was relatively quiet, with only a few sporadic and milder self-destructive outbursts.

No self-destructive behavior occurred in the succeeding sessions, until session twelve. At this session the mask was removed and Kevin bit himself twice, but time-outs quickly extinguished this behavior. During session seventeen there were two incidents as the mother observed through the one-way observation screen, and during the eighteenth session, when Kevin's hands were completely untied, two more incidents occurred.

Figure 8.8 shows the frequency of times that Kevin did not answer a question by the teacher before she asked the next question. As can

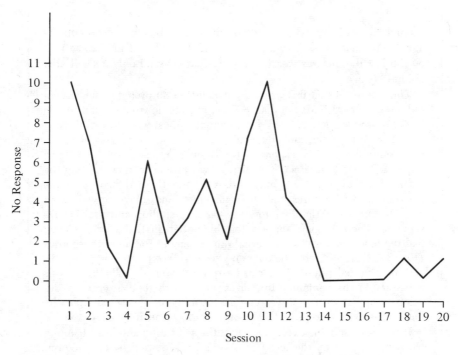

Figure 8.8.   Number of times that Kevin did not respond to a question from the teacher

be seen, toward the later sessions Kevin responded to nearly every question asked.

Further evidence that Kevin would work for social reinforcement was that the session itself was used as a reinforcer for other behaviors. The requirements for participation in the session were gradually increased. From the second session on, Kevin had to remove the box from his head in order to gain admission. Later, this requirement was extended even more, so that he did not wear the box at all while at school, although he wore it occasionally at home. At the sixth session, his hands were required to be in front of him, and on each subsequent day the bindings were loosened slightly more than they had been on the previous day. At session fifteen they were untied completely for part of the time. This was done so that he could be taught to write. On the day of the last session, his hands were untied for the entire stay at school, and his mother reported that they were untied for part of the time at home. Beginning with session six, Kevin was permitted to wear either a cap or a mask, but not both. His mother had purchased a small baseball cap, which made quite an improvement in his appearance. The mask that he wore was gradually reduced in size, so that on the last day he was wearing a mask that covered only a small area around his eyes.

The use of food at first probably had little reinforcing value. Kevin did not eat the M & Ms but placed them in a cup in front of him. When M & Ms were no longer used, little change appeared in Kevin's behavior. The only indication of any effect was that at session eleven a greater number of "no responses" by Kevin were recorded. Insofar as the M & Ms had an effect, however, it was probably in controlling the teacher's behavior. Social approval is frequently a difficult variable to control, and the presentation of an object may have served as an S^D (Discrimative Stimulus) for the teacher's smiling and praising responses. There is some support for this notion in that session eleven had the lowest percentage of verbal reinforcement for correct responses (Fig. 8.3). At any rate, the data on sessions eleven to twenty-one indicate that verbal praise alone can be quite powerful. Whether it was necessary in the beginning to pair approval with food in order to develop approval as a positive reinforcer cannot be answered from the data. However, it appears that it may not have been.

It seems reasonable to conclude that the self-biting and head-banging were maintained by the social consequences provided by the environment. The change in the consequence provided for these responses resulted in the rapid extinction of these behaviors, both in the sessions and elsewhere at school. These responses were probably developed in order to produce the responses the child desired of others. In addition, there is strong, though not conclusive, evidence that it is possible to develop new, desirable behaviors through procedures of social reinforcement.

The instructional content of the session was left to the teacher, since this was her area of expertise. The sessions concentrated for the most part on phonics, which included the making of proper vowel and consonant sounds and the sounding and spelling of simple words. Some arithmetic and writing were also introduced. It is difficult to quantify the material, since adequate baselines were not established. However, Figure 8.9 indicates that the number of correct responses tended to increase as the sessions progressed. Figure 8.10 indicates a slight increase in the percentage of correct responses, which would take into account the variation in the number of questions asked in different sessions. Because new materials were periodically introduced, the data were difficult to interpret. Besides, it was sometimes difficult to ascertain what constituted a correct response for phonics. By the end of the sessions, however, Kevin could pronounce most sounds distinctly, recognize and spell small words like *house, boy,* and *bee,* and write the alphabet.

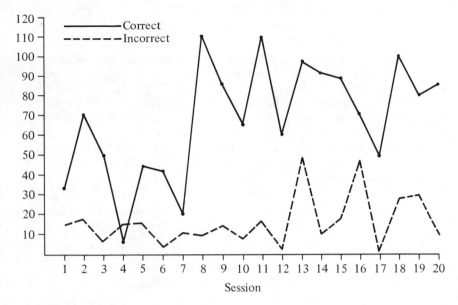

Figure 8.9. Number of correct and incorrect responses made by Kevin during the fifteen-minute sessions

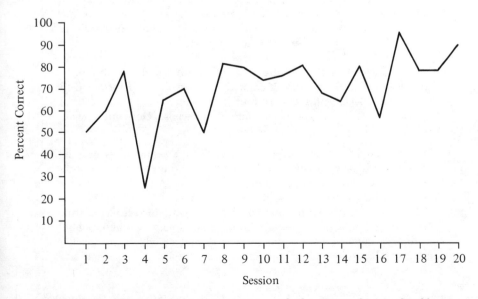

Figure 8.10. Percent correct responses made by Kevin during the fifteen-minute sessions

Summary

Twenty fifteen-minute sessions between an autistic boy and a teacher were conducted for a period of four weeks. The sessions were conducted in line with the principles of operant conditioning. Data indicate a reduction in the total number of aversive behaviors emitted by the subject and an increase in various verbal skills. Data on the teacher's behavior indicate that she was able to learn the basic principles of operant conditioning and to use them to bring the behavior of the subject under the control of her social reinforcement. There are some indications of changes in the subject's and teacher's behavior in other situations as well.

Behavorial Case Study Two: Modification of Reading Behaviors*

Method

Subjects. Four elementary school boys (grades five, four, four, and three), severely disabled in reading but average or above average in intelligence, were diagnostically evaluated by the experimenters as one to five years retarded in reading skills. Entering reading behaviors are categorized in Table [8.1] under entering grade level, word recognition level [determined] from the Gates-McKillop Diagnostic Reading Tests, instructional reading level determined by informal basal reading tests, and placement in Sullivan Programmed Reading Books determined by the Sullivan Placement Test. All four boys presented reading skills at the primer level in Sullivan Programmed materials. Only one boy, R, read above the primer level in a basal reader.

Materials and apparatus. Reading materials were sequentially ordered in frames with answers adjacent to each presentation to allow for individual progress and effective sequencing of skills. A slider covered the answer until a written response was completed.

The highly structured reading environment contained a teacher station, four student stations, and a reinforcement area. A podium behind the four students served as the teacher station at which the teacher performed her observations and made verbal contact with each boy

---

*This case study is quoted from Norris G. Haring and Mary Ann Hauck (1969a).

Table 8.1. Entering and Terminal Levels of Reading Skills of Subjects

Student			Entering Levels		Terminal Levels	
	Grade	Programmed Material	Basal Reader	Word Rec-ognition	Basal Reader	Programmed Material
RD	5	Primer	Primer	2.8	4-1	4.2
M	4	Primer	Primer	2.5	3-1	3.9
R	4	Primer	3.1	3.1	4-2	4.5
P	3	Primer	Primer	2.5	2-2	3.5

SOURCE: Haring and Hauck 1969a.

through a microphone to the headsets worn by each boy. She whispered instructions, provided directional prompting cues during oral reading, and manipulated switches to reinforce oral responses throughout the experiment. At the student stations, students completed all written and oral reading work, and manipulated a switch at the outside edge of their carrels to record correct and incorrect written responses.

The reinforcement area contained edibles, trinkets, and toys priced at various point values based on actual retail value. Items with retail value of fifteen cents or more had point values based on 400 points per fifteen cents. Five cent items were valued at 200 points, ten cent items at 350 points, and one cent items at fifty points. Pellets of candy, gum, and peanuts were valued at twenty-five points. Reinforcers were packaged separately except for pellets of candy and gum which were bottled for dispensing one at a time.

Design and procedures. Obtaining continuous evaluation and making ongoing decisions for the development of terminal behaviors required that the effects of reinforcement variables on written and oral reading responses be continuously measured through each change in variables. The five periods of the design included two baseline periods and three modification periods (See Table [8.2]). The study continued for ninety-one days with a sixty-five minute session each day—the students' only formal reading period. Reading material remained constant throughout the five periods except that content became progressively more complex.

Two types of responses from each student were measured: written responses and oral responses. A written response was defined by the response requirement of each programmed frame: (a) circling the correct word or picture, (b) drawing a line to the correct word or picture, (c) writing one letter or several letters, or (d) writing a whole word. Each constituted one written response. One oral response was defined as each word read orally from (a) lists of new words, (b) word discrimination groupings, and (c) sentences appropriate to each unit in the programmed books.

Table 8.2. Baseline and Modification Periods of Experiments

Independent Reinforcement Variables	Periods					
	A	**B**	**C**	**D**	**E**	**F**
	Without answers	With answers	Counters	Continuous reinforcement token reinforcement	Variable ratio token reinforcement	Variable ratio token reinforcement
Material	Programmed Material			Programmed Material		Basal reader
Period Type	Baseline periods			Modification periods		

SOURCE: Haring and Hauck 1969a.

The four boys served as their own controls in two ways. First, each brought with him an academic history exhibiting from one to four years of low rates of performance in reading. Secondly, during the first two weeks of the experiment, the students made reading responses to the programmed material without receiving any reinforcement beyond what the programmed format offered, i.e., immediate confirmation of answers and/or appropriate sequencing of textual material. These measures, especially the latter, were considered as representing the number of correct reading responses each student made under conditions prior to the experimental conditions—response data which served as a baseline from which to compare behavior change.

Prior to the first baseline period, four days of adaptation introduced procedures for: (a) written responding to programmed reading; (b) oral responding to appropriate stimuli from cards and teacher directions through earphones; and (c) switch use.

Period A—during the four days of Period A, answer columns were stapled together, visible answers were blacked out, and verbal correction of oral responses was not given. Under these conditions, which approximated classroom assignments for which answer feedback is often delayed, each response was followed by the next frame and movement of a switch by the student to record his response.

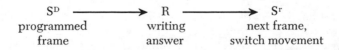

$$S^D \longrightarrow R \longrightarrow S^r$$

programmed frame	writing answer	next frame, switch movement

Period B—the seven days of this period provided a typical programmed format. After making each written response, the student obtained answer confirmation from the adjacent answer column. Verbal correction of oral responses was given by the teacher. The student recorded the accuracy of his answer by moving a switch at his carrel to the right if he was correct and to the left if incorrect.

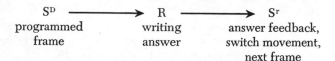

$$S^D \longrightarrow R \longrightarrow S^r$$

| programmed frame | writing answer | answer feedback, switch movement, next frame |

During this period the programmed format was modified permanently to avoid misuse of answers. This enabled measurement of responses emitted before answers were known. Answers were cut from the books, perforated at the top, and hung backwards on hooks in front of the student. The cut pages were stapled into books. The modified format required the student to write responses to a complete page of frames, remove the answer column from the hook, place it next to the corresponding frames, and correct his written responses.

Period C—following the baseline period, a counter, which tallied the number of correct responses being made, was installed at each carrel and functioned as the only change in variables for the next twelve days.

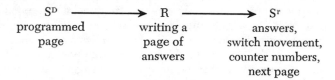

$$S^D \longrightarrow R \longrightarrow S^r$$

| programmed page | writing a page of answers | answers, switch movement, counter numbers, next page |

This running account of the number of correct responses emitted proved to be important for both the student and his neighbor.

Although the counter directly influenced behavior, the more important process for modification of the student's skills was the systematic application of reinforcement using two basic procedures: acquisition and maintenance reinforcement. During the initial modification procedures (Period D), when each student's correct reading responses occurred at a very low rate, it was necessary to reinforce each correct reading response. When each student had exhibited a high, stable rate of correct reading responses over a number of sessions, reinforcement was presented only intermittently (Period E), but no less systematically, to maintain the high output of correct responses each boy was exhibiting.

Period D—throughout the twenty-one days of Period D, counter numbers functioned as points (token reinforcement) with exchange value for edibles, trinkets, and more expensive items. Correct responses were reinforced continuously. Each correct written or oral response immediately earned one point, and each student set up his own chained reinforcement schedule of continuous reinforcement (CRF) components by his choice of the reinforcers for which he would work. During the first week, points had exchange value for store items varying from 25 points to 1,000 points. During the second week, expensive items were introduced for purchase requiring point-saving over many days or several weeks.

Period E—correct responses during the forty-seven days of Period E were reinforced intermittently. Arrangements for reinforcement changed progressively from presentation following a variable ratio (VR) of every two responses (VR 2) to VR 4, VR 5, VR7, VR 10, VR 15, and VR 25, without instruction to the student. For example, arrangements for presenting points on a variable ratio of two correct responses entailed presenting points variably, sometimes after one correct response and sometimes after two correct responses. Arrangements for presenting points on a variable ratio of ten correct responses meant that on the average each tenth correct response received a point, although in fact sometimes a marble would be earned after one response, or after three responses, or sometimes only after twenty correct responses.

The objective in using intermittent reinforcement was to maintain, as the number of reinforcements per responses progressively decreased, the high stable rate of performance which developed during continuous reinforcement. Intermittent reinforcement of correct responses initially was very frequent, but progressively became less frequent as responding appeared to stabilize with each change in schedule. Except for the initial instructions indicating that sometimes, following a number of correct responses, the student would earn a marble worth ten points, no instructions were given when reinforcement arrangements changed.

Marbles worth ten points each took the place of counter points as token reinforcement to give the experimenters the flexibility necessary for intermittent reinforcement with crude, nonautomatic equipment. The series of numbers within a ratio schedule was determined randomly to permit randomly varied reinforcer presentation controlled from the teacher's podium. Following a predetermined number of correct responses registered on a student's counter at the teacher's podium, the teacher flipped a microswitch which activated a stimulus light at a student carrel indicating to the student he had made enough correct responses to earn a marble. The boy responded to the stimulus light by manipulating an apparatus, attached to his carrel, which dispensed a marble.

Period F—this month of transition was designed as another step in the reinforcement of successive approximations to the terminal behavior— "normal reader functioning under natural contingencies." The independent variables which changed were the instructional materials. As Figure 8.11 indicates, a three-component chained sequence of responding required (a) reading a word list, (b) reading a story from

A

Word List

| Silent reading for | opportunity to read orally for points | $--\rightarrow$ | *B* |

Basal reader

| Silent reading for | opportunity to read orally for points | $--\rightarrow$ | *C* |

Choice

| Silent reading for | opportunity to read orally for points | $--\rightarrow$ | points earned could be spent upon completion of this chain |

Figure 8.11. Chained sequence of responding required in Period F. From Haring and Hauck 1969a

the basal reader, and (c) making a choice between reading in a basal book or a library book. Silent reading preparation preceding the opportunity to read orally for points constituted the basic procedure in each component. The points earned and the reinforcement given for correct oral reading were credited to the student contingent on daily completion of all three components. Words not known [to the students] during silent preparation or oral responding were grouped [into study lists] to emphasize common word parts, derivations, and/or syllable division. Comprehension was measured by responses to oral questions from the teacher after oral reading and by answers to written multiple choice questions following story completion.

Initially, the students were assigned to read only one basal reader page silently before having the opportunity to read orally for points.

But within one week, this requirement had changed to silently reading three pages before oral reading and, finally, students were required to read a complete story. Initially, when a student orally read a randomly selected paragraph for points, he earned one point per word in each line of print read correctly. But within a week, reading the total paragraph correctly was required before any points were earned. This incorporated an essential feature of skill development: progressive increase in task difficulty as performance data indicate readiness.

Reinforcement was provided only for correct oral responding, as follows: (a) from the word list, five points per word within each group of similar words read correctly, but no points for words in a group if errors occurred within it; (b) from the basal reader, initially one point per word from a line of print read without error and later from a paragraph read without error, but no points if any errors were made in either instance; (c) during the "choice" component, two points per word from a paragraph read without error if the basal reader was chosen, and one point per word from a paragraph or page if a library book was chosen. All material to be read orally was randomly selected from pages already read silently, except the words on the word list. Correct oral answers to oral comprehension questions received five points. Correct written answers to written comprehension questions received ten points. Following Period F, the same reading procedures were continued but under the direction of the teacher in the student's public school classroom.

Teacher Instruction

The teacher paced the students together through side one of the Sullivan Primer the first two days of the adaptation period to establish the procedural chain for functioning in the experimental environment. From that time on each student progressed individually.

All other reading instruction from the teacher was given during oral reading in the Sullivan material for Periods A through E and in the basal readers and word lists during Period F. When a student mispronounced a word while reading orally, the teacher directed him to the word for another try by repeating the word immediately preceding the word mispronounced. With this cue, the student returned to the mispronounced word for a second try. If he failed on this try, the teacher provided directional cues highlighting the beginning, middle, or ending of the word. For example, the teacher would say, "Look at the beginning of the word again." If the student failed with this cue, he was told the sound of the part missed, and finally told the word, if necessary. The first cue was often sufficient; the latter two were rarely needed. Mispronounced words were programmed for a word list the next day.

For diagnostic purposes, the teacher recorded mispronunciations during oral reading. With microswitches she recorded the interval and content of her verbal interaction with a student as well as the number of correct oral responses a student was making. The latter data also registered on the student's counter.

Teacher Communication

Teacher communication was almost totally preplanned and prepared in script form. Scripts controlled teacher communication for: (a) giving initial procedural directions, (b) repeating directions upon request or upon teacher observation of improper responding to directions, (c) requesting oral reading, (d) stopping behavior harmful to others or to equipment, (e) dispensing final reinforcers, and (f) commencing or dismissing class.

The two basic procedures for the students entailed writing answers in their programmed books and orally reading from word cards at the teacher's requests. Oral reading was programmed to correspond with progress in the books.

During reinforcement periods, points earned, spent, and saved were recorded in common bank savings books. At any time a student had earned enough points or marbles to make a purchase, he had the option to make a purchase, although students usually waited until the session ended.

A twenty pen event recorder automatically recorded the occurrence of correct oral responses, and the occurrence and content of teacher communication as well as correct and incorrect written responses. A daily check of the student's switch use was obtained from a book count of the actual number of correct and incorrect written responses.

Results

Results will be discussed under three categories: (a) comparison of response data between baseline and modification periods, (b) reading skill progress and (c) reinforcer preference.

Baseline performance. Response data for both baseline periods (Period A, with no answer confirmation given, and Period B, with immediate answer confirmation given) were similar for all four students. Whether or not the student was provided immediate confirmation of answers, the total number of correct responses made daily was low. Correct responding, which occurred at the rate of about four per minute when the child was reading, was irregularly interspersed with responding to stimuli other than reading materials. Almost half of each session was spent in behavior incompatible with making reading responses, resulting in an overall average of 2.8 correct responses per session. Over the last few days of baseline period, a rapid decrease in the number of reading responses and a rapid increase in the amount of time spent not reading were evident. Figure 8.12 exhibits for each stu-

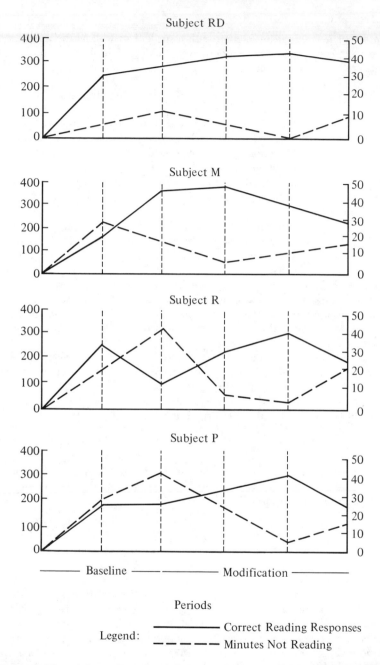

Figure 8.12.   Average number of correct responses and average number of minutes spent not reading per period. From Haring and Hauck 1969a

dent the average number of correct responses made each session and the average number of five minute intervals spent not making reading responses.

Counters (Period C). After counters were installed, dramatic changes occurred in reading performance. Students who made correct responses at the baseline rate of four per minute now typically made over 300 each session, resulting in an overall rate of 4.5 responses per session. Responding became stable throughout the session with very few five minute intervals when the student was not making reading responses. Although response rate varied extremely over sessions for each student, compared to rate during continuous reinforcement (Period D), counters did function as conditioned reinforcers. Average response rates were significantly higher for three of the four boys compared to baseline rates. Misuse of the programmed format by the fourth boy, M, before answers were clipped from the frames prevented accurate comparison of his overall baseline rate with rates between other periods. Comparison between his rate during Period A when he could not misuse the answers and his rate during any modification period, however, indicates a very significant difference.

Acquisition reinforcement (Period D). Systematic application of reinforcers following each correct response during the first week of this modification period resulted in: (a) establishing stable reading rates throughout each session; (b) accelerating response rates to 6.2 and 8.5 correct responses per minute; and (c) producing daily rates as high as 400 to 550 correct responses. Table 8.3 exhibits the significantly higher average response rates which occurred for three of the four students under continuous reinforcement compared to baseline conditions.

Table 8.3. Comparison of Average Total Responses per Period

Subjects	Average Total Responses				
	Baseline Periods		Modification Periods		
	A	B	C	D	E
RD	115	228	335*	334*	316*
M	121	335ᵃ	337*	267	240
R	219	94	295*	319*	209*
P	180	174	221*	297*	213*

SOURCE: Haring and Hauck 1969a.
* Chi square test revealed a significantly higher ($p < .001$) average total response.
ᵃ Misuse of answers.

Two boys, P and RD, averaged about 100 more correct responses every session, while R averaged almost 200 more correct responses. It may be of importance to note that M responded during Period D almost as fast as he misused the answers during the baseline conditions of Period B.

Expensive reinforcers, introduced the second week and requiring long term saving, were not effective in maintaining high response rates. Rates either decelerated or stabilized at a lower rate until the middle of the third week of Period D when three of the four students, short of the points necessary for very expensive items for which they had been saving, spent all points they had. At that time, responding again accelerated to near the high level observed the first weeks of Period D. A reinforcer too far removed from the response—too far in time from the final reinforcer—does not maintain the desired response (Kelleher and Gollub, 1962).

Maintenance reinforcement (Period E). As the average number of reinforcements given decreased gradually from one for every two correct responses to an average of one for every twenty-five responses, without instruction to the student over forty-seven days, the significant difference between baseline response rates and changes in response rates during Period D modification procedures was maintained. A chi square test revealed that total responses under variable ratio schedules were significantly higher (.001 level) than baseline rate for three of the four boys, although significantly lower than rate under continuous reinforcement for two of the four boys.

Although research has demonstrated that response rates are characteristically higher under intermittent reinforcement than under continuous reinforcement (Ferster and Skinner, 1957; Kelleher and Gollub, 1962; Staats, Finley, Minke, and Wolf, 1964), there are several reasons why this failed to occur in the present study. During continuous reinforcement, the student probably responded near his physiological limit as he moved through the chain of requirements for writing, correcting, and recording the answer. Secondly, response requirements had become more complex, requiring much more silent reading per written response. RD and M, for whom response requirements changed greatly during Period C but not during Periods D and E, exhibited average daily responses not significantly different between these two periods. R and P, for whom response requirements changed greatly, exhibited significantly lower rates in Period E.

Observation of the number of minutes spent reading when learning conditions were motivating reveals a marked decrease in the number of intervals spent avoiding reading. When reading was reinforcing, the reading performance of the four students exhibited both higher rates and more intervals of reading during each session. The increase in minutes spent not reading during Period E for R and P is evidence of weakening reinforcers. Certainly for R the data indicate the effect of a visit by his mother two weeks before the end of the period; she told him he must not buy any more candy or other edibles. For R, edibles had been the strongest reinforcers; consequently, his rate rapidly decelerated, but all points he did earn were spent on candy.

Maintenance reinforcement during transition (Period F). The chain of three silent and oral reading components, through which the child had to respond each session, using reading materials typical of the classroom, proved very effective in maintaining stable rates during the final nineteen days in the experimental setting and the final three weeks of responding in the regular classroom. Only once out of the nineteen days of the period did each boy fail to silently prepare his reading lesson carefully before having the opportunity to read orally for points. A lesson poorly prepared silently meant few points earned during oral reading.

This same three-component chained assignment was used during the final three weeks of school within the regular classroom with equal effectiveness. At the time the students returned to the classroom, R moved out of the state. A followup letter from his mother stated he was reading above grade level in his classroom, and at home was reading "everything he could get his hands on." Reading performance back in the regular classroom actually occurred at a higher average rate than was observed during the last week in the experimental setting. In the classroom, a student helper or the classroom teacher listened to the oral reading, tallied the number of words read correctly, and recorded the information in a common bankbook. The total number of correct responses was converted into "points to spend"; the same intermittent purchases were permitted according to reinforcement schedules used in the experimental procedures. Twice a week each student was presented a supply of store items from which to make purchases. Plans for the final phase of the project required maintenance of these efficient, accurate reading performances, using systematic programming of learning conditions natural to the classroom.

Reading Progress

Change in reading performance was not only remarkable because of the amount of change in rate of making correct responses every day and the number of five minute intervals spent reading, but also because of the amount of measurable skill development. Overall changes in the instructional reading levels of the four boys ranged from one and one-half years to four years, following five months of instruction (Table 8.1). Comparison of pre- and postmeasures of instructional basal reading levels indicated: (a) RD progressed from primer to book 4–1; (b) M progressed from primer to book 3–1; (c) R progressed from book 3–1 to book 4–2; and (d) P progressed from primer to book 2–2 by the time the transition period began. Each student read his final programmed book with less than a 5 percent error rate during both oral and silent reading.

Reinforcer preference. Of the three types of reinforcers available for purchase, the preferred reinforcers were generally edibles and expensive items, although individual preference patterns differed. The typical daily pattern for point spending included purchases of 50 to 200 points worth of edibles and saving of the remainder toward purchase of an expensive item valued between 500 and 1,500 points.

Summary and Conclusion

Learning conditions were individually programmed in a group setting to provide sequential arrangement of reading material and systematic presentation of reinforcing events to optimize each child's performance. Arrangements of reinforcing events were designed first to accelerate performance rate, then to maintain the high rate. Learning conditions were considered optimal when the child's performance rate accelerated and stabilized at a higher rate and/or when the number of minutes spent avoiding reading greatly decreased.

When learning conditions were individually appropriate, each child averaged between 100 and 200 more correct responses every day and spent very few minutes avoiding reading. The students not only made more correct responses daily and worked longer, but also progressed in instructional reading levels from one and one-half to four years over five months of instruction. Behavior and performance in other academic areas within the regular classroom also improved markedly, according to *unsolicited* comments from the classroom teachers.

Conditions for learning were evaluated, through direct and continuous measurement of the student's performance under specified conditions, (a) in terms of effectiveness of the conditions for reading, and (b) for functional, ongoing decisions about future arrangements of these conditions.

Behavioral Case Study Three:
Modification of Social Behaviors in a
Head Start Classroom*

Townsend was four and one-half years old when he was transferred to the [Head Start] Demonstration Class. Beginning at seven months

---

* This case study is quoted from Allen, Turner, and Everett (1970).

of age he had been in a series of foster homes, each of which ,had reported great difficulty in managing him. Townsend's teachers described him as excessively disruptive, hyperactive, noncompliant with adults, and aggressive toward children. Frequent emission of these maladaptive behaviors in the homeroom were confirmed by [the observer]. The Head Start bus system for several months had refused to transport Townsend because of his uncontrollable behaviors, and, therefore, he was privately transported each day by his social worker in her own car.

Collection of data (according to the system described by Bijou, Peterson, Harris, Allen and Johnston, 1969) continued after his transfer to the Demonstration Class, where the teachers were instructed during the baseline period to replicate as nearly as possible the homeroom teachers' methods of handling Townsend: rechanneling his disruptive activities, comforting him during catastrophic outbursts, physically restraining him when he attacked other children, [and] verbalizing his feelings. The maladaptive behaviors continued at a high rate during baseline conditions.

Tantrum Behavior

On Townsend's eleventh day in the Demonstration Classroom a first step in behavior modification procedure was initiated. All tantrums, regardless of duration or intensity, were to be ignored, that is, put on extinction. Absolute disregard of the tantrum, no matter how severe it might become, had to be thoroughly understood by the teachers inasmuch as there are data (Hawkins, Peterson, Schweid, and Bijou, 1966) which indicate that when tantrums are put on extinction, extremes of tantrums may temporarily ensue. Townsend's data were no exception to the classic extinction curve. His first tantrum under the nonattending contingency lasted twenty-seven minutes (average duration of previous tantrums had been five minutes), becoming progressively more severe up to the twenty-minute point. The classroom was cleared of all children and adults when it became obvious that the tantrum was going to be lengthy. The children were taken to the playground by a teacher and a volunteer while the other teacher stationed herself immediately *outside* the classroom door. When Townsend quieted down, the teacher opened the door to ask in a matter-of-fact voice if he was ready to go to the playground. Before the teacher had a chance to speak, Townsend recommenced his tantrum. The teacher stepped back outside to wait for another period of calm. Twice more Townsend quieted down, only to begin anew at the sight of the teacher. Each time, however, the episodes were shorter (six, three, and one minute, respectively). Finally the teacher was able to suggest going out of doors. This she did in a thoroughly neutral fashion with *no* grimaces or recriminatory comments on the tantrum or the shambles in which she found the room.

On the second day of tantrum intervention there was one trantrum of fifteen minutes with two two-minute followup tantrums when the teacher attempted to re-enter the room. On the third day there was one mild four-minute tantrum. No further tantrums occurred in the Demonstration Class nor was there a recurrence when Townsend returned to his regular Head Start class.

Disruptive Behaviors

Modification of behaviors categorized as generally aggressive and disruptive—hitting and kicking children, spitting, running off with other children's toys—was instituted on the sixteenth session. Disruptive episodes of this type had been averaging nine per session. On the first day of modification the teachers were instructed to give their undivided attention to the child who had been assaulted while keeping their backs to Townsend. Nine episodes of aggressive behavior were tallied on this day. During the next eleven sessions, there was a marked decrease (to an average of three per session). During the twelfth session, there was an upswing to seven episodes with a gradual decrease over the next four sessions until finally no more grossly aggressive or disruptive acts were observed. A zero rate was recorded for the remainder of the session.

During this period of withdrawal of adult attention for the two classes of maladaptive behaviors, Townsend began dumping his lunch on the floor and then smearing it around with his feet or hands. The teachers handled the situation the first few days by getting sponges and towels for Townsend and instructing him to clean up the mess. However, a teacher always participated in the cleanup. The food-dumping and smearing continued day after day with the teachers obviously not realizing that their insistence on the cleanup and their assistance in the task were maintaining the food-dumping at a steady rate of one plate and one glass per day. The teachers were, therefore, instructed to ignore the entire episode and to give their undivided attention to the other children who were attending to the meal. Songs were to be sung if necessary to override peer comments calling attention to Townsend's behavior. On the first session of extinction Townsend himself called attention to the episode repeatedly: "Hey, looka I done." "I make a mess." "Get a sponge, we gotta scrub." The teachers failed to "see" or "hear" any of this. Instead, they sang a bit more lustily, calmly finished lunch with the children, and helped them get ready for outdoors. When Townsend came over to the wrap area, he was matter-of-factly helped with his clothing, with no acknowledgment of his continuing suggestions that "We gotta clean up a big mess." On the following day he again dumped his plate; teachers followed the procedure of the previous day. That session marked the end of the food-dumping except for one isolated episode two and a half months later, which the teachers again ignored.

Bus Program

Another behavior modification project with Townsend involved the use of consumable reinforcers. As mentioned earlier, Townsend had been banned from the Head Start bus. The children were required by the bus system to stay in their seats and keep their seat belts fastened. Staying buckled in a seat belt was a behavior incompatible with the disruptive behaviors that had caused Townsend to be banned: attempting to open the doors while the bus was in motion, playing with the instrument panel, and throwing himself upon the bus driver while the latter was driving. Therefore, staying buckled in the seat belt was the target behavior in the following program aimed at reinstating Townsend as an acceptable bus rider.

Day 1. Townsend was prepared in advance for the bus trip. The teacher explained to him that he would be expected to sit quietly and keep his seat belt buckled. "I don't keep no seat belt on me," Townsend replied. The teacher ignored the remark. When the bus arrived, the teacher got on the bus with Townsend. The bus driver snapped Townsend's seat belt in place and the teacher immediately put a peanut in Townsend's mouth commenting, "Good, you are sitting quietly, all buckled up snug in your seat belt." She then quickly dispensed peanuts to every child on the bus with approving comments about their good bus-riding habits. Continuous rounds of peanut dispensing and approving comments were continued throughout the fifteen-minute bus ride.

Day 2. The same procedure as on Day 1 except that one peanut was dispensed to each child at longer intervals—two to three minutes.

Days 3, 4, 5. Peanuts—several at a time—were given only three times at variable intervals. Townsend's social worker alternated with the teacher in riding the bus and dispensing the consumables.

Days 6, 7, 8. One or the other of the adults continued to ride the bus but told the children that the peanuts would be saved until they got off the bus.

Day 9. With the exception of the bus driver, no other adult rode the bus. Both the teacher and the social worker were stationed at Townsend's bus stop. The driver had been cued to praise the children for their good bus-riding behavior as he let them off the bus. In Townsend's case he was to say nothing if Townsend had not stayed buckled. When the teacher and social worker heard the bus driver praise Townsend, they voiced approval, too, and gave him a small sucker as they accompanied him to his house.

Day 10. The same as Day 9 except that this day only the teacher met Townsend at his bus stop.

Day 11. Only the social worker met Townsend. Instead of a consumable reinforcer she presented him with a small toy.

Days 12 and 13. The social worker met Townsend but gave only social reinforcement for his good bus-riding behaviors.

Days 14, 15, and 16. No one met Townsend, but the bus driver was reminded to give him praise and a hug as he lifted him off the bus.

From then on Townsend was on his own, although the social worker occasionally met the bus if she were doing a routine call on the family. If she had brought clothing or play materials for Townsend, she presented these to him as she took him off the bus. The teachers also continued to intermittently praise his independent bus-riding.

Shaping Play Skills

Establishing appropriate behaviors incompatible with his maladaptive behaviors was the area to which teachers gave the greatest time, energy, and planning in Townsend's program. Data from the home classroom indicated that he had few play skills. Out of doors he was unsuccessful at tricycle riding, climbing, jumping, and ball-throwing activities. Frequently the unsuccessful attempt precipitated a tantrum. Indoors, the only sustained play activity in which he engaged was isolate play in the housekeeping corner. Investigation of the data revealed that he did not build with blocks, paint, do woodworking, use puzzles or other manipulative toys except to dump them out, scatter them about, or grab them away from other children. Also, he had an exceedingly low rate of interaction with other children. They avoided him, apparently, because of his deficient play skills and his high rate of noxious behaviors.

It seemed futile to attempt to build cooperative play with children until Townsend had acquired some play skills. Therefore, the teachers began a step-by-step program of teaching play with each of the materials considered important in a regular preschool program. For example, a teacher helped Townsend to duplicate what at first were exceedingly simple block models. If he refused to participate in a play "lesson" he simply forfeited the attention of all adults in the classroom. The moment he returned to the play materials, the attention of the teacher was again immediately forthcoming. In order to avoid Townsend's acquiring only stereotyped play patterns, he was also reinforced for all divergent or unique uses of materials and equipment as long as the divergence was within the broad limits acceptable to preschool teachers. Throwing blocks, while surely a divergent use, was considered inappropriate. This program of shaping play skills was concurrent with the extinction of maladaptive behaviors previously described. Therefore, even though the consequence of any one of Townsend's maladaptive behaviors was immediate withdrawal of adult social reinforcement, social reinforcement was readily and unstintingly available to him for any approximation to appropriate behavior.

Between sessions six and twenty-six Townsend acquired an excellent repertoire of play skills with a variety of materials and equipment. It was decided, therefore, to change reinforcement contingencies: adult social reinforcement would be available only when Townsend engaged in constructive use of play materials *and* interacted appropriately with another child. The change in contingencies appeared to have a positive effect. Between sessions twenty-six and thirty-two (Fig. 8.13) there was a steady increase in the rate of cooperative play.

Return to Home Classroom

Analysis of the data at this point indicated that it was an appropriate time to return Townsend to his home classroom. Townsend's original teachers had visited the Demonstration Classroom and had also been informed on each phase of the modification program. A joint staff meeting was held several days prior to the transfer in which all guidance procedures and supportive data were reviewed. A member of the ... research team was assigned to Townsend's home classroom to continue the data collection and to provide necessary coaching of the teachers in maintaining the reinforcement contingencies. Coaching was supplied on sessions thirty-three to thirty-six (Fig. 8.13) at which point the data indicated that Townsend's teachers were able to carry forward on their own. Not only were there no incidents of disruptive behaviors, but Townsend's social skills also continued to hold at a high stable rate as measured by the amount of cooperative play (Fig. 8.13, sessions thirty-seven–forty-one). Several postchecks were made throughout the remainder of the school year. Townsend continued to be a "normal" outgoing little boy, working and playing happily with an assortment of play materials and with a variety of children while requiring no more than an average share of the teacher's attention.

Case studies do not necessarily have to be long. The following one describes a very simple modification procedure in a regular classroom.

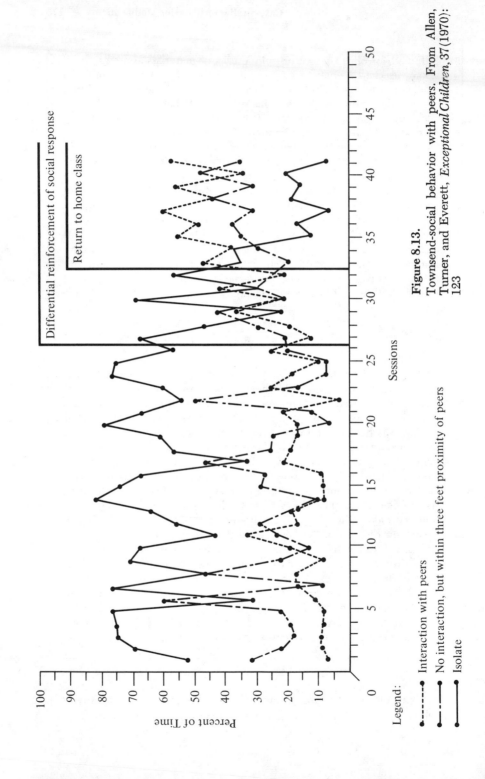

Figure 8.13.
Townsend-social behavior with peers. From Allen, Turner, and Everett, *Exceptional Children, 37* (1970): 123

Legend:

•------• Interaction with peers

•—·—• No interaction, but within three feet proximity of peers

•——• Isolate

Percent of Time

Sessions

Differential reinforcement of social response

Return to home class

Behavioral Case Study Four:
Modification of Aggressive Behavior*

This project involved two boys in a regular second-grade class who fought with each other. These fights were observed daily for 345 minutes. During a five-day baseline phase, the median rate of fighting was about .02 fights per minute. During phase B an "etch-a-sketch" was introduced. Prior to the recess each day the two boys were seated with the etch-a-sketch and were told to draw or write the word "friends." When the boys had successfully written the word "friends" they were given an ice cream cone. The data revealed that during this five-day intervention phase the median rate of fighting was .003 per minute. A second intervention phase was established in which the boys had to write the word "friends" on their etch-a-sketch within ten minutes before they were given ice cream. A withdrawal phase (no ice cream) was then instituted. The data revealed that throughout this five-day phase the boys did not fight. The results of this project are shown in Figure 8.14. (Note that the data [are] graphed on six-cycle log paper.)

References

Allen, K. Eileen, Keith D. Turner, and Paulette M. Everett. "A Behavior Modification Classroom for Head Start Children with Problem Behaviors." *Exceptional Children,* 37 (1970): 119–27.

Bijou, Sidney W., Robert F. Peterson, Florence R. Harris, K. Eileen Allen, and Margaret S. Johnston. "Methodology for Experimental Studies of Young Children in Natural Settings." *The Psychological Record,* 19 (1969): 177–210.

Ferster, C. B., and B. F. Skinner. *Schedules of Reinforcement.* New York: Appleton-Century-Crofts, 1957.

Haring, Norris G., and Mary Ann Hauck. "Improved Learning Conditions in the Establishment of Reading Skills with Disabled Readers." *Exceptional Children,* 35 (1969): 341–52.

Haring, Norris G. and Thomas C. Lovitt. "The Application of Functional Analysis of Behavior by Teachers in a Natural School Setting." Final Report, Grant No. 0EG-0-8070376-1857 (032), U. S. Department of Health, Education, and Welfare, Office of Education, Bureau of Research. Washington, D. C., November, 1969.

Hawkins, Robert P., Robert F. Peterson, Edda Schweid, and Sidney W. Bijou. "Behavior Therapy in the Home: Amelioration of Problem Parent-Child

* This case study is taken from Haring and Lovitt (1969).

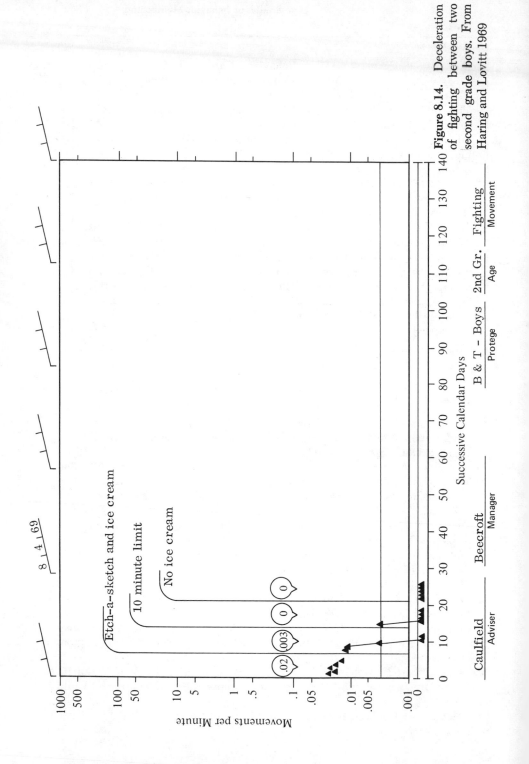

Figure 8.14. Deceleration of fighting between two second grade boys. From Haring and Lovitt 1969

Relations with the Parent in a Therapeutic Role." *Journal of Experimental Child Psychology,* 4 (1966): 99–107.

Holland, James G., and Skinner, B. F. *The Analysis of Behavior: A Program for Self-Instruction.* New York: McGraw-Hill Book Company, 1961.

Kelleher, Roger T., and Lewis R. Gollub. "A Review of Positive Conditioned Reinforcement." *Journal of the Experimental Analysis of Behavior,* 5 (Suppl., 1962): 543–97.

Norman, Mary Alice. "Child Development and Mental Retardation Center." *University of Washington Magazine* (Seattle, Wash.), 1 (1969): 3–4.

Staats, Arthur W., Judson R. Finley, Karl A. Minke, and Montrose Wolf. "Reinforcement Variables in the Control of Unit Reading Responses." *Journal of the Experimental Analysis of Behavior,* 7 (1964): 139–49.

Appendix

The Experimental Education Unit at the University of Washington uses daily event sheets on which to record classroom data. Each event sheet represents one hour of the school day divided into sixty columns and features ten major column headings (see Fig. A). The titles of the columns and explanations of them are:

1. *Contingency Code and Program Cycle.* The contingency code, i.e. 514, is a numerical code, each number of which refers to a specific interval or ratio. The program cycle is the name of the event programmed for the allotted time (i.e. Botel Spelling).
2. *Time.* The teacher marks that number in the time column showing the minute she has contacted the pupil or the pupil has contacted her. For example, if the pupil raises his hand at 9:45 and the teacher goes to him, she marks the block numbered 45 on the first sheet.
3. *Contact Initiation.* This column is for marking the kind of contact which occurred between teacher and pupil.
4. *Movement Cycle.* Under this column the teacher notes the precise movement cycle (the writing of numbers, the saying of words, etc.) that is being recorded.
5. *Errors.* The number of errors made in the work during a given amount of time are recorded here.

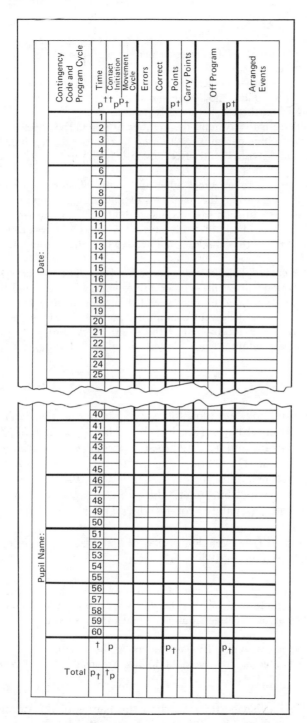

Figure A. Experimental Education Unit event sheet

6. *Correct.* The number of correct responses made in the given time are recorded here.
7. *Points.* The recorder circles the appropriate letter (p or t) indicating who set up the contingency arrangement. A slash is made in the appropriate box when the teacher awards points.
8. *Carry Points.* In this column the number of points the child has earned within a given time period is recorded. The points may be totaled whenever the child wishes and used toward free time or the arranged contingency.
9. *Off Program.* There are times when the pupil will not be attending to the program, e.g., when the teacher is explaining an assignment or correcting answers. In such cases, a line should be drawn under "Off Program" through the number of minutes when the child was disengaged. The same procedure should be followed when the student takes free time.
10. *Arranged Events.* This is the column for recording the nature of an arranged subsequent event. For example, it may be arranged that if a student earns free time, he may spend it playing pool. This would be written in the arranged event column as "play pool." Space for totaling data is provided at the bottom of the event sheet. Rates are then calculated and the information is plotted on six-cycle log paper.

Six-Cycle Log Paper

One of the more important tools for viewing data on behavior is six-cycle semi-logarithmic chart paper (see Fig. B). This type of graph, developed by Dr. O. R. Lindsley and his students, features six exponential increments on the vertical axis. The vertical axis represents 0–1000 movements per minute broken down into six cycles—.001–.01, .01–.10, .10–1.0, 1.0–10, 10–100, 100–1000—which encompass the ordinary range of human responding. The horizontal axis allows for 140 days (twenty weeks) of graphing.

The advantages of six-cycle log paper, as listed by the American Society of Mechanical Engineers (1960), are noted below.

1. It presents a picture that cannot be shown on an arithmetic-scale chart.
2. It converts absolute data into a relative comparison, without computing.
3. It shows the relative change from any point to any succeeding point in a series.
4. It retains the actual units of measurement of the absolute data.
5. It reveals whether or not the data follow a consistent relative change program.

The graph provides space for recording the names of the program manager, the student or protégé, the protégé's age and label, and the identification of the behavioral movement.

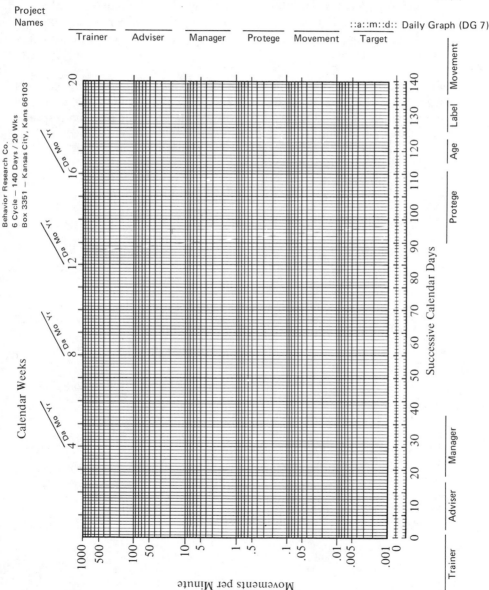

Figure B. Six-cycle semi-logarithmic paper

Rate Plotter

A rate plotter (fig. C) is a simple transparent plastic tool upon which are imprinted lines corresponding to the horizontal lines on the six-cycle log paper. On the rate plotter, numbers of minutes are written beside the horizontal lines. In order to obtain the response rate quickly without laboriously dividing the frequency of answers by the time taken to do the task, one locates the total task time (number of minutes) on the rate plotter and aligns that line and number over the number of task answers on the graph paper. The response rate for the task can be read at the point of the arrow.

For example, if the time of the session was ten minutes and twenty answers were completed, the 10 on the rate plotter is aligned with the 20 on the graph paper. By reading from the arrow, one observes that the response rate is two per minute (Lovitt 1968, p. 40a).

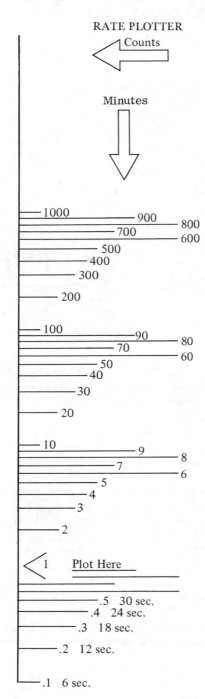

Figure C.   Rate plotter

Bibliography

Allen, K. Eileen. "The Strengthening of Adjustive Behaviors through Systematic Application of Reinforcement Procedures." In *International Convocation on Children and Young Adults with Learning Disabilities Proceedings*. Pittsburgh, Pa.: Home for Crippled Children, 1967.

Allen, K. Eileen; Hart, Betty; Buell, Joan S.; Harris, Florence R.; and Wolf, Montrose M. "Effects of Social Reinforcement on Isolate Behavior of a Nursery School Child." *Child Development* 35 (1964): 511–18.

Allen, K. Eileen; Turner, Keith D.; and Everett, Paulette M. "A Behavior Modification Classroom for Head Start Children with Problem Behaviors." *Exceptional Children* 37 (1970): 119–27.

American Society of Mechanical Engineers. *American Standard Time-Series Charts* (ASA X15.2). New York, 1960.

Becker, Wesley C.; Madsen, Charles H., Jr.; Arnold, Carole Revele; and Thomas, Don R. "The Contingent Use of Teacher Attention and Praise in Reducing Classroom Behavior Problems." *The Journal of Special Education* 1 (1967): 287–307.

Bereiter, Carl, and Engelmann, Siegfried. *Teaching Disadvantaged Children in the Preschool*. Englewood Cliffs, N. J.: Prentice-Hall, 1966.

Berkowitz, Pearl H., and Rothman, Esther P. *The Disturbed Child: Recognition and Psychoeducational Therapy in the Classroom*. New York: New York University Press, 1960.

Bijou, Sidney W. "Application of Experimental Analysis of Behavior Principles in Teaching Academic Tool Subjects to Retarded Children." In *The Learning Environment: Relationship to Behavior Modification and Implications for Special Education,* coordinated by Norris C. Haring and Richard J. Whelan. Symposium sponsored by the School of Education, University of Kansas, 1965. *Kansas Studies in Education,* **16,** no. 2 (1966): 16–23.

Bijou, Sidney W., and Baer, Donald M. *Child Development.* Vol. 1: *A Systematic and Empirical Theory.* New York: Appleton-Century-Crofts, 1961.

Bijou, Sidney W., and Baer, Donald M. "Operant Methods in Child Behavior and Development." In *Operant Behavior: Areas of Research and Application,* edited by Werner K. Honig. New York: Appleton-Century-Crofts, 1966.

Bijou, Sidney W.; Peterson, Robert F.; Harris, Florence R.; Allen, K. Eileen; and Johnston, Margaret S. "Methodology for Experimental Studies of Young Children in Natural Settings." *The Psychological Record* **19** (1969): 177–210.

Bijou, Sidney W., and Sturges, Persis T. "Positive Reinforcers for Experimental Studies with Children—Consumables and Manipulatables." *Child Development* **30** (1959): 151–70.

Birnbrauer, J. S.; Wolf, M. M.; Kidder, J. D.; and Tague, Cecilia E. "Classroom Behavior of Retarded Pupils with Token Reinforcement." *Journal of Experimental Child Psychology* **2** (1965): 219–35.

Bloom, Benjamin S., ed. *Taxonomy of Educational Objectives.* Handbook 1: *Cognitive Domain.* New York: David McKay Company, 1956.

Buchanan, Cynthia Dee. *Programmed Reading.* St. Louis–New York: Webster Division, McGraw-Hill Book Company, 1964.

Burchard, John, and Tyler, Vernon, Jr. "The Modification of Delinquent Behaviour through Operant Conditioning." *Behaviour Research and Therapy* **2** (1965): 245–50.

Burns, Richard W. "Measuring Objectives and Grading." *Educational Technology* **8,** no. 18 (1968): 13–14.

Carter, Joseph B. "Learning Laboratories in North Carolina." *Educational Technology* **8,** no. 18 (1968): 5–10.

Chalfant, James; Kirk, Girvin; and Jensen, Kathleen. "Systematic Language Instruction: An Approach for Teaching Receptive Language to Young Trainable Children." *Teaching Exceptional Children* **1** (1968): 1–13.

Charp, Sylvia, and Wye, Roger E. "Philadelphia Tries Computer Assisted Instruction." *Educational Technology* **8** no. 9 (1968): 13–15.

Clark, Marilyn; Lachowicz, Joe; and Wolf, Montrose. "A Pilot Basic Education Program for School Dropouts Incorporating a Token Reinforcement System." *Behaviour Research and Therapy* **6** (1968): 183–88.

Dechert, Charles R., ed. *The Social Impact of Cybernetics.* New York: Simon and Schuster, Clarion Book, 1967.

Engelmann, Siegfried, and Bruner, Elaine C. *Distar Reading: An Instructional System.* Chicago: Science Research Associates, 1969.

Ferster, C. B. "Positive Reinforcement and Behavioral Deficits of Autistic Children." *Child Development* **32** (1961): 437–56.

Ferster, C. B. "Operant Reinforcement of Infantile Autism." In *The Improve-*

ment of Instruction, edited by Norris G. Haring and Alice H. Hayden. Seattle, Wash.: Special Child Publications, 1971.

Ferster, C. B., and DeMeyer, Marian K. "The Development of Performances in Autistic Children in an Automatically Controlled Environment." *Journal of Chronic Diseases* 13 (1961): 312–45.

Ferster, C. B., and DeMyer, Marian K. "A Method for the Experimental Analysis of the Behavior of Autistic Children." *American Journal of Orthopsychiatry* 32 (1962): 89–98.

Ferster, C. B., and Skinner, B. F. *Schedules of Reinforcement*. New York: Appleton-Century-Crofts, 1957.

Girardeau, Frederic L., and Spradlin, Joseph E. "Token Rewards in a Cottage Program." *Mental Retardation* 2 (1964): 345–51.

Glynn, E. L. "Classroom Applications of Self-determined Reinforcement." *Journal of Applied Behavior Analysis* 3 (1970): 123–32.

Goldiamond, Israel, and Dyrud, Jarl E. "Reading as Operant Behavior." In *The Disabled Reader: Education of the Dyslexic Child*, edited by John Money. Baltimore, Md.: Johns Hopkins Press, 1966.

Hall, R. Vance; Lund, Diane; and Jackson, Deloris. "Effects of Teacher Attention on Study Behavior." *Journal of Applied Behavior Analysis* 1 (1968): 1–12.

Haring, Norris G. *Attending and Responding*. San Rafael, Calif.: Dimensions Publishing Co., 1968.

Haring, Norris G. "Experimental Education: Application of Experimental Analysis and Principles of Behavior to Classroom Instruction." In *Behavioral Intervention in Human Problems*, edited by H. C. Rickard. London: Pergamon Press, Ltd, in press.

Haring, Norris G., and Hauck, Mary Ann. "Improved Learning Conditions in the Establishment of Reading Skills with Disabled Readers." *Exceptional Children* 35 (1969a): 341–52.

Haring, Norris G., and Hauck, Mary Ann. "Contingency Management Applied to Classroom Remedial Reading and Math for Disadvantaged Youth." *Proceedings of the Ninth Annual Research Meeting* (cosponsored by the Department of Institutions, Division of Research, State of Washington, and the University of Washington, School of Medicine, Department of Psychiatry) 2, no. 2 (1969b): 41–46. Seattle, Wash.: University of Washington Press, 1969.

Haring, Norris G., and Hayden, Alice H. "The Contributions of the Experimental Education Unit to the Expanding Role of Instruction." *The College of Education Record* (University of Washington, Seattle, Wash.) 34 (1968): 31–36.

Haring, Norris G., and Kunzelmann, Harold. "The Finer Focus of Therapeutic Behavioral Management." In *Educational Therapy*, Volume 1, edited by Jerome Hellmuth. Seattle, Wash.: Special Child Publications, Inc., 1966.

Haring, Norris G., and Lovitt, Thomas C. "Operant Methodology and Educational Technology in Special Education." In *Methods in Special Education*, edited by Norris G. Haring and Richard L. Schiefelbusch. New York: McGraw-Hill Book Company, 1967.

Haring, Norris G., and Lovitt, Thomas C. *The Application of Functional Analysis of Behavior by Teachers in a Natural School Setting.* U. S. Department of Health, Education, and Welfare, Office of Education, Bureau of Research. Final Report of Grant No. OEG–0–8–070376–1857–(032), 1969.

Haring, Norris G., and Phillips, E. Lakin. *Educating Emotionally Disturbed Children.* New York: McGraw-Hill Book Company, 1962.

Haring, Norris G., and Ridgway, Robert W. "Early Identification of Children with Learning Disabilities." *Exceptional Children* 33 (1967): 387–95.

Harris, Florence R.; Johnston, Margaret K.; Kelley, C. Susan; and Wolf, Montrose M. "Effects of Positive Social Reinforcement on Regressed Crawling of a Preschool Child." *Journal of Educational Psychology* 55 (1964): 35–41.

Harris, Florence R.; Wolf, Montrose M.; and Baer, Donald M. "Effects of Adult Social Reinforcement on Child Behavior." *Young Children* 20 (1964): 8–17.

Hart, Betty M.; Allen, K. Eileen; Buell, Joan S.; Harris, Florence R.; and Wolf, Montrose M. "Effects of Social Reinforcement on Operant Crying." *Journal of Experimental Child Psychology* 1 (1964): 145–53.

Hawkins, Robert P.; Peterson, Robert F.; Schweid, Edda; and Bijou, Sidney W. "Behavior Therapy in the Home: Amelioration of Problem Parent-Child Relations with the Parent in a Therapeutic Role." *Journal of Experimental Child Psychology* 4 (1966): 99–107.

Herrnstein, R. J. "Superstition: A Corollary of the Principles of Operant Conditioning." In *Operant Behavior: Areas of Research and Application,* edited by Werner K. Honig. New York: Appleton-Century-Crofts, 1966.

Hewett, Frank M. "Educational Engineering with Emotionally Disturbed Children." *Exceptional Children* 33 (1967): 459–67.

Hewett, Frank M. *The Emotionally Disturbed Child in the Classroom: A Developmental Strategy for Educating Children with Maladaptive Behavior.* Boston: Allyn and Bacon, Inc., 1968.

Holland, James G. "Teaching Machines: An Application of Principles from the Laboratory." *Journal of the Experimental Analysis of Behavior* 3 (1960): 275–87.

Holland, James G., and Skinner, B. F. *The Analysis of Behavior: A Program for Self-Instruction.* New York: McGraw-Hill Book Company, 1961.

Homme, Lloyd E. "Human Motivation and Environment." In *The Learning Environment: Relationship to Behavior Modification and Implications for Special Education,* coordinated by Norris G. Haring and Richard J. Whelan. Symposium sponsored by the School of Education, University of Kansas, 1965. *Kansas Studies in Education,* 16, no. 2 (1966): 30–39.

Homme, L. E.; deBaca, P. C.; Devine, J. V.; Steinhorst, R.; and Rickert, E. J. "Use of the Premack Principle in Controlling the Behavior of Nursery School Children." *Journal of the Experimental Analysis of Behavior* 6 (1963): 544.

Jastak, J. F.; Bijou, S. W.; and Jastak, S. R. *Wide Range Achievement Test,* rev. ed. Wilmington, Del.: Guidance Associates, 1965.

Kelleher, Roger T., and Gollub, Lewis R. "A Review of Positive Conditioned Reinforcement." *Journal of the Experimental Analysis of Behavior* 5, Suppl. (1962): 543–97.

Keller, Fred S. *Learning: Reinforcement Theory*. New York: Random House, 1954.

Keller, Fred S., and Schoenfeld, William N. *Principles of Psychology*. New York: Appleton-Century-Crofts, 1950.

Kuypers, David S.; Becker, Wesley C.; and O'Leary, K. Daniel. "How to Make a Token System Fail." *Exceptional Children* **35** (1968): 101–109.

Lent, J. R. "The Application of Operant Procedures in the Modification of Behavior of Retarded Children in a Free Social Situation." Paper delivered at the American Association for the Advancement of Science Annual Meeting, Berkeley, California, December 1965. Mimeographed.

Lindsley, Ogden R. "Direct Measurement and Prosthesis of Retarded Behavior. *Journal of Education* **147**, no. 1 (1964): 62–81.

Lippman, Hyman S. *Treatment of the Child in Emotional Conflict*, 2d ed. New York: McGraw-Hill Book Company, 1962.

Long, Nicholas James; Morse, William C.; Newman, Ruth G., eds. *Conflict in the Classroom: The Education of Emotionally Disturbed Children*. Belmont, Calif.: Wadsworth Publishing Company, 1965.

Lovaas, O. Ivar. "Some Studies on the Treatment of Childhood Schizophrenia." In *Conference on Research in Psychotherapy*, Vol. 1, edited by J. M. Shlien. Washington, D. C.: American Psychological Association, 1968, pp. 103–21.

Lovaas, O. Ivar; Freitag, Gilbert; Gold, Vivien J.; and Kassorla, Irene C. "Experimental Studies in Childhood Schizophrenia: Analysis of Self-Destructive Behavior." *Journal of Experimental Child Psychology* **2** (1965): 67–84.

Lovaas, O. Ivar; Schaeffer, Benson; and Simmons, James Q. "Building Social Behavior in Autistic Children by Use of Electric Shock." *Journal of Experimental Research in Personality* **1** (1965): 99–109.

Lovitt, Tom C. "Classroom Management: An Empirical Approach." Unpublished manuscript, Experimental Education Unit, Child Development and Mental Retardation Center, University of Washington, Seattle, Wash., 1968.

Lovitt, Thomas C., and Curtiss, Karen A. "Academic Response Rate as a Function of Teacher- and Self-imposed Contingencies." *Journal of Applied Behavior Analysis* **2** (1969): 49–53.

Margulies, Stuart, and Eigen, Lewis D. *Applied Programed Instruction*. New York: John Wiley and Sons, 1962.

McKenzie, Hugh S.; Clark, Marilyn; Wolf, Montrose M.; Kothera, Richard; and Benson, Cedric. "Behavior Modification of Children with Learning Disabilities Using Grades as Tokens and Allowances as Backup Reinforcers." *Exceptional Children* **34** (1968): 745–52.

Michael, Jack. *Laboratory Studies in Operant Behaviors*. New York: McGraw-Hill Book Company, 1963.

Nolen, Patricia A.; Kunzelmann, Harold P.; and Haring, Norris G. "Behavioral Modification in a Junior High Learning Disabilities Classroom." *Exceptional Children* **34** (1967): 163–68.

Norman, Mary Alice. "Child Development and Mental Retardation Center." *University of Washington Magazine* **1**, nos. 3 and 4 (1969).

O'Leary, K. Daniel, and Becker, Wesley C. "Behavior Modification of an Adjustment Class: A Token Reinforcement Program." *Exceptional Children* **33** (1967): 627–42.

O'Leary, K. Daniel; Becker, Wesley C.; Evans, Michael B.; and Saudargas, Richard A. "A Token Reinforcement Program in a Public School: A Replication and Systematic Analysis." *Journal of Applied Behavior Analysis,* **2** (1969): 3–13.

Orme, Michael E. J., and Purnell, Richard F. "Behavior Modification and Transfer in an Out-of-Control Classroom." In *Behavior Modification in the Classroom,* edited by George A. Fargo, Charlene Behrns, and Patricia Nolen. Belmont, Calif.: Wadsworth Publishing Company, 1970.

Packard, Robert G. "The Control of 'Classroom Attention': A Group Contingency for Complex Behavior." *Journal of Applied Behavior Analysis,* **3** (1970): 13–28.

Patterson, Gerald R., and Gullion, M. Elizabeth. *Living with Children: New Methods for Parents and Teachers.* Champaign, Ill.: Research Press, 1968.

Patterson, G. R., and Reid, J. B. "Reciprocity and Coercion: Two Facets of Social Systems." In *Behavior Modification in Clinical Psychology,* edited by C. Neuringer and J. L. Michael. New York: Appleton-Century-Crofts, 1970.

Pavlov, Ivan Petrovich. *Conditioned Reflexes.* Edited and translated by G. V. Anrep. London: Oxford University Press, 1927.

Pearce, Lucia. "Environmental Structure: A Third Partner in Education." *Educational Technology* **8,** no. 17 (1968): 11–14.

Premack, David. "Toward Empirical Behavior Laws: 1. Positive Reinforcement." *Psychological Review* **66** (1959): 219–33.

Premack, David. "Reinforcement Theory." In *Nebraska Symposium on Motivation,* edited by David Levine. Lincoln, Nebraska: University of Nebraska Press, 1965, pp. 123–80.

Quay, Herbert C.; Werry, John S.; McQueen, Marjorie; and Sprague, Robert L. "Remediation of the Conduct Problem Child in the Special Class Setting." *Exceptional Children* **32** (1966): 509–15.

Rath, Gustave J. "Non-CAI Instruction Using Computers and Non-instructional Uses of CAI Computers." *Educational Technology* **8,** no. 3 (1968): 11–13.

Raygor, Alton L.; Wark, David M.; and Warren, Ann Dell. "Operant Conditioning of Reading Rate: The Effect of a Secondary Reinforcer." *Journal of Reading* **9** (1966): 147–56.

Reese, Ellen P. *The Analysis of Human Operant Behavior.* Dubuque, Iowa: Wm. C. Brown Company Publishers, 1966.

Sidman, Murray. *Tactics of Scientific Research.* New York: Basic Books, 1960.

Silverman, Robert E. "Using the S-R Reinforcement Model." *Educational Technology* **8,** no. 5 (1968): 3–12.

Silvern, Leonard C. "A Cybernetic System Model for Occupational Education." *Educational Technology* **8,** no. 2 (1968): 3–9.

Skinner, B. F. *The Behavior of Organisms: An Experimental Analysis.* New York: D. Appleton-Century Company, 1938.

Skinner, B. F. *Science and Human Behavior.* New York: Macmillan/Free Press, 1953.

Skinner, B. F. *Verbal Behavior.* New York: Appleton-Century-Crofts, 1957.

Skinner, B. F. "What is the Experimental Analysis of Behavior?" *Journal of The Experimental Analysis of Behavior* 9 (1966): 213–18.

Skinner, B. F. "Teaching: The Arrangement of Contingencies Under Which Something is Taught." *The Improvement of Instruction,* edited by Norris G. Haring and Alice H. Hayden. Seattle, Wash.: Special Child Publications, in press, 1971.

Staats, Arthur W.; Finley, Judson R.; Minke, Karl A.; and Wolf, Montrose. "Reinforcement Variables in the Control of Unit Reading Responses." *Journal of the Experimental Analysis of Behavior* 7 (1964): 139–49.

Suppes, Patrick, and Suppes, Joanne. *Sets and Numbers.* New York: L. W. Singer Co. (subsidiary of Random House), 1968.

Terrace, H. S. "Stimulus Control." In *Operant Behavior: Areas of Research and Application,* edited by Werner K. Honig. New York: Appleton-Century-Crofts, 1966.

Thomas, Don R.; Becker, Wesley C.; and Armstrong, Marianne. "Production and Elimination of Disruptive Classroom Behavior by Systematically Varying Teacher's Behavior." *Journal of Applied Behavior Analysis* 1 (1968): 35–45.

Thomson, James C., Jr. "From Reason to Technology." *Educational Technology* 8, no. 6 (1968): 3–8.

Tyler, Vernon O., Jr., and Brown, G. Duane. "The Use of Swift, Brief Isolation as a Group Control Device for Institutionalized Delinquents." *Behaviour Research and Therapy* 5 (1967): 1–9.

Warren, A. Bertrand, and Brown, Robert H. "Conditioned Operant Response Phenomena in Children." *Journal of General Psychology* 28, second half (1943): 181–207.

Watson, John B., and Rayner, Rosalie. "Conditioned Emotional Reactions." *Journal of Experimental Psychology* 3 (1920): 1–14.

Williams, Carl D. "The Elimination of Tantrum Behavior by Extinction Procedures." *Journal of Abnormal and Social Psychology* 59 (1959): 269.

Wolf, M. M.; Giles, D. K.; and Hall, R. Vance. "Experiments with Token Reinforcement in a Remedial Classroom." *Behaviour Research and Therapy* 6 (1968): 51–64.

Wolf, Montrose, Risley, Todd; and Mees, Hayden. "Application of Operant Conditioning Procedures to the Behaviour Problems of an Autistic Child." *Behaviour Research and Therapy* 1 (1964): 305–12.

Index

N

F